Spanish and Basc

Translated and adapted by

Richard Marsh

Legendary Books
Dublin

Legendary Books Series 2
Spanish and Basque Legends
ISBN 0-9557568-1-2 / 978-0-9557568-1-8

Published by
Richard Marsh
15 Fontenoy Street
Dublin 7, Ireland
Phone 353-1-8827941
www.RichardMarsh.ie
Richard@RichardMarsh.ie

Trade enquiries to CMD BookSource

© 2010 Richard Marsh text and photos

Also by Richard Marsh:
The Legends and Lands of Ireland, Sterling, 2004
Tales of the Wicklow Hills, Legendary Books, 2007
Saints and Gore and Fairy Lore: Irish and Basque Legends (CD 1997)
The Tower of Breogán: Irish and Spanish Legends and Tales (CD 2003)

Title page: detail of the pillar at the bridge in Hospital de Órbigo, León, commemorating the Paso Honroso of Don Suero de Quiñones (page 172).

Cover background: the Mezquita in Córdoba.

Front cover: Fernán González on the 16th-century Arco de Santa María, Burgos (page 64).

Back cover: statue of Guzmán el Bueno, Tarifa (page 156); unattributed public domain painting of the Lovers at the Peña de los Enamorados, Antequera (page 169).

All photos by Richard Marsh except author photo by Isabel Severing. Design consultant Christine Warner.

"In the present day, when popular literature is running into the low levels of life, and luxuriating on the vices and follies of mankind; and when the universal pursuit of gain is trampling down the early growth of poetic feeling, and wearing out the verdure of the soul, I question whether it would not be of service for the reader occasionally to turn to these records of prouder times and loftier modes of thinking; and to steep himself to the very lips in old Spanish romance."

Washington Irving, from the "Spanish Romance" chapter in *Tales of the Alhambra*, 1832.

"Traditional narrations ... [are] a fundamental part of our cultural heritage and our collective memory, although they are not made of stone and they cannot be seen in a museum."

Professor Eloy Martos Núñez, Universidad de Extremadura, in the Prologue to *Cuentos y Leyendas de España y Portugal / Contos e Lendas de Espanha e Portugal*, I Seminario Internacional [1996], Editorial Regional de Extremadura, 1997.

"Legends are the sentimental chronicle of the people; they are almost the true history, because it is the people who create, mould and decorate them and spread and live with them."

José Calles Vales, *Leyendas Tradicionales*, Editorial LIBSA, Madrid, 2003.

3

Contents

Late Middle Ages (11-16th centuries)

Modern Times

Timeless Tales

Ballads

Foreword by Pilar Alderete-Diez

People like you enrich the dreams of the worlds, and it is dreams that create history. Ben Okri

Before I read these tales, my imagination wondered about which stories of the old Iberian Peninsula I would encounter. I thought back to my old schoolbooks, when as a child I was more interested in the heroes in my class than the ones that blew the horn of our glorious past.

Today – as these tales have travelled through the years and through languages, from their original to this English version by Richard Marsh – I found my imagination ignited by names I had overheard but had overlooked: Fernán González (whose mention filled me with an inexplicable sadness, until I re-read the tales); El Cid (who RTVE – our national television station – had converted into a little boy in a 1980s cartoon series called "Ruy, el pequeño Cid," where he never fully managed to become the legendary warrior). These tales resurrected places that I visited over and over again but never fully understood: El Paso Honroso or the Aqueduct of Segovia.

Tales like these contribute to pinning their protagonists to locations that anyone interested in the cultures of Spain should attempt to visit: San Andrés de Teixido (they'd better) or Almanzor, the highest mountain in the Central Range. When visiting Spain after reading these tales, you will be walking through layers of meaning and transiting through historic periods cocooned in these locations. When reading the records in our monuments, these characters will come alive and whisper in your ear their words that we claim as our tradition. The dialogue that the author has established with the locals will also provide you with the weapon of a sharpened Spanish wit. There is a story that I particularly like, which highlights the importance of this dialogue: "The Lovers of Teruel". I like it not so much because of the story itself, but for the well-known Spanish proverb used in response to the tale: "los amantes de Teruel, tonta ella y tonto él" (the lovers of Teruel, silly her and silly him); for a community is portrayed not only by their stories but also by the collective – and personal – responses given to them.

Personal and collective memory meet at a crossroads in these tales, and Richard's craft presents us with a sumptuous blend of historical narrative, legendary tales and anecdotal evidence. These three main

7

ingredients are richly seasoned by the diversity of the peoples that gave shape to these stories. At the same time, these ancient – or simply far away – neighbours take shape before our bewildered eyes, thanks to these tales that have captured them for today's readers. The accurate historical background, carefully detailed by the author, contributes to the mixture of these stories with the essential ingredient of history remembered by the people who recorded them originally as historians or storytellers, crafts that have overlapped throughout history. The combination of different sources provides Richard's translations with the prismatic light reflected by these multiple perspectives.

There has been enough talk about the differences between the distinct communities inhabiting the land now called Spain at any given moment in time: Christians, Moors, Celts, Basques, Jews, Mediterranean traders … Many of these characters are the protagonists of the older tales; whereas in Modern Times, our legends seem to focus on the mysteries, our well-known picaresque spirit or regional stereotypes in which the other world and the physicality of our worldly experience are not at odds but overlap with or without a purpose.

Bridges (the Aqueduct, Soravilla and Oiartzun) seem to captivate our imagination, probably as a symbol to emphasize that these distinct cultures have shared rivers of wealthy history and folklore. They have sung the same ballads together and had similar points of view. And these bridges extend beyond the shores of the Iberian peninsula towards the lands to which these peoples have been attracted, including Ireland.

The author concludes his collection with the sweet cruelty of our ballads. We learned them at school or heard them from our mothers, warning their daughters against the follies of love, chanting them to sleep. These beautiful songs finish up the book, leaving a legendary world behind, to walk into the realm of our dreams, which as Okri reminds us, create history; infected by the symbols and the adventures of lands – so far so near – joined by the bridge of our collective imagination.

Pilar Alderete-Diez was born in Castilla in 1975. She has been a teacher in Spanish at the National University of Ireland, Galway, since 1999. Her main interests are translation and language learning. She writes stories and other forms of fiction under the pseudonym of Irma Mento.

Introduction

"Se non è vero è ben trovato – even if it isn't true it's plausible." – said of Dante's *Inferno*

Myth is the embodiment of the abstract. Sacred myths tell how the world began and how humans and animals were created. "Aetiological legends seek to explain the origins of various things. They are often fanciful and do not pretend to give true reasons to account for how particular things came into being. They are, however, based on a kind of keen observation of nature and of other facets of life" (Sean O'Sullivan, *Legends from Ireland*). Historical legends are history in fancy dress or "disputed history" or the past selectively recalled, and are based on real people and events and set in identifiable places. Folk tales are often scraps of myth imperfectly remembered and understood, but they endure because they retain the magic and psychological truth of their source.

Many traditional stories contain elements of all these categories. The characters in legends often have gods for parents, are born in miraculous or magical circumstances, and attract universal folk tale motifs. Christian saints have taken on characteristics of ancient heroes and wizards, and migratory international folk tales have become attached to them as pagan daring and magic were converted into Christian faith and miracles.

This collection of legends (broadly defined) is meant to be representative rather than comprehensive. As a Basque saying goes, "A small fountain quenches your thirst as well as a big one." I have selected the stories based on period, place, theme and type. Galicia and the Basque Country are especially rich in local tales, Burgos (Old Castile) in medieval historical legends. During the Christian Reconquest of Moorish Spain between AD 718 and 1492, there is a concentration of accounts of courage and compassion, cruelty and outrage at action hot spots such as Toledo and Seville and throughout the shifting borderlands.

Most of the legends have come to me from multiple sources. I have compiled my versions of these in a straightforward manner in the style I feel is best suited to each story, giving precedence to the narrative while reflecting the often formal tone of the older sources. Historical and background information necessary to the appreciation of each story is provided in a brief introduction or incorporated in the text. Additional information is in the Notes section in the back of the book.

The two 19th-century literary legends, Arturo Campión's "Orreaga" and Antonio de Trueba's "Jaun Zuria", are a combination of direct translation and paraphrase, retaining the styles of the authors as far as possible. The medieval accounts of "The Coming of the Almujuces", "The Death of Munso López", "The Goat-foot Lady", and the Portuguese version of "Ramiro and Aldonza" possess certain charms that I wished to preserve intact, and so I have translated these with minimal editing. I have lightly edited the 16th-century English of "How the Basques Discovered Ireland".

The understandably biased view of the Jesuit historian Father Juan de Mariana, in reporting the long struggle between Christians and Muslims during the Reconquest, provides a subtle insight into the transmission of historical legend. However, his overall fairness and his scrupulous attempt to present an accurate account of the complex history of Spain make his contribution to this collection of legends invaluable. I quote and paraphrase his 1592 *Historia General de España* frequently in the medieval sections.

Mariana's responsible approach to the sometimes impossible task of differentiating between fact and fancy reflects the attitude of the first historians: the traditional oral storytellers and the anonymous composers of the ballads that were used as sources for the first histories set down in Spanish. This approach is summed up in the disclaimer at the end of his chapter on El Cid (Book 10, Chapter 4):

Some take most of this narration for mere legend; I have recounted more things than I believe, because I neither dare to pass over in silence what others affirm, nor do I wish to state as certain what I doubt.

Washington Irving, who used Mariana as one of his sources, takes that sentiment a step further in the Preface to his 1866 *Spanish Papers*:

To discard, however, everything wild and marvellous in this portion of Spanish history [the sometimes fanciful chronicles], is to discard some of its most beautiful, instructive, and national features; it is to judge of Spain by the standard of probability suited to tamer and more prosaic countries.

I kept Mariana's and Irving's words in mind while I made these translations and adaptations, and my inner eye frequently glanced at the inscription on the reconstructed clock tower in the Galician village of A Pobra de Trives. When the 17th-century church of San Bartholomé was demolished in 1928, the bell/clock tower was left standing, but was then torn down in 1968. In response to popular demand, it was rebuilt in 1996.

Como me vedes, xa fun [As you see me, so I was] 1928
Deixademe para sempre asi [Leave me always thus] 1996

Here are details of two medieval sources used for some of the stories in this book.

Livro das Linhagens (Book of Lineages), also called *Nobiliario de Linajes* and *Nobiliario del Conde Don Pedro*, Don Pedro Alfonso de Barcelos, 14th century.

The author (1288?-1346) was the son of Denis, King of Portugal. The book had two main purposes: the tracing of lineages among the nobility to avert prohibited marriages between close relatives and to prove legitimate descent in order to substantiate claims for the inheritance of property and titles; and the celebration of the heroism of those who fought against the Moors. A further unstated purpose was to assert (often falsely) the absence of the "taint" of Jewish or Moorish blood in families descended from Gothic nobility. The 1344 *Crónica General de España* is also attributed to Don Pedro.

Istoria (or *Libro*) *de las Bienandanzas [Prosperities] e Fortunas*, Lope García de Salazar, c. 1474.

A member of the minor nobility and a swash-buckling adventurer and faction-fighter himself, Don Lope devoted his spare time to scouring the libraries of the aristocracy and listening to oral accounts in order to chronicle the lives and trace the lineages of heroes and rulers of the distant and recent past. He began writing this anecdotal Who's Who in 1471 to pass the time and take his mind off his problems when he was

11

imprisoned "by those who I engendered, nourished and raised, and fearful of being poisoned". He died in 1476, apparently poisoned by one of his sons. Don Lope also wrote *Crónica de Siete Casas de Vizcaya y Castilla*, 1454.

All translations are mine, except where otherwise indicated.

Acknowledgements

Thanks are due to the helpful staff at many public and private libraries, especially José Lozano at the Institución Fernán González in Burgos, Pili at the Municipal Library in San Sebastián, and those who allowed me to browse a 16th-century edition of *Las Siete Partidas* at the University of Salamanca library.

My special gratitude goes to Fermín Leizaola Calvo, president of the Department of Ethnology of the Aranzadi Society of Sciences, San Sebastián, for insight into Basque traditions and for the story of the Bridge of Oiartzun; to Patricia Aristondo (who tried to teach me Basque) and her cousin Jaione Alkorta Aldazabal of Ondarroa for introducing me to Leokadi; and to Rosa María Perclomo of Fuerteventura, who told me about the Fire of Mafasca.

About the Author

Richard Marsh is a storyteller specialising in Irish, Spanish and Basque legends. He tells in Ireland, Spain, the USA and elsewhere and collects stories on his travels to tell in other countries. In Ireland, he is also a Legendary Tours guide, taking people to the places where the legends happened and telling them on site.

List of Colour Plates

Prehistory and Early Christian Era

The Coming of the Almujuces
(Galicia)

This is a close translation from the 13th-century *Estoria de España* (14), compiled by King Alfonso X the Wise. The Almujuces were apparently Phoenicians.

About the time of the Fall of Troy in the 13th century BC, the Almujuces arrived in Spain. They were fire worshippers. When a child was born, they passed it through a dry-wood fire north, south, east and west, like a baptism. They came mainly from Caldea. They stayed until Nabucodonosor and Xerxes destroyed them in the 5th century BC, and some fled to the cold islands such as Norway, Dacia and Prussia.

Then they built ships and became powerful on the sea and conquered England with all its islands: Scotland, Ireland and Wales. Then they came to Bayona south of Vigo in Galicia in this manner. They knew that in the tower of La Coruña there was a mirror with which the people watched for ships coming over the sea. So the Almujuces covered some ships with green trees standing up, so that the inhabitants took them for small islands. The invaders thus avoided discovery, and they were able to reach the mountains, from where they threw stones with ballistas and broke the mirror. Then they signalled the rest of their fleet to come and capture the town.

How the Basques Discovered Ireland

Paraphrased and quoted from *The New Chronicles of England and France* by Robert Fabyan, 1516.

Moliuncius was the first king of Britain. Belynus and Brennius were his sons. Gurguncius, son of Belynus, became king of Britain in 356 BC. The Danes had been withholding an agreed tribute, and Gurguncius mounted an expedition to Denmark to give the Danes a reason to reinstate payments. Having whipped them into submission, Gurguncius was on his way back to Britain, when he encountered a fleet of 30 ships full of men and women beside the Orkney Isles. The chief Captain, Bartholomew, told the king that they were Basques exiled from Spain and had been sailing a long time in search of some prince who would give them a dwelling place, and they would become his subjects and hold the land of him. Bartholomew beseeched the king to have compassion on them and grant them a place to inhabit, so they need not continue to live on their ships.

"The king with the advice of his barons granted unto them a void and vast country, which was and is the farthest isle of all isles toward the west, the which isle as sayeth the English Chronicle was then named Ireland ..."

How the Celts of Spain Discovered Ireland
(Galicia)

This story is common to Irish and Spanish mythological history and is widely known in Galicia, where the *Hino da Galiza* – the Galician anthem – mentions Breogán in every chorus. The full account, which is based on fact, is told in the 12th-century *Lebor Gabála Érenn*, the *Book of Occupations of Ireland*. When the Gaelic lords were forced to flee Ireland following failed rebellions in the 16th and 17th centuries, they used this tradition to claim Spanish citizenship.

In Egypt at the time of Moses, Scota, daughter of the Pharaoh, and Neil, son of Fenius the inventor of the Irish language, had a son named Gaedhael. Gaedhael was the progenitor of the group of Celts who became the Irish. When he was a young boy, he was bitten by a snake. Moses cured his snakebite and said, "God commands and I command that this boy's descendants will live in a land free from snakes." Depending on how you look at it, that is why there are no snakes in Ireland, or why Gaedhael's people eventually settled in Ireland, where there were no snakes.

But first they stopped off in Spain for a few hundred years. Gaedhael's people came from Scythia, lived in Egypt for a time, were

15

evicted from there, and then dominated the Iberian Peninsula and the rest of Europe.

The lighthouse in La Coruña in Galicia, on the northwest coast of Spain, is part of the city's coat of arms. It is called the Tower of Hercules, because it was built by Hercules over the bones of the giant Gerión after he killed him in combat. But long before that, in the fifth century before Christ, Breogán, one of Gaedhael's descendants, built a tower on the same site.

At that time, the king of Spain was Mil. One day, Breogán's son Ith, nephew of Mil, was standing on top of the Tower of Breogán, and he saw land on the horizon 600 miles (1000 km) north of La Coruña.

Ith and his family got into a boat and set off to investigate this strange island. When they arrived at what was then called Inis Ealga – the Noble Island – but is now known as Ireland, they met the inhabitants, the Tuatha Dé Danann, who possessed magic arts.

Ith made a serious mistake. First he admired the beauty and fertility of the country, and then he gave the Tuatha Dé Danann advice on how to run it. This made the Tuatha Dé Danann think that Ith wanted to take over Ireland for his own people – and perhaps that was true – so they killed him. When Ith's family went back to Spain and told the other Celts what had happened, a large group – the Sons of Mil or the Milesians – returned to invade Ireland.

The druids of the Tuatha Dé Danann covered the country with a cloud, so the Milesians couldn't see the land. The Milesians circled the island three times to break the spell, and when they landed they met the three queens of the Tuatha Dé Danann – Banba, Fodhla and Éire. Each of them asked the Milesians to name the country after her, if they were victorious in the coming battle.

They promised that they would, and even though the Tuatha Dé Danann had magic powers, they were Bronze Age people, with bronze weapons, and the Iron Age Milesians, with their superior iron weapons, defeated them. So now Ireland's official name in Irish is Éire, but Fodhla and Banba are still used as poetic names.

Why February Has 28 Days
(Basque Country)

A shepherd in the hills of Euskal Herria on the exposed north coast of the Iberian Peninsula always lost a number of ewes and lambs each lambing season, which comes during the worst weather of the year – February and March. But one year, March Weather was so mild the shepherd didn't lose a single sheep all month, and he was very grateful.

"March Weather," he said, (a shepherd lives close to the elements and can understand and talk with them), "you didn't kill any of my sheep this year, and I want to thank you."

But March Weather was proud of his fierce reputation as a killer, and he was angry to think that he might lose it, so he snatched two days of weather from his neighbour, February, and killed all the sheep in the shepherd's flock. And ever since then, February has had only 28 days.

Saint John's Eve Bonfires
(Cataluña)

Saint John's Eve, 23 June, in Spain is like Halloween in English-speaking countries, and bonfires are lit in celebration. This story of the origin of the custom comes from Sabadell, near Barcelona in Cataluña.

The mothers of Jesus Christ, Saint John the Baptist and Saint Judas were close friends when they were girls, and they lived only a short distance from one another after they were married. They agreed that the first one to give birth would light a bonfire on top of a hill near her house to announce the event to the other two. Saint John's mother was the first, and she lit a fire to signal the others.

It is interesting to speculate that this story may have been brought to Spain by Mary the mother of Jesus herself. She probably passed through Barcelona on her way to Zaragoza, where she joined the apostle Saint James the Greater (Santiago) to found a church on the site of the present Basilica of the Pillar. Zaragoza tradition affirms that she came in person – *en carne mortal* – and that this was not an apparition. It was the only time she was known to have left her homeland. As proof that the story is

17

true, the pillar she stood on is displayed in the Basilica. (See "Santiago" chapter.)

When the Pyrenees Were Green
(Cataluña)

The Pyrenees were once soft and green. This is how they came to be covered with rocks and snow.

It was a cold, rainy night, and a group of shepherds were crowded into a small hut with a fire to keep warm, while their sheep found shelter outside. There was a knock on the door. One of the shepherds opened it, and a man was standing there dressed in rags and shivering with the cold, looking exhausted.

"Can I come in to rest and get warm?" he asked.

"No," the shepherd said. "There isn't enough space here for another person."

"But I'm very tired and cold," the stranger said. "I've come a long way."

"Well then, you'll just have to go back where you came from," said the shepherd with a heartless laugh.

"Yes," said the stranger. "I suppose I'll have to."

With that, his clothes turned white, and his body began to glow so that a halo surrounded him, and his feet lifted slowly off the ground. Higher and higher he rose into the air until he disappeared. Suddenly, there was a flash of lightning and a crash of thunder, and the rain turned to snow and sleet and hail. Bolts of lightning continued to pound the earth like a blacksmith's hammer, and the shepherds huddled together in fear as thunder shook their hut.

Finally, all the thunders the world had ever heard seemed to come together in one tremendous explosion. In the morning, if anyone had been alive, they would have seen that the green pastures were now a rocky wasteland covered in snow, and all the shepherds and their sheep had been turned into stones.

San Martín Txiki and the Basajauns
(Basque Country)

Long ago, only the basajauns (lords of the woods) knew how to plant, harvest and mill wheat to make flour. The basajauns kept this knowledge to themselves, but San Martín worked out a plan to steal the secret of agriculture and give it to the human race. ("Txiki", pronounced "cheeky", is Basque for "little" and is used in an affectionate sense. San Martín is often called simply "Samartitxiki" in the stories.)

San Martín challenged the basajauns to see who could jump over the heaps of wheat they had harvested. The basajauns laughed at San Martín, because they knew that a mere human would be no competition for them, and they laughed at his big floppy shoes. They all jumped over the wheat easily, but when San Martín tried, he landed on top of one of the heaps, and the basajauns laughed again.

Then San Martín laughed, and he laughed last and best, but quietly, because his trick had worked. The basajauns are big and slow-witted, but when they saw San Martín walking away home, with his big, floppy shoes full of grains of their wheat, they realised that they had been tricked. When they stopped laughing, San Martín began to run for his life, and it's a good thing that he did.

He was already a kilometre away when one of the basajauns threw a hatchet. The lords of the woods may be slow, but they are strong. San Martín saw the hatchet coming, and he ducked behind a chestnut tree just in time, because the hatchet struck the tree and split it in half.

San Martín now had the seeds, but he didn't know the right time of the year to sow them. Fortunately, a man was passing by the cave of one of the basajauns, and he heard him singing:

> "If the humans knew this song
> They'd be well informed.
> When the leaf is in the bud
> Then you sow the corn.
> When the leaf falls off the trees
> Then you sow the wheat.
> When San Lorenzo's feast comes round
> Sow the turnip in the ground."

19

The man told San Martín what he heard, and San Martín told all the humans, and that is how cultivation spread through the world. (The Feast of San Lorenzo is 7 February.)

According to a story from Oiartzun (Gipuzkoa), San Martín wanted to know how to make a saw, so humans could cut down trees as the basajauns did and make mills to grind the wheat to make flour. The basajauns wouldn't tell, because they wanted to keep all their secrets to themselves. So San Martín sent a man to the basajauns to tell them that he had discovered the secret of making a saw.

"So he has seen the leaves of the chestnut tree, has he?" the basajaun said.

That is how San Martín learned to use the chestnut leaf as a model for making a saw blade, and humans were able to cut down trees and build flour mills. But there was a problem. The axles of the mills kept wearing out, and a lot of time was wasted in replacing them. So San Martín sent a man to tell the basajauns that he had learned how to keep the axles from wearing out.

"So he's learned to polish the axles smooth, has he?" one of the basajauns said.

[Variant: "So he's learned to make the axles of alder-wood, has he?"]

And again, when men started to work with metals and needed to know how to weld pieces of iron together, San Martín sent a man to tell the basajauns that he had learned how to weld.

"So he knows how to sprinkle the iron with clayey water, does he?" was the response.

Perhaps it was because the basajauns admired the humans for their great cleverness that they used to give the shepherds warning of a coming storm by whistling.

The Lagoon of Antela
(Galicia)

In the district of Xenza de Limia about 20 miles (34 km) south of Ourense, there was once a town called Antioquía at the confluence of the rivers Limia, Nocelo and Faramontaos. Its inhabitants were notable for their belligerence and meanness. God decided to send a flood to

20

punish them for their sins, but first he sent Jesus to see if there was anyone worth saving in the town. Disguised as a beggar, Jesus walked the streets of Antioquía and knocked on doors asking for alms, but all He got for His pains was abuse and threats.

Passing through an oak grove on His way out of the town, He noticed a hovel, and by the smoke rising from the chimney He knew that there was one more person to test. The old woman who lived there had no possessions but a goat and a chicken, but as soon as she heard the beggar's voice at the door, she invited Him in, served Him a glass of milk and a piece of pie, and gave Him her own humble bed of rags to sleep in.

In the morning, Jesus led the woman to the door and said, "See what has become of Antioquía."

A lake which is now called the Lagoon of Antela covered the town, and none survived but the woman who had invited a beggar into her house and fed Him. They say that on the morning of Saint John's Day, when the first ray of the rising sun strikes the surface of the lake, the sound of the submerged church bells rings over the water, and on Christmas Eve at midnight you can hear the roosters crow.

Early Middle Ages (8-10th centuries)

Most of the legends in this section deal with the Moorish Conquest of Spain and the first centuries of the Reconquest.

King Rodrigo and the Losing of Spain
(Toledo)

AD 711. The Moors are encouraged by Musa to invade Spain, though the initial move is taken by the Christian governor of [Ceuta], who has a quarrel with Roderick, the last Visigoth king of Spain. Led by the Moorish chief Tariq, the Moorish army lands near Gibraltar (the Mountain of Tariq) and at the battle of Lake Janda (July) decisively defeats Roderick, who is probably killed in the battle. (*Chronology of the Ancient World*, Mellersh)

By that sparse historical entry hangs a central tale in the legendary history of Spain, the Moorish Conquest, which is the seedbed of the many individual tales and cycles of stories that make up the nearly 800-year saga of the Reconquest.

The Goths had established themselves as the dominant power in the Iberian Peninsula by AD 575. Vitiza "the Wicked" became the Gothic ruler in 701. He imprisoned and blinded Teodofredo, a perceived threat to his rule, and killed Favila, the father of Pelayo, the leader who would initiate the Reconquest in 718. Vitiza was deposed, imprisoned and blinded by Teodofredo's son, Rodrigo, the "plague and disgrace" of Spain, in 710. Although some of the legends present him in a sympathetic light, Rodrigo (Roderick) is blamed for the Losing of Spain and the ushering in of the Moorish Conquest.

Yesterday I was King of Spain, today I have nothing at all.
Yesterday I had houses and castles, today not even a hall.
Yesterday I had servants aplenty, and people to work in my home.
Today not even a turret that I can claim for my own.
Unfortunate was the hour, unfortunate was that day

That I was born to inherit such a great kingdom as Spain,
For now I have lost all I had, all in only one day.
(from "The Destruction of Don Rodrigo", anonymous ballad)

The Seduction of the Cava

Count Julián was the above-mentioned Christian governor of Ceuta, the Spanish colony on the north coast of Africa, which served as a bulwark against Moorish invasion across the Straits of Gibraltar. The southern Pillar erected by Hercules stood on (or was) the present Mount Sidi Moussa at Ceuta. The northern Pillar was called Calpe and is now known as the Rock of Gibraltar, from Gibel Tariq – Mountain of Tariq – after the leader of the Moorish invasion.

Julián's wife was a sister of Vitiza, but Julián pragmatically switched allegiance to Rodrigo. As a token of trust, and following the custom of nobles sending their young sons and daughters to the court to be educated, Julián left his 16-year-old daughter, Florinda, in Rodrigo's care at the royal seat in Toledo. By chance, Rodrigo noticed Florinda bathing nude in a stream next to his palace. The place is marked by the remaining tower of a bridge destroyed in 1203 next to the Bridge of San Martín and is called the Baño de la Cava. His passions inflamed, he tried to seduce her. Up to this point in the story, historians and storytellers are in agreement.

What happened next has long been a matter of hotly contested opinion.

If you ask which of the two
deserves the greater blame,
men will say the Cava;
Rodrigo, women name.
(from an anonymous ballad in a 1679 collection)

Those who believe that Florinda was a willing accomplice in her downfall refer to her as the "Cava", a derogatory term like "slut". (Cervantes said that the name "Florinda" was thereafter used only for dogs, as no Spaniard would give it to a daughter.) Others insist she was raped by Rodrigo.

She never wanted to do what the king commanded of her,
And so he took her by force, and it was against her desire.
(from "The Seduction of the Cava", 15th-century ballad)

In either case, Julián was informed of the event in a note sent secretly by Florinda, her version being that she was raped. (Three Moorish accounts say that she was not allowed to write to her father, but she sent him presents, among which was a rotten egg, from which he deduced what had occurred.) Julián was outraged by this betrayal of his trust. In the words of Washington Irving in his *Legends of the Conquest of Spain*, he "meditated against his native country one of the blackest schemes of treason that ever entered into the human heart. The plan of Count Julian was to hurl King Roderick from his throne, and to deliver all Spain into the hands of the infidels."

Pretending ignorance of his daughter's deflowering, Julián visited Rodrigo in Toledo and advised him to move the bulk of his troops to Ceuta and the border with Gaul, it not being necessary to protect the south and centre of Spain. Julián then evacuated his wife and daughter to Ceuta, mobilised his family and that of Vitiza, including Oppas, Vitiza's brother and bishop of Seville (who had Rodrigo's confidence), and enlisted the aid of his erstwhile adversary, Musa, the commander of the Moorish forces in Northern Africa, over whom he had just celebrated a major victory. The legendary incident of the Cave or Tower of Hercules is set during the time of Julián's secret manoeuvres.

The Cave of Hercules

In some versions, the Cave is approached from under a tower outside the walls of Toledo; in others it is located in or accessed from the crypt beneath the since-demolished church of San Ginés, which replaced a successor to the 13th-century BC tower at the top of the prominent rock on which Toledo is built. Both versions are credible in the context of the legend. Present-day residents confirm that Toledo is honeycombed with centuries-old subterranean rooms and passages, and stories are told of people becoming lost in the labyrinth and on their eventual escape finding themselves miles outside the city.

Some say the Cave was built by Túbal, others by the same Hercules of Libya who liberated Spain from the giant Gerión and built the Tower in La Coruña and the Pillars of Hercules, or Hercules Alcides, the Theban Greek, but all agree that the builder concealed his treasure in it. It is also believed that long before the Goths made Toledo their capital in the 6th century AD, the Cave was the repository of all the arcane knowledge in the world. Like the Cave of Salamanca / San Cipriano, it is rumoured to have once been the home of a school for the black arts – "las artes toledanas". The Scottish wizard Michael Scot (c. 1175 - c. 1235) is said to have studied in Toledo.

When Rodrigo established himself as king and took the throne in Toledo in 710, two old men called to the palace and told him about the cave built by Hercules, who "finished it with magic art, shutting up within it a fearful secret, never to be penetrated without peril and disaster. To protect this terrible mystery he closed the entrance to the edifice with a ponderous door of iron, secured by a great lock of steel, and he left a command that every king who should succeed him should add another lock to the portal; denouncing woe and destruction on him who should eventually unfold the secret of the tower" (*Legends of the Conquest of Spain*). These two men, guardians of the Tower, told Rodrigo that some kings had opened the door but had been killed or repulsed and "hastened to reclose the door and secure it with its thousand locks". They had come to tell him about the custom of each newly crowned king adding one more lock, and that it was his duty to do this now.

The impulsive and capricious Rodrigo, who had been fascinated from childhood by rumours of Hercules's treasure, told Urbino, the archbishop of Toledo, that he intended to seek out the mystery of the cave.

"Beware, my son," said Urbino. "There are secrets hidden from man for his good. Seek not then to indulge a rash and unprofitable curiosity. Do not disturb a mystery which has been held sacred from generation to generation within the memory of man, and which even Caesar himself, when sovereign of Spain, did not venture to invade."

"Of what importance are the menaces of Hercules the Libyan?" Rodrigo replied. "Was he not a pagan? And can his enchantments have aught avail against a believer in our holy faith? Besides," he continued, scenting hidden treasure, "my coffers are exhausted. Surely it would be an acceptable act in the eyes of Heaven to draw forth this wealth which lies buried under profane and necromantic spells, and consecrate it to religious purposes."

Rodrigo led his courtiers to the Cave, where they read the inscription over the entrance: "The king who opens this door and uncovers the marvels it contains will discover good and bad things."

Urbino again implored him: "Whatever is within this tower is as yet harmless, and lies bound under a mighty spell; venture not then to open a door which may let forth a flood of evil upon the land."

And he added this warning:

"Nor shall it ever ope, old records say,
Save to a King, the last of all his line,
What time his empire totters to decay ..."
(from "The Vision of Don Roderick", Walter Scott, 1811)

But instead of adding one more lock as ritual and custom demanded, Rodrigo ordered his locksmith to open the 24 locks that had been put in place over the centuries. This took time, but eventually the last lock was prised off. The bold young warriors put their shoulders to the rusted iron door but were unable to move it. Rodrigo ordered them to stand back, and as soon as he set his hand on the door it swung open with a groan. Dank, fetid air carried the stench of decay into their faces, and they could hear a rhythmic pounding from within the cave. A few of the more adventurous warriors trouped into the darkness with torches, but no sooner had they turned the first corner than they came running back pale and gibbering with fright. They managed to stammer that they had seen something so horrible they couldn't begin to describe it.

The king cursed them for their cowardice. He grabbed the nearest torch and plunged into the shadows, inviting anyone who was brave enough to follow him. As they rounded the corner they saw a large room lavishly decorated, in the middle of which stood a huge bronze mechanical figure viciously striking the floor with a whirling mace. On the breast of the metal beast was a sign that read simply: "I do my duty." Rodrigo told the guardian that he had only come to find out what was hidden in the cave and did not intend to violate a sanctuary. The statue ceased moving. Rodrigo and his entourage passed the figure safely and entered another large chamber. There were no windows, but the room

26

seemed to be illuminated by the precious gems that covered the walls. On a table in the centre of the room lay a golden casket with these words inscribed on the cover:

"In this coffer is contained the mystery of the tower. The hand of none but a king can open it; but let him beware, for marvelous events will be revealed to him, which are to take place before his death."

Again the archbishop begged the king to turn back and not tempt fate.

"What have I to dread from a knowledge of the future?" Rodrigo said.

He broke the mother-of-pearl lock on the chest and found inside a linen cloth folded between two tablets of copper. He unfolded the cloth. On it were figures of mounted warriors dressed in the Arab fashion. Above them was an inscription in Greek: "Rash monarch, behold the men who are to hurl thee from thy throne, and subdue thy kingdom!"

Rodrigo was taken aback, and as he and his followers gazed on the scene it seemed as if the figures began to move. A faint sound of warlike tumult arose from the cloth, at first as if from far off, then growing louder – a blast of trumpets, a roll of drums, the clash of swords and axes – as the cloth itself spread until it filled the hall and its texture was no longer visible. The figures of the warriors now seemed a vision or an army of ghosts, and Rodrigo found himself witnessing a fierce battle between Moors and Christians. He watched as the standard of the Cross was brought down and the Christians routed.

He recognised himself in the figure of a warrior wearing a crown and dressed in his own armour, mounted on his own warhorse, Orelia. As the Christians fled, the royal warrior was unhorsed, and he disappeared in the confusion of the rout.

Terrified, Rodrigo and his followers rushed from the hall. The monstrous sentinel was missing from his post, but when they reached the entrance they found the ancient guardians lying dead, crushed by a mighty blow. A thunderstorm had just broken out, and rain and hail poured down. Rodrigo ordered the door closed, but it was now immovable, and the din of battle still sounded from within.

The king and his party fled back to the palace, pursued, it seemed, not only by the elements of an angry Nature, but also by the phantom warriors of the linen cloth, for they were surrounded by the shouts of men fighting and the cries of men dying and the thunder of galloping hooves. The River Tajo overflowed and trees were uprooted.

The following morning, with the storm abated and Nature calm again, Rodrigo ventured once more to the tower, this time with a great multitude, to try to close the iron door. Washington Irving describes the scene that confronted them when they reached the tower:

"An eagle appeared high in the air, seeming to descend from heaven. He bore in his beak a burning brand, and, lighting on the summit of the tower, fanned the fire with his wings. In a little while the edifice burst forth into a blaze, as though it had been built of rosin, and the flames mounted into the air with a brilliancy more dazzling than the sun; nor did they cease until every stone was consumed, and the whole was reduced to a heap of ashes. Then there came a vast flight of birds, small of size and sable of hue, darkening the sky like a cloud; and they descended, and wheeled in circles round the ashes, causing so great a wind with their wings that the whole was borne up into the air, and scattered throughout all Spain, and wherever a particle of that ash fell it was as a stain of blood. It is furthermore recorded by ancient men and writers of former days, that all those on whom this dust fell were afterwards slain in battle, when the country was conquered by the Arabs, and that the destruction of this necromantic tower was a sign and token of the approaching perdition of Spain."

The Destruction and Penitence of Don Rodrigo

In 713, Rodrigo and a force of Goths numbering more than 100,000 opposed the Moors led by Count Julián and Tariq at the Guadalete (River of Death) near Jerez. On the eighth and final day of the battle, Bishop Oppas and the sons of Vitiza took their troops over to the side of the Moors. The ruling Goths had forgotten the arts of war during the preceding 150 years of peace since they had consolidated their domination of Spain, and they were quickly defeated. Don Rodrigo was last seen fighting valiantly, and then:

Rodrigo the king is nowhere seen, and nobody knows where he is. ...
The lord king has been lost, and nothing is known of his fate.
(from "The Vengeance of Don Julián", anonymous ballad)

Rodrigo's crown, his clothes and shoes embroidered with gold and jewels, and his horse, Orelia, were found in a swamp next to the Guadalete. It is generally accepted that he died in the battle, and his body was removed by his own people. Centuries later a tomb was found in Saint Michael's church in Viseo, Portugal, with the inscription: "Here lies Rodrigo, the last king of the Goths." The earliest mention of this in writing comes from the 13th century.

Thus far history, but the legend of "The Penitence of Don Rodrigo" sprang up in the 14th century to assert that the king survived the battle and fled to Portugal, pursued by the Moors. He escaped and was sheltered and fed by a shepherd. When he was given brown bread, a sign of poverty and hardship, Rodrigo was unable to contain his tears. But worse, much worse, was to come.

Directed by the shepherd to a religious hermit, Rodrigo told the holy man who he was and that he wished to do penance for his sins. The hermit prayed for guidance, and after three days God advised him to tell Rodrigo to go to a fountain, take a two-headed snake he would find there, raise it to adulthood, and then lie naked in a closed tomb with the snake. When Rodrigo heard this, he "was full joyful and content and pleased therewith, and gave many thanks to our Lord, for that he should now complete his penance and save his soul."

The serpent did nothing for three days. At the end of the third day, "the serpent rose from his side, and crept upon his belly and his breast, and began with the one head to eat at his nature, and with the other straight toward his heart. And at this time the Elder came to his tomb, and asked him how he fared, and he said, 'Well, thanks to God, for now the serpent has begun to eat.'"

The hermit later returned to see if the king was still living;
He found that he was praying; he heard him groaning and grieving.
He asked him how he was. "Now God is helping me,"
Responded the good Rodrigo. "The snake is starting to eat –
Which I completely deserve – it's eating me in that portion
Where was the start and the reason for all my great misfortune."
With the hermit giving him courage, there the good king did die.
So ended the king Rodrigo; straight to heaven his spirit did fly.
(from "The Penitence of Don Rodrigo", anonymous 16th-century ballad)

The Fate of Count Julián and his Family

Having betrayed his king, Julián fled from the Moors to collect his wealth so he could begin to organise a resistance against them. He was heading for Aragón, but they caught up with him in Guadalajara Province at Taravilla south of Molina de Aragón. He threw all his treasure into the lake at Taravilla, where it is said people still recover pieces of it today. The Moorish leader Alahor then imprisoned Julián at Loarre north of Huesca, where he was tortured to death or tortured and beheaded and buried in unhallowed ground.

Alternatively, Julián escaped from Loarre and took refuge in a castle at nearby Linás de Marcuello, where the tower of the castle fell on him and killed him. Washington Irving reports, "We are told that the castle is no longer inhabited on account of the strange and horrible noises that are heard in it; and that visions of armed men are seen above it in the air; which are supposed to be the troubled spirits of the apostate Christians who favored the cause of the traitor."

One tradition has Florinda throwing herself from a tower in Málaga in grief for her part in the Conquest, saying before she did so, "Let this city be henceforth called Malacca, in memorial of the most wretched of women, who therein put an end to her days." (Málaga was originally a Phoenician colony called Malaca conquered by the Romans in the 3rd century BC.) But a more romantic version brings the story full circle to say that she returned to Toledo to drown herself in the River Tajo near the Baño de la Cava, where Rodrigo had spied her naked. For a long time, her wailing spectre was seen haunting the banks of the river, but following an exorcism some centuries ago the peaceful ghosts of the king and Florinda are still seen strolling along the riverbank in friendly conversation.

Julián had sent his wife, Frandina, and son, Alarbot, to Ceuta. Frandina's brother, Bishop Oppas, having just died while a prisoner of insurgent Christians at Covadonga, appeared to her as a ghost to warn her that her son's life was in danger. Emir Alahor stormed the citadel, and when it was obvious that it would be taken, Frandina took the boy to the chapel, where she concealed him in the tomb of his sister, whose body had been brought there from Málaga.

When Alahor demanded to know where her son was, she swore that he was buried among the dead. Alahor did not know what to make of her words, but his more astute astrologer, Yuza, sensed a hidden meaning and said, "Leave this to me. I will find the child."

Yuza led a group of soldiers on a search through the fortress, keeping Frandina with him and watching her reaction. They looked round the chapel without success, but as they were leaving Yuza noticed a gleam of joy in the face of the countess. Recalling her words "among the dead", he ordered the tombs opened and found the boy. Frandina pleaded with Alahor to no avail and was dragged away to the dungeon.

On Alahor's orders, Yuza led Alarbot to the tower that stood high above the sea where Hercules had raised one of his Pillars and told him there was nothing to fear. He asked him if he knew what the land across the water was. The boy said, "Spain, the land of my parents."

"Then stretch forth your hands and bless it," said Yuza.

When Alarbot took his hands away from the wall, Yuza pushed him over the edge.

The following morning, Frandina was led into the presence of the Christian defenders of the citadel who had been captured in the attack. He ordered them to stone her to death, threatening to stone to death anyone who refused. They all obeyed.

Some say that Rodrigo and Florinda had a son and that he grew up in the castle of Torrejón el Rubio in Trujillo, Cáceres, which had belonged to his grandfather, Julián. He tried to organise an army to eject the Moors and restore the reign to the Gothic line in the person of himself. He used to waylay and kidnap boys at a place called Calleja (Lane) de la Cava in order to press-gang them into his army – and continued to do so after his death. The Calleja became a place where mothers forbade their sons to go after dark.

Rationalising that "for the purposes of poetry, it is immaterial whether the story be true or false," the English Poet Laureate Robert Southey, in his 1814 poem "Roderick, the Last of the Goths", brings Rodrigo, Julián and Florinda together for a romantically tragic farewell. Rodrigo and Florinda have already become reconciled and would like to marry, but Rodrigo's wife is still living and unhappily married to a Moorish leader. Julián has been wounded and is dying. He orders his troops to join the resistance under Don Pelayo, and with his dying breath informs Rodrigo of his wife's death. Rodrigo and Florinda, who is also on the point of death, are now free to marry. They embrace ...

... and round his neck she threw
Her arms and cried, My Roderick! mine in Heaven!
Groaning, he claspt her close, and in that act
And agony her happy spirit fled.

Other authors have been equally flexible with the (supposed) truth. In Pedro Montengón's 1793 epic ballad *El Rodrigo*, Rodrigo defeats a warrior on the battlefield and then discovers it is Florinda. Holding her dying in his arms, he says: "Oh, Florinda, oh eternal love of the most unfortunate of kings!" Florinda turns her head away and welcomes death. In *Florinda: A Tragedy in Three Acts* by María Rosa Gálvez, 1804, Florinda has been saved by Rodrigo from murder at the hand of her uncle, Tulga. Then she kills herself after receiving the spoils of the disappeared Rodrigo: his crown, dagger and cloak. The long poem *Florinda* (1826) by the Duke of Rivas has Julián defeating Rodrigo in single combat. He is then prevented from killing him by an unknown warrior who takes on Julián. During the fight, Julián splits the warrior's helmet, revealing Florinda, who shouts, "Father." Julián flees.

"Florinda" as the Cava's name appears for the first time in a novel by Miguel de Luna in 1592, *The True History of King Don Rodrigo*, which the author claimed was a factual translation from the Arabic. In the 1773 poem "Letter from Florinda to her Father Count Don Julián after her Disgrace" by Don José Cadahalso, Florinda says: "He was the king, and young and loving, / and I a woman, beautiful and unknowing." On the other hand, in an anonymous 17th-century ballad, Florinda states bluntly, "It wasn't love, it was rape."

Pelayo, the Saviour of Spain
(Asturias)

This king Don Pelayo, serving the Creator,
guarded well the land, there was no one greater.
(from Poema de Fernán González*)*

When Chindasvinto, the Gothic king of Spain, died in 653, he was succeeded by his son Recesvinto. Recesvinto died in 672 without a male heir, and the nobles installed Wamba as king. Chindasvinto's daughter had married a Greek named Ardebasto, and their son Ervigio followed Wamba as king. Ervigio had a daughter Cijilona, who married Egica, who was king after Ervigio. Cijilona and Egica's son was Vitiza the Wicked, who was assassinated at the instigation of Rodrigo, the last of the Gothic kings, with the apparent support of the nobles. Vitiza's brother was the traitor Oppas, archbishop of Seville and later of Toledo.

Favila, a son of Chindasvinto, was Duke of Cantabria and Vitiza's captain of the guard in Galicia while Vitiza was living there before he became king. After Vitiza ascended the throne, there was a falling-out, probably because Vitiza coveted Favila's wife, and the king killed the duke with one blow of his staff. Vitiza also blinded and imprisoned Favila's brother Teodofredo, who he saw as a possible threat to the throne. Favila's son, Pelayo, moved to Cantabria to be out of the way of Vitiza, and he went on pilgrimage to Jerusalem.

Thus far history according to Mariana and other sources. But the fantastical tale of Rodrigo and the Losing of Spain needs to be balanced by an equally imaginative and mythic account of the beginning of the Reconquest, and legend, supported by older histories now considered factually unreliable, supplies that.

The Birth of Pelayo

Egica was king in Toledo. Teodofredo was the father of the future king Rodrigo, and his brother Favila was the Duke of Cantabria. Luz was the daughter of the daughter of Chindasvinto, and so the niece of Teodofredo and Favila. Favila and Vitiza son of Egica were in love with Luz. Luz rejected Vitiza's advances because she was in love with

33

Favila, but such was the power of the king's son that Luz and Favila had to keep their love secret. Since they could not marry openly, they pledged their union privately before an image of the Blessed Virgin.

Luz soon became pregnant. She tried to hide the fact, but the palace was buzzing with rumours. The penalty for being an unmarried mother was burning at the stake. Vitiza was unable to accuse her openly, so he waited until she gave birth. Meanwhile, he exiled Favila. As soon as her son was born, Luz wrapped him in a richly decorated cloth and with the aid of a faithful servant placed him in a small ark with a generous amount of money and a note saying that the child's name was Pelayo and he was of noble birth. The ark glowed with a miraculous light as they set it on the currents of the River Tajo with a prayer for the boy's safety.

The Justice of God

Vitiza discovered the birth too late to present the baby as proof of Luz's guilt, but there was enough circumstantial evidence to make a public accusation. In those days, an accused person could submit to the Justice of God in a trial by combat. If the champion of the accused defeated the champion of the accuser, the divine verdict was interpreted as "not guilty". No one in the court could be found to defend the honour of Luz, but Favila arrived in time from Cantabria to challenge and kill the champion named by Vitiza and save Luz from the stake. The couple were then married formally and retired to Cantabria, ignorant of the fate of their son.

The Finding of Pelayo

The blinded and now exiled Teodofredo, uncle of Luz, was living in Alcántara in Extremadura on the Tajo downstream from Toledo. The ark bearing Pelayo was fortuitously caught in the rushes on Teodofredo's property and brought to him, and he raised the child as if he were his own son and had him instructed in the arts of a warrior and gentleman.

With the passing of Egica, Vitiza was crowned king, and all the nobles, including Favila, were summoned to Toledo for the ceremony. Teodofredo brought the boy Pelayo to Toledo and introduced him to the nobles in hope of finding him a position as a page. (One version of the legend gets round the political improbability of Teodofredo appearing in the royal court by making Pelayo's adoptive father a more distant relative, a retired knight named Count Grafeses.) Favila was much taken with the boy's charm and bearing and brought him home to Cantabria. Teodofredo had ordered the rich cloth that lined the ark made into a fine suit, and when Luz saw the young man dressed in the material in which she had wrapped her infant, she fainted. When she recovered, questions were asked and answered, and a joyful reunion ensued.

Legend has thus filled the historical gap in the early life of Pelayo. From here, history and legend are in substantial agreement about the major events.

Covadonga, the Cradle of Spain

Within two years of the invasion, the Moors had solidified their Conquest throughout most of the peninsula and pushed the Christians to Galicia, Asturias and Bizkaia, which remained relatively free of Moorish occupation. Bands of nobles native to the region were joined by those forced from their lands in the south to mount an unorganised and ineffectual resistance.

Munuza was the leader of the Moors occupying Gijón, and Favila, like others, was forced to pay him tribute. About 718, Munuza sent Pelayo to Córdoba on a mission of feigned importance to the welfare of the Christians, and he took advantage of the young man's absence to rape (some say marry) Pelayo's sister, Lucinda. When Pelayo returned and discovered what had occurred, he rescued his sister from Munuza and fled with her to the fastness of the Asturian mountains.

Here he unfurled his banner at Covadonga, also called the Cave of Santa María, 12 miles (20 km) from the sea at Monte Auseva in the Picos de Europa massif near Cangas de Onís. This became his rallying point from where he organised damaging raids against the Moors. Munuza requested reinforcements from Tariq in Córdoba, saying that Pelayo was in revolt. Tariq sent 140,000 men along with Archbishop Oppas, who was instructed to order Pelayo to cease his rebellion. If he refused to submit to Moorish authority, he was to be brought to Córdoba in chains.

When Pelayo learned of the coming invasion, he sent a call throughout the north and assembled a thousand select warriors at

35

Covadonga, and stationed thousands more in the surrounding mountainside. The cave, now a religious and political shrine, is secure from frontal attack. The entrance is narrow and well above ground level, and difficult of access without modern stairways.

The Moorish army arrived through the narrow valley that runs north to Soto de Cangas and camped in front of the cave. Oppas approached and spoke to Pelayo.

"Don Pelayo, you know how the power of the Goths conquered the Romans and the barbarians. But God willed that they should be conquered and their power destroyed. If even King Rodrigo and his army were annihilated by the Moors, what do you think you can do with so few people in that cave? Submit to Tariq, who has never been defeated, and save your life and goods and those of your followers."

Pelayo replied, "You and your brother Vitiza and your sons have awakened the anger of God by your pact with that servant of Satan, Don Julián. God may have punished us Christians for our sins, but He does not wish us to remain subject to the Moors. We are confident that the mercy of Jesus Christ and the Blessed Virgin will liberate us. We may be few, but from tiny seeds grow fields of grain."

Oppas turned to the Moors and said, "This man means to fight to the end. Attack the cave, for only through force will he surrender."

The Moors attacked with slings and arrows and javelins, but God, showing mercy to the Christians who trusted in Him, made the weapons turn back against the Moors. Twenty thousand were killed by this miracle. A standard with a white cross on a red field and inscribed with the name "Jesus" was placed in Pelayo's hand, and where it came from he never knew. An unknown voice cried out, "Arouse your strength; go forth in the name of Jesus Christ, and you will conquer." Wherever the standard was placed in the ensuing battle, the Moors fell before it as if struck by an unseen hand, and they began to flee in panic. The Christians pursued them and slaughtered many.

The survivors fled south over the mountains to the Valley of Liébana on the banks of the Deva, where the mountain collapsed on them and fell into the river. Nearly all were either crushed or drowned. Bishop Sebastián of Salamanca, who blessed Fernán González before his first battle in 925, recorded that even in his day, when the river flooded, bones and weapons of the Moors were recovered.

Oppas was taken prisoner, and Pelayo placed a flaming mitre on his head and threw him off a cliff. Pelayo was proclaimed king. This beginning of the Reconquest is usually dated 722.

On Pelayo's death in 737, his only son, Favila, reigned for two years until he was killed by a bear.

Orreaga
(Navarre)

Cer nahi zuten gure mendietaric Norteco guizon horiec?
Certaco jin dira gure baekaren nahastera?
Jaungoicoac mendiac eguin dituenean nahi izan du hec guizonec
ez pasatcea.

What would they in our hills, these Northern men?
Why come they here our quiet to disturb?
God made the hills intending none should pass.
(from Altabiskarco Cantua – The Song of Altabiskar*)*

In 778, Charlemagne was returning over the Pyrenees to France after ravaging the Basque province of Navarre. The famous paladin Roland was commanding the rearguard when they were ambushed by Basques and Saracens at the mountain pass of Orreaga (Juniper Place) north of the village of Roncesvalles in Navarre. Roland waited too long to sound his trumpet to call for help, and he and the flower of Charlemagne's cavalry were massacred.

In this poetic literary legend by Arturo Campión (1877) inspired by the Basque ballad *Altabiskarco Cantua*, Charlemagne and his army are camped in Espinal, four miles southwest of Roncesvalles, on the road from Pamplona. Orreaga is flanked by the hill of Altabiskar and the Forest of Irati on the east and the hill of Ibañeta on the west. Tomorrow they will march through that pass.

It is midnight. There is no moon, no stars in the sky. In the distance bonfires gleam on the tops of Altabiskar and Ibañeta. The Franks are singing in the town. The wolves howl on Altabiskar. The Basques are sharpening their axes and arrows on the stones of Ibañeta.

37

Charlemagne, deeply worried, is not asleep. Next to his bed his young page is reading an adventure story. Nearby, Roland the brave is cleaning the famous sword Durandarte, while the good archbishop Turpín is praying to the Holy Mother of God.

"My page," says King Charlemagne, "what is that murmuring that breaks the silence of the night?"

"Lord," the page answers, "those are the leaves of the Forest of Irati moving with the wind."

"Ay, dear boy. It sounds like the cry of death, and my heart is frightened."

There is no moon, no stars in the sky. The bonfires now gleam in the middle of the mountains. The Franks are sleeping in Espinal; the wolves howl on Altabiskar; the Basques are sharpening their axes and arrows on the rocky slopes of Ibañeta.

"What noise is that?" again asks Charlemagne. His page is asleep now and does not answer.

"Lord," says the brave Roland, "it is the torrent of the mountain, it is the bleating of the sheep of Andresaro."

"It sounds like a groan," says the king of the Franks.

"So it is," answers Roland. "This land weeps when it thinks of us."

Charlemagne is restless, still awake; the land and the heavens are now without light; the wolves continue to howl on Altabiskar; the axes and arrows of the Basques gleam among the oak trees of Ibañeta.

"Ah," sighs Charlemagne. "I cannot sleep. I am burning with fever. What is that noise?" Roland is asleep and does not answer.

"Lord," says the good Turpín, "pray, pray with me. That clamour you hear is the *irrinzi*, the war-chant of the Basques, and today is the last day of our glory."

The sun is shining on the mountain; Charlemagne has been conquered and is fleeing "with his red cape and black-plumed cap". The children and the women are dancing in Ibañeta. No longer are there foreigners in the Basque Country, and the irrinzi is raised to the heavens by the mountain people.

Santiago
(Galicia)

¡Santiago, y cierra España!
(Christian war cry during the Reconquest)

The apostles James the Greater and John the "beloved disciple" were the sons of Zebedee and Salomé, who is believed to have been the sister of Mary, the mother of Jesus. As Santiago, James is the patron saint of Spain. His support of Christian warriors against the Moors has earned him the title of Matamoros: "Moor-slayer".

After the Ascension, James spent seven years spreading the gospel in Spain, travelling from Andalucía through Portugal to Galicia, thence to Aragón and Cataluña. In the year 40, the Blessed Mother joined him in Zaragoza to help him found a church on the site of the present Basílica del Pilar. The pillar she stood on is kept in the basilica, and part of it is exposed so the faithful can kiss it. Local tradition is firm that this was not a mere apparition. The Blessed Mother came to Zaragoza in person – *en carne mortal* – the only time she is known to have travelled outside the Holy Land.

James returned to Judea, where he encountered the magicians Hermógenes and Fileto, whose tricks and spells attracted those who had been converted to Christianity. Challenged by Hermógenes, James defeated him and his attendant demons, threw his magic books into the sea and converted him and Fileto. In AD 44, Herod Agrippa ordered James's execution. As he was being led by the scribe Josias to the headsman, James cured a paralytic man. Josias was so impressed he asked to be baptised, and both were beheaded together.

James's disciples, Anastasius and Theodore, accompanied by Hermógenes and Fileto, took the body to the coast, where they saw a crewless boat rigged and ready to sail. They put his body on board to take it to Galicia for burial, and the boat sailed off, directed by the hand of God. One of James's followers who wanted to accompany them arrived too late to embark and, seeing the boat sailing away without him, spurred his horse off the dock and into the water. The men in the boat fell asleep, and the boat arrived six days later at Padrón on the River Sar, 12 miles (20 km) from the present town of Santiago de

39

Compostela. The horseman and his horse emerged from the sea just behind the boat, covered with scallop shells. This is one of the reasons that the scallop shell is the symbol of pilgrims to Compostela.

For the scallop shows in a coat of arms,
That of the bearer's line
Some one, in former days, hath been
To Santiago's shrine.
(from "The Pilgrim to Compostella", Robert Southey, 1829)

As James's followers disembarked, his body floated up into the air to the sun. An angel led the followers to where the body landed 12 miles inland, a sign that he was to be buried there. They laid the body on a large stone, and the stone melted as if it were soft wax to conform to the shape of the body.

They were in the kingdom of a powerful woman, Queen Lupa (Wolf), who knew nothing of Christianity and worshipped demons. They went to her sumptuous palace and asked her for enough land to provide a suitable resting place for their master. She sent them to the neighbouring King of Duyo, who was aware of the new religion and hated all Christians. He imprisoned the disciples, but they were freed by an angel. The king's soldiers pursued them into a cave, where the roof fell and killed the soldiers, sparing the Christians.

They returned to Queen Lupa, who had heard what happened to the king's men. She was afraid to oppose the disciples openly and resorted to a trick to get rid of them. She told them to go to nearby Monte Ilcino and bring back the herd of tame oxen they would find there. These were, in fact, fierce wild bulls, which she hoped would kill the Christians. She also knew of the dragon they would encounter on their way. This dragon, with its putrid breath, had devastated the countryside for miles around and left it uninhabitable.

Confronted by the dragon, the disciples made the Sign of the Cross, and it vanished in a puff of smoke. The same sacred sign tamed the bulls, which they yoked to a cart in which they bore James's body to Lupa's palace. Convinced by these prodigies, she relinquished her own palace for a tomb and sanctuary and became a Christian. She is said to be buried with all her treasures beneath A Moa, the peak of the pink granite massif of Monte Pindo, which is known as the Olimpo Celta (Celtic Olympus), near Fisterra.

There were pilgrimages to James's burial site until the third century, when the emperor Vespasian put a stop to them. The location of the tomb was then forgotten until the year 813, when a hermit noticed a star shining brightly over a hill. This led to the discovery of the sarcophagus inscribed with the saint's name and with a decapitated body inside. Since then, Santiago de Compostela has been the third most important Christian shrine in the world, next to Jerusalem and Rome.

> Meu santo Apóstol Santiago,
> este ano alá non vou;
> po-la falta d'o diñeiro
> moita xente se quedou.

> My holy Apostle Santiago,
> this year I'm not going;
> for the lack of money
> many people stay home.

Statues and paintings often depict Santiago Matamoros mounted on a white horse in the act of trampling or spearing a Moor. During the Reconquest, he frequently (38 times, according to one source) led angelic warriors to the rescue of the Christian armies when they were in danger of being defeated by the Moors. His first intervention was in the Battle of Clavijo, near Logroño, in 844 (see next chapter). He was in Coimbra with Fernando I in 1064 and in Mérida with Alfonso IX in 1230. He also took part in the Battle of Otumba in Mexico in 1520 as Santiago Mataindios. Santiago's appearances in the battles of Simancas and Hacinas are recounted in the chapter "Fernán González".

"Cierra España" in the war cry "¡Santiago, y cierra España!" is ambiguous. Sancho Panza asked Don Quijote, "Is it that Spain is open and needs to be closed, or what ceremony is it?" (*Don Quijote II*, 58). Don Quijote affirmed that Santiago had been seen many times in battles attacking and destroying the Moors, but he did not answer Sancho's question. The phrase has been interpreted two ways: "Close Spain (to the Moors)" and "(Warriors of) Spain, close with, ie, attack, the enemy."

41

The Tribute of the Hundred Maidens:
The Battle of Clavijo, AD 844
(La Rioja)

Modern history says this most famous battle took place at Albelda south of Logroño during the reign of Ramiro I's son Ordoño I (850-866), but legend and older histories know it as the Battle of Clavijo with Ramiro as the hero. (Some say the first encounter was at Albelda and the second at nearby Clavijo.) History and legend are otherwise in substantial agreement.

Aurelio, king of Asturias and León 768-774, was forced to pay a tribute to the Moors consisting mainly of servants and peasants. An ensuing revolt was put down, and the tribute continued under Silo, the Christians being too weak to resist. Mauregato (783-788) was the son of a Moorish woman and a Christian man. It may be for this reason that he receives the blame for the annual tribute now consisting of a hundred maidens, half of whom were to be of noble lineage and the other half of common stock. The women were taken to the Moorish capital of Córdoba to serve as wives and prostitutes. This situation persisted through the reigns of Bermudo I and Alfonso II, but when Emir Abd al-Rahman II (822-852) demanded the Tribute from Ramiro I (842-850), the Christians felt themselves powerful enough to refuse. Mariana continues the story.

"Abd al-Rahman sent ambassadors to threaten Ramiro with war if he did not obey. Great was the horror of the people, but greater was the insult of this diplomatic mission, so the ambassadors were dismissed. The Law of Nations served them well, and they were not punished as their mad audacity and unworthy and intolerable demand deserved.

"After this all who were of age in the kingdom were forced to enlist and take arms, apart from some few who remained to work the fields, for fear that if farming ceased the Christians would be adversely affected no less by hunger than by war. Great was the doubt of all, though the action was just, whether they had any hope of emerging with victory. To gain respect and show that they did voluntarily what had been forced upon them, they decided to attack first and rushed to enemy territory, in particular to La Rioja, which was at that time in the power of the Moors.

42

"Battle was joined at Albelda [in 844] with a Moorish army numbering 200,000. The Christians were outnumbered and losing on all sides, and nightfall was the only reason they were not defeated on the first day. That night, Ramiro had a dream in which the Apostle Santiago appeared in a form of majesty and grandeur greater than human. He ordered Ramiro to take heart, because with the help of God he should have no doubt of victory, and that he would be victorious the following day for certain.

"In the morning, Ramiro told his troops about the dream and urged them to lift their hearts and throw off all sadness and hopelessness. The Christians closed with the enemy calling out with loud voices the name of Santiago. This was the beginning of the custom that Spanish soldiers even today [1592] follow to invoke his help at the time they want to attack. ["¡Santiago, y cierra España!"]

"The barbarians were turned by the daring of our forces, something unthinkable for them, as they had already taken us for vanquished. Then terror from the sky suddenly overcame them. The Apostle Santiago, as he had promised Ramiro, was seen captaining our people from a white horse and carrying a sword in one hand and in the other a white flag with a red cross in the middle of it. At this sight, the strength and vigour of our warriors grew, and the barbarians on all sides could not withstand the charge we gave them and were put to flight dismayed. The Christians pursued them as far as the Ebro, and 70,000 Moors were beheaded."

Tradition adds that the indelible hoof prints of Santiago's horse remain stamped on the mountains where he galloped from peak to peak on his way to Clavijo. This event is commemorated by the Feast of the Apparition of Saint James on 23 May, the date of the battle. The annual Fiesta de las Cantaderas (Singers) that takes place in August in León celebrates the ending of the Tribute.

"A Toledan Night"
(Toledo)

Ask a Spanish friend why he looks tired, dishevelled and half-dead, and if he moans, "Una noche toledana (a Toledan night)," you know that he is suffering from a massive hangover. The expression originates in a 9th-century party in which "half-dead" does not adequately describe the condition some of the guests were left in.

One of many realignments of power among the quarrelling Moorish leaders resulted in Emir Al-Hakam taking Toledo from his uncles Suliman and Abdallah. Al-Hakam named Jussuf, the son of one of his generals, as governor of the city. The inexperienced young man lost no time in alienating the people with his capricious and unjust domination to the extent that the disaffected citizenry were soon gathering to stone the castle. The nobles of Toledo marched Jussuf to Al-Hakam and demanded that they be given another governor. The emir consented, and he installed Jussuf's father, General Amrú in his place.

Humiliated by his son's treatment, Amrú decided to avenge himself on the nobles. He bided his time, patiently gaining the confidence of those who had deposed Jussuf until the opportunity arose to take action. This came when Al-Hakam's young son and successor, Abd al-Rahman II, paid a ceremonial visit to Toledo with all his entourage. Amrú ordered a great banquet in honour of the occasion, which the nobles of the city were invited to attend. The castle was specially decorated with pennants and streamers and illuminated for the festivities.

The guests arrived and were greeted with all due courtesy, but once inside the door they were divided into two groups. Some were conducted into the banquet hall, while others – the nobles of Toledo – were led, with apparent respect and honour, to the dungeons, where their heads were cut off. No one in the banquet hall was aware of what was happening beneath their feet.

The following morning, Toledo awoke to the sight of 400 heads adorning the walls of the castle. It is said that the shock of this scene caused a twitch in the face of Abd al-Rahman, which afflicted him the rest of his life.

44

The Jaun Zuria Cycle

The following four stories deal with Jaun Zuria, the first Lord of Bizkaia, and some of his family and descendants.

Jaun Zuria – The Golden-haired Lord
(Bizkaia)

Lémor was the son of Morna, King of Tara, the sacred and royal centre of Ireland. As with all who live in those sun-starved Atlantic islands, Lémor's skin was as white as the snow that from time to time lightly blankets the Hill of Tara in the middle of winter. His hair was the rich gold that the teasing afternoon sun of the short winter days uses to promise a clear day to follow, a promise rarely fulfilled. And the eyes that sparkled in the pale face through the tousled golden strands of hair even on a dull, misty day – they were like the hardy bluebells that sprinkle skylight across the dark floor of the forest. Lémor was the favourite son of the well-beloved Morna, and all accepted him as the future king, when Morna's life would have run its full course.

One day, as King Morna and Prince Lémor and the warrior-heroes set off from Tara, no tears fell from the eyes of the women, and no frowns of anxiety creased the faces of the warriors. For they marched not to war but to the hunt, and the beast they sought, for all his long tusks and sharp bristles, should have been no match for their light javelins and arrows and, if those failed, the heavy war spears. All expected to return safely to Tara, bearing the weight of enough wild boars for a feast.

No sooner had the hunters left the rich, cultivated plains of the royal province of Meath and entered the dense forest than they were swallowed up in the thick clouds that hang low in the hills around Lough Leane. Almost at once, a king of boars rushed in amongst them, savaging the dogs and scattering the men, until each warrior was an island in a sea of mist. If one or two of the younger warrior-apprentices found themselves perched like birds in the trees, it was no shame to them, for the wild boar is the most terrifying instrument of destruction designed by nature.

45

Even the brave Lémor stood with his back to a tree and his war spear butted firmly against it, straining his eyes through the mist for the expected sudden rush of tusked death. Then a trumpet warned Lémor that the beast was coming in his direction, and he fitted an arrow to his bow.

Suddenly, there was a stir in the mist in front of him, and the monstrous head of the boar appeared in the thicket. Lémor sent his arrow flying. The mist closed in again, and a pitiful cry echoed through the forest. But when Lémor ran to the bushes to finish the boar, he heard the cry coming from further away. It was not the sound of a beast in death-agony, but a man.

The cry led him deeper into the mist to where he found his father, Morna, lying on the ground with Lémor's arrow protruding from his breast.

The wise men of Morna's council agreed that the death of Morna was an accident, but they further declared that it was not right for Lémor to assume a blood-stained kingship. They put Lémor and a few companions into a rudderless boat and set it adrift on the sea with provisions for a week, a form of exile that suggests a verdict of not necessarily "guilty" but not completely "innocent" either.

The hardships endured by the band of exiles in the weeks that followed are not told in the story, but they can be imagined. It was long after they had lost any sense of their location, and the days were uncounted since any water but the salt sea had wetted their lips. Land appeared on the horizon, and when they were close enough to distinguish the features of the landscape, they knew that wherever the winds had delivered them, it was not to Ireland.

If they were disappointed, at least it was dry land, with green hills rolling back into the interior, and, miraculously, a fountain burbling in a shady grove of trees. They leapt from the boat as soon as it reached shore and cooled their parched lips with water as cool and sparkling-clear as that which flows through the cave of Santimamiñe, just a few miles from where they had landed in Busturia in the province of Bizkaia in the land of the Basques. And then they slept.

An *etxeko-jaun* (clan chief) of Busturia happened to be watching from the top of a hill. When he saw the exiles approaching the shore, he rushed to their aid, but by the time he reached them, they were already in the sleep of relief and exhaustion. When they awoke and learned what land had saved them from death:

"Iberia!" Lémor said. "The land of our ancestors. Our people came to Ireland from here."

"Through here," corrected the etxeko-jaun. "The Celts came from across the Mediterranean to dominate this peninsula called Iberia, which includes our country, Euskal Herria [the Basque Country]. After a few centuries, they were pushed by the Phoenicians into Galicia in the northwest, and most of them emigrated from there to Ireland. That was not so long ago – a little over thousand years – and the same blood flows in our veins."

Lémor and his companions enjoyed hospitality under the roof of the etxeko-jaun, but it was not long before word had spread among the Euskaldunak (Basque People) that a son of a king was among them. This was a wonder to the fiercely independent Euskaldunak, for they had no lord to whom they gave allegiance. Nor did they recognise any laws apart from those written in the conscience of their elders. And besides the hierarchies of virtue and intelligence and antiquity, there was only one hierarchy among the Basques. They elected a battle leader to lead them in combat whenever their free land was invaded, and for more than half a century that title had rested on the worthy shoulders of Lekobide. He was a descendant of that famous Lekobide who had humbled Caesars and defied the power of Rome, and who was celebrated in the popular songs of the Basques.

Lekobide sent messengers to Lémor, inviting him to make his home with him in the valley of Padura. Padura is a short distance south and east of Bilbao, but you will not find it on the map by looking for "Padura", for this story tells how its name was changed to Arrigorriaga – the Place of the Blood-red Stones.

If Lémor was impressed by the solemn air of majesty that surrounded the venerable head of Lekobide, he was even more taken with the innocent aura of beauty that radiated from the young face of Lekobide's daughter, Argi (Light). Months passed in peace, but south of the Ebro the Moors were on the march. Lémor, good Christian warrior that he was, felt ashamed to sit in idleness while the Holy Cross was being trampled underfoot by the sons of Agar. He wanted to offer his sword arm to Fernán González, the brave Count of Castile, but Lekobide

47

and Argi begged him not to go. And another voice, a new voice deep inside, also held him back.

Lémor occupied himself with battle practice and the hunt. Every time he left Padura for the mountains to follow the wild boar and other game, he found himself turning back to look at Lekobide's house, and every time he looked back, he saw Argi watching from the window. And on his return, he would also see her at the window, as if she had never moved from it.

One day, runners from the mountains arrived breathless at Padura: "Lekobide, a huge army is marching towards Euskal Herria from the south, and they have crossed the cordillera of Orduña. It will be the worse for the Basque people if the *irrinzi* [battle cry of the Basques] is not heard."

These strangers were not the brave warriors of León and Castile who had often planted the Holy Cross over the destroyed tents of the Moors, but base adventurers led by Ordoño the Wicked, usurper of the crown of Sancho the Stout of León. Having been expelled from León, Ordoño planned to establish a new throne in the mountains of Euskal Herria, and install himself on it.

"Sound the war trumpets on the five mountains of Euskal Herria," Lekobide ordered. "Light the signal fires in the hills."

When the etxeko-jaunak from the mountains assembled in Padura to hear the news, they demanded that Lekobide lead them into battle.

"Hand me the coat of armour I've worn," he said, "and the spear of war I've carried into combat for the past fifty years."

But when Lekobide put on the heavy coat, he sank beneath its weight, and when he took the great spear, his arm could not lift it. The brave heart and young soul of Lekobide had forgotten the age of his body.

"Prince of Ireland," he said to Lémor, "you will wear my battle coat and carry my war spear and take my place at the head of the warriors of Euskal Herria. The invaders are led by a prince of the royal blood of León, and it is right and just for a prince to lead our army."

"I am ready to fight against the enemies of the country that has given me welcome and hospitality," Lémor replied, "but I will fight as a warrior alongside the Basque warriors. You must find a more worthy man to lead your army."

The assembled etxeko-jaunak of twenty valleys spoke with one voice, and as they spoke, they invested Lémor with the title he would thenceforth be known by:

"Jaun Zuria [Golden-haired Lord], the free and independent people of Euskal Herria, who have never recognised a lord, will grant you lordship if you will be our battle leader."

But again Lémor declined the honour.

More runners arrived to announce that the invaders had now passed the tree Malastu at Luyando, which marks the border between Bizkaia and the lands to the south.

"Prince of Ireland," Lekobide said. "Lead our army and drive these invaders from our land, and my house will be your house, and I will call you my son."

Lémor glanced at Argi. A look passed between them, and something in her face melted his heart. He put on the armoured coat and took up the heavy war spear.

"Lekobide," he said, "God willing, when this battle is finished, I will sit in your house and hear from your own lips the name of 'son'."

The war trumpets resounded through the mountains, and they were echoed by the yodelling irrinzi from the valleys. Every man who could shoot an arrow, cast a spear or swing a sword or axe poured into Padura in answer to their country's call. The invaders had marched up the long Valle de Ayala from Luyando and were now approaching Padura to personally defy Lekobide, for they knew he made his home there.

Jaun Zuria rode at the head of the Basques into the hills around Padura. Clouds of arrows obscured the sun. Huge rocks hurled by the mighty arms of the Basques rained down on the heads of the hosts of Ordoño, scattering and slaughtering them. The axe, the spear and the sword of the Basque patriots sowed the heads of the strangers like seeds in the slopes of Padura and fertilized the soil with their blood. Ordoño grew desperate.

"Kill the battle leader of the Euskaldunak," he cried, "and victory will be mine."

He sought out Jaun Zuria, and soon the would-be king of the Basques and the son of the king of Ireland met in single combat. It was not long until the great war spear of Lekobide, wielded by Jaun Zuria, pierced the breast of Ordoño, and a roar like that of a wounded lion rang through the Basque mountains.

49

At this, the invaders fled in disorder, and the Euskaldunak pursued them to the foot of Luxa. There, wearied of battle and seeing that the enemy had been driven back across the border and their land was once again free, they lay down to rest and celebrate their victory in the shade of the tree Malastu. Jaun Zuria drove a dagger into the trunk of the great oak and left it there as a warning to other would-be invaders.

More than eleven centuries have passed since the Basques, led by an Irish prince in defence of their homeland, saturated the fields of Padura with the blood of invaders.

Ask in Arrigorriaga – formerly known as Padura – how it came to be called the Place of the Blood-red Stones, and the old people will tell you that for centuries after the battle the stones in the area still bore the stains of the blood shed by the hordes of Ordoño the Wicked.

Go to the parish church in Arrigorriaga and ask who is buried in the stone sepulchre that stands next to the holy water font, and the villagers will say that there lies the body of a prince called Ordoño the Wicked, who thought he could rob the Basques of their independence and make himself king over them, and who was killed by Jaun Zuria, the first Lord of Bizkaia.

Then examine the dusty archives in the church, and if you can read the ancient and eternal Euskara, you will learn from the yellowed pages that in that church the daughter of Lekobide and the son of a king of Ireland were united in marriage.

The Death of Lekobide
(Bizkaia)

Lekobide, the chosen battle leader of the free and independent Basque people for more than fifty years before he passed that responsibility on to Jaun Zuria, had now reached the age of one hundred. One morning he awoke at dawn, knowing that he had come to the end of his days. He awoke his great-granddaughter, Oria, the only remaining survivor of his numerous family in those violent and perilous times, and asked her to help him climb to the top of the mountain that rose above Arrigorriaga.

At the summit, they rested and watched the sun rise in all its brilliance, a sight Lekobide knew he was seeing for the last time, a symbol of the continuation of life of which his great-granddaughter was an example.

Lekobide said, "In a dream last night, I saw my father calling to me with open arms, and I know that this will be my last day on earth. And so I now give my blessing to you and all of your descendants."

This made Oria sad, and she began to cry. Then she asked Lekobide to leave her with some of his profound wisdom, because the Basques put great store in the final words of those who are about to die.

"What are you most interested in?" he asked her.

"I want to know: of all the peoples who are fighting for domination, which one is the chosen people of God, and which peoples will be destroyed, and which will eventually be the dominant one?"

With a serene smile, and speaking haltingly, Lekobide replied: "God did not create humans so that they could destroy each other, but so that they would cooperate to walk the road to happiness and perfection together. I have travelled East and West, and I have seen that all peoples consider themselves the Chosen of God, but they are all wrong. To God, all peoples are not only equal, they all have the same rights and responsibilities."

This answer did not seem to satisfy Oria, because the Basques would not like to hear that they would never be the Chosen People. So she decided to ask Lekobide, "Can you give me some advice that will guide our people after you are gone?"

Lekobide pondered on the virtues and shortcomings of the Basques, whose independent nature meant that they refused to unite under a king. They only agreed to a temporary battle leader whenever the Basque Country was threatened with invasion. The old man and his great-granddaughter remained for some time in silence, until Oria, unable to contain her grief at the imminent death of her people's wisest advisor, burst into tears and threw her arms around him.

With a great effort and in a trembling voice, Lekobide said to Oria, "I am leaving my people a master teacher, one who taught me all I know. Thanks to this infallible master, many things that have for the past hundred years appeared good to me now appear hateful, and what I have seen as unjust I now see as just. My teacher has finally allowed me to have a glimpse of reality."

Lekobide seemed to fall asleep, and Oria begged him to tell her the name of this great master. With the last of his strength, Lekobide whispered, "The greatest and best teacher in life is Time."

With that, the old man breathed his last. Oria began to walk down to the village to tell the people that Lekobide was dead. She repeated his final words to herself slowly, unable to comprehend them.

The Death of Munso López
(Bizkaia)

This is a direct translation from Lope García de Salazar's *Libro de las Bienandanzas e Fortunas* (1474), Book XX.

On the death of Don Zuria, his legitimate son, Munso [var. Muño, Manso, Nunso] López, became Lord of Bizkaia. Serving under the Counts of Castile, he was taken prisoner by the Moors. When his wife heard that, she called Don Íñigo Esquirra ("Left-handed"), her husband's handsome young son by his first wife, and said to him, "Since your father is a captive and won't escape, marry me and we will be Lord and Lady of Bizkaia."

He rejected her proposition, and she left the room scratching her face and saying in a loud voice that he had tried to rape her. When he saw that, he went to the frontier to release his father. Fortunately, he was able to exchange him for a Moor that he had captured. When they arrived home, Íñigo didn't want to go into the house with his father.

"Lord father," he said, "don't believe anything bad about me that they may tell you before you know the truth."

When Munso's false wife saw him, she ran to him scratching her face and told him that Don Íñigo Esquirra had tried to dishonour and rape her. When he heard this, Munso went in search of his son and found him in Meazaur. Íñigo saw that his father did not credit the truth, and he said:

"Lord, because falseness is worth more to you than the truth is to me, I will put the matter to the Justice of God. We will fight, you armed and I unarmed, you with a steel-tipped lance and I with a plain spear shaft."

That was agreed, and so it was done. The blunt end of Íñigo's spear shaft passed straight through his father's armour and killed him, and he is buried there in the church in Meazaur.

The Goat-foot Lady
(Bizkaia)

This is a close translation from the 14th-century Portuguese *Livro das Linhagens* by Don Pedro Alfonso de Barcelos. Similarities between this and the previous story are discussed in the Notes section.

Diego López, fourth Lord of Bizkaia, was a fine horseman, and one day when he was boar-hunting he heard the sweet voice of a woman singing from the top of a mountain. He followed the sound and discovered a beautiful, well-dressed lady, well shaped in every way except that she had one foot that was cleft like a goat's foot. She told Don Diego that she was of high birth, but her name is not mentioned. He immediately fell in love with her, and he told her that he was lord of all the land and asked her to marry him. She accepted his proposal on condition that he would never make the Sign of the Cross in her presence, to which he agreed.

They lived happily and had a son named Íñigo Ezquerra and a daughter whose name is given simply as Doña. They used to sit at dinner together with Íñigo next to Don Diego and Doña next to her mother. One day Don Diego went to the mountains and killed a large pig and brought it home for dinner. As they were eating, he threw a bone on the floor. Suddenly, two dogs appeared, a Great Dane-greyhound crossbreed called an *alano* and a small hound called a *podenca*, and they began to fight over the bone. The little podenca grabbed the alano by the throat and killed it. When Don Diego saw this he took it for a miracle and made the Sign of the Cross, saying, "Who ever saw such a thing? Holy Mary, save us!"

His wife, when she saw this, took hold of the boy and the girl and started to run off, but Don Diego held his son so that she couldn't take him. The woman grabbed the girl and fled through the garden and went to the mountains. The story says that they were never seen again, but that is not completely true.

Years later, Don Diego was fighting against the Moors and was captured and taken prisoner to Toledo. His son, Íñigo, grieved at this, and he asked the people of his land for advice on how to free him. They told him that the only way was to go to the mountains and find his mother, and she would tell him how to rescue his father. He mounted his horse and went alone to the mountains. When he reached the summit, he heard a voice: "Son Íñigo Ezquerra, come to me, for I am the one you seek."

He went to her, and she said, "You have come to ask how to get your father out of prison."

Then she summoned a horse that roamed wild on the mountain, calling it by its name, Pardallo, and she said to her son:

"Pardallo is yours for the rest of your life. He does not need a saddle or bridle or shoes, nor does he have to be fed or watered. Whenever you ride him into battle you will win. Now mount, and Pardallo will take you to Toledo, and he will stop at the door of the place where your father is being held. When you find your father, grasp him by the hand as if you are greeting him, and quickly pull him onto the horse and hold him in front of you. You will be back in Bizkaia before nightfall."

And that is exactly what happened. After some years, Don Diego López died and left his land to his son Don Íñigo Ezquerra.

Guifré the Hairy and Charles the Bald
(Cataluña)

Guifré I el Pelós (Wilfred the Hairy) was the first independent Count of Barcelona 879-897. He was invested in his first counties in 870 by the emperor Charles the Bald of France, son of Louis the Pious and grandson of Charlemagne, the Marca Hispanica in the northeast of Spain being under French control at the time. Although Guifré is well deserving of fame for his military and political accomplishments, time has further turned him into an almost mythic culture hero of Cataluña. This may be due partly to the fusion in stories of his character with his father's, which explains why one version of the blood-striped flag legend, as illustrated by a 19th-century painting, features Charles the Bald's father, Louis the Pious, who was long dead by the time of the incident.

The Dragon

Repelled from the Mediterranean coasts of Spain and France, the Moors retreated to Africa and planned vengeance. They searched the mountains and found a young dragon, part bird and part reptile, and sneaked it into Sant Llorenç del Munt near Barcelona, where it made its home in what is still called Cova del Drac, the Cave of the Dragon. As the beast grew in size and appetite, so its depredations spread wider until it was the terror of the region. Guifré sent a troop of knights to deal with the problem. Dismounting as they neared the dragon's lair, the warriors cautiously and quietly moved to the entrance of the Cave. The dragon first swooped toward the horses, which stampeded in fright and fell into a gorge known as Salt dels Cavalls, Horses Leap. Then the monster made short work of the knights.

Guifré armed himself with a sword and a stout oak log and challenged the dragon, which quickly broke the log in two and grasped Guifré in its talons and started to fly away with him. Guifré searched for a vulnerable spot in the beast's belly and sank his sword in to the hilt, killing it.

The pieces of the broken log had fallen in the form of a cross, for which that place is named, and the dragon's hide was stuffed with straw and put on public display. The skeleton of a large animal, purportedly the dragon but probably a whale, was preserved for many years afterwards.

The Blood-striped Flag of Cataluña

During Guifré's term as Count of Barcelona and other territories, first as a subject of Charles the Bald and later as a sovereign ruler, the Mediterranean coasts of Spain and France were constantly assailed by Vikings and Moors. Guifré was very much to the fore in the defence of the coasts, and when France was attacked one time by Vikings his aid was requested by Charles. Guifré repelled the invaders but was seriously wounded by an arrow. Charles visited him while he was convalescing and asked what reward he would like for his service.

"I want nothing of spoils or riches, lord," said Guifré. "I only regret that we have shed our blood for France, and yet we have no blazon or shield on our flag in recognition of that."

At that time the flag of Cataluña was solid yellow. Charles placed the fingers of his right hand into Guifré's wound and drew four bloody stripes across the flag, and that is the origin of the present-day flag of Cataluña.

The Maimed Maidens of Simancas
(Valladolid)

When Fernán González, Count of Castile, and Ramiro II, King of León, defeated the Moors at Zaragoza, the Moorish leader Abd al-Rahman III raided Castile and León in retaliation. His demand of a tribute of a hundred maidens was rejected, and Moorish and Christian forces met in battle at Simancas on 1 August 939. (See "Fernán González: The Battle of Simancas".)

The legend of the Maimed Maidens may have occurred in this period or at any time during the perilous years when Simancas formed part of the frontier between lands reconquered and tenuously repopulated by the Christians and lands still in Moorish hands.

On one occasion when the people of Simancas, which was then called Bureva, learned that the Moors were coming, seven young women of rare beauty determined to avoid the outrages that were all too common, in fact were to be expected, during such raids. They made a daring pact to cut off their hair and their left hands, and then they smeared their blood over their faces. This so disfigured the women that the Moors wanted nothing to do with them, and so they were saved from a worse fate. They all then entered a convent.

In memory of that brave deed, the *escudo* or coat of arms of Simancas, whose name is derived from "siete mancas – seven maimed women", bears a gold tower on a red field dominated by a star with seven hands.

Ramiro and Aldonza
(León, Galicia, Portugal)

The kingdom of León in the early 10th century encompassed much of the northwest quadrant of the Iberian Peninsula, roughly corresponding to the Roman Province of Galaecia: Galicia, Asturias, León, Burgos, Cantabria, the present Basque provinces of Bizkaia and Álava, and the north of modern Portugal south to Porto. (Castile, subject to León at this time, comprised Burgos, Cantabria, and parts of present-day León, Bizkaia and Álava.)

Fruela II, King of León, died of leprosy in 925 after reigning little more than a year. His nephew Alfonso IV the Monk succeeded him but in 930 abdicated in favour of his brother, Ramiro II, to join a monastery. When Alfonso changed his mind and tried to reclaim the throne in 931, Ramiro put out his eyes and imprisoned him. Fruela's sons posed a threat merely by being Ramiro's cousins and met the same fate. Ramiro is regarded as the greatest of the León kings (reigned 931-951), for under his leadership and with the support of Fernán González of Castile and Queen Toda of Navarre, the Christians consolidated their hard-won territorial gains and pushed back the Moorish frontier.

A cultural note: in medieval Christian society, a man might take a Moorish wife if she converted to Christianity, but it was not acceptable for a Christian woman to marry a Moor.

Most of the action in this story takes place in what is now Portugal, in Vila Nova de Gaia on the south side of the River Douro opposite Porto. The version below closely follows the account in the 14th-century Portuguese *Livro das Linhagens* (Book of Lineages) by Don Pedro de Barcelos.

Ramiro was married to Aldonza (also called Teresa or Tarasia), the sister of García Sanchez II the Trembler, King of Navarre. Their son was Ordoño III, who would succeed his father as King of León. Ramiro had heard about the beauty of a Moorish girl, the great-granddaughter of that Aboalli who had conquered the land in the time of King Rodrigo (711). She was the sister of Alboazar Albucadam, who had fought, and generally lost, many battles against Ramiro, but remained lord of all the land from Gaia to Santarém near Lisbon. During a period of peace between Moors and Christians, Ramiro made a friendly approach to

Alboazar and told him that he had heard about his sister and wanted to meet her. Alboazar agreed to this, and Ramiro and his retinue sailed to Gaia in three galleys. He met the girl and told her he loved her and wanted her to become Christian so he could marry her.

Alboazar objected: "You already have a wife by whom you have children, and you are a Christian. How can you marry twice?"

Ramiro said that this was true, but as he was a close blood relative of his wife, Doña Aldonza, the holy church would grant an annulment.

Alboazar refused to allow the marriage, so Ramiro kidnapped the girl and took her to his castle at Salvaterra de Miño in Galicia, on the modern border with Portugal, and then to his capital, León. He had her baptised with the name Ortiga ("Stinging Nettle"), which at that time meant well bred and educated and possessing all riches.

Alboazar learned that Aldonza remained at Salvaterra de Miño, so he "seized" her and took her to his castle at Gaia. All evidence indicates that she collaborated enthusiastically in her abduction. When Ramiro heard about this, it made him so sad and angry he was like a madman for 12 days. When he recovered, he ordered his son Ordoño and some of his vassals to disguise themselves as galley slaves and prepare five small galleys camouflaged with green cloths. They stood small trees in the boats to conceal their military purpose.

They sailed from Salvaterra down the River Miño to the sea and followed the coast to the mouth of the Douro. A short distance up the river near Sam Joaõ de Furado, at a fishing quarter known today as Afurada, they pulled in to the right bank on the sea-side of the bend in the river, where they lay concealed by a clump of trees out of sight of Alboazar's nearby hilltop castle. Ramiro donned his suit of mail and slung his sword and battle horn around his neck, and he covered them with beggar's clothes and daubed his face with mud so that he looked like a leper. He told his men to follow him quietly and hide in the trees outside the castle, and to be prepared to rush in when they heard him blow his horn. Before dawn, Ramiro went to the castle and sat next to the well and waited.

As was her custom, Aldonza's French serving-maid, Perona, went to the well early in the morning to draw water. She saw Ramiro lying near the fountain, but she didn't recognise him.

"Is Alboazar at home?" Ramiro asked her, disguising his voice.

"No. The master's gone off to the mountains hunting."

"Give me some water, please, for the love of God. I'm too weak to get up."

She handed him the pitcher to drink from. When Ramiro and Aldonza were engaged, they had broken a cameo ring and each kept a half. Ramiro had secreted his half of the ring in his mouth, and now as he drank he dropped it into the pitcher.

When Perona gave the pitcher to Aldonza and she poured out the water, she saw the half-cameo and said to the maid, "Who put this cameo in the cup?"

"No one."

"You're lying."

"There was a sick leper at the well, and I gave him some water. He must have done it."

Aldonza sent the maid to bring the beggar to her room secretly. When Ramiro entered she recognised him and said in an unwelcoming manner, "Ramiro, what brings you here?"

"My love for you."

"You look like a corpse in those clothes."

"Little wonder. I did this for the love I have for you."

"You don't have any love for me. You took Ortiga from here, and you prize her more than me. But get into this closet, and I'll dismiss my maids and servants, and then I'll go with you."

As soon as Ramiro was in the closet, she put a big lock on it.

Just then Alboazar arrived home and came to her room. Aldonza said, "What would you do if you had Ramiro here?"

"I would kill him with great tortures."

"Well, he *is* here. I locked him in this closet, and now you can avenge yourself as you wish."

Ramiro heard this, and when he realised that he had been betrayed by his wife, and that he would not be able to escape without some trick, he decided it was time to call on his cunning.

"Alboazar Albucadam," he said in a strong voice, "I know I have done you wrong, pretending friendship in order to take away your sister who is not of my religion. I have admitted this sin to my confessor, and the penance he gave me was to come and place myself in your power in the meanest way possible. And if you wish to kill me, he ordered that I ask you, since I committed such a grave sin against such a person as yourself and against your people in seizing your sister, while showing

59

you good love, that it would be good if you give me a shameful death in a public place like your communal corral with its grand acoustics. And, because so great is the sin that I have committed that it has been sounded throughout the land, that besides that you should make my death announced by a horn and displayed to all your people. And now I ask that since I'm going to die you call your sons and daughters and relatives and the people of this town and make me go to this corral and set me in a high place and let me play my trumpet, which I have brought for this purpose, until the breath and soul leave my body. Thus will you have your revenge on me, and your children and relatives will be entertained, and my soul will be saved. For you know that your religion says you must do all you can to save the souls even of those of other religions."

He said that to make all Alboazar's children and relatives come to the corral so that he could avenge himself on them, for in no other way could he reach them, and because the corral was high-walled and had but one gateway. Alboazar thought about what Ramiro had requested, and he was seized by compassion. He said to Aldonza, "This man has repented of his sin, and besides, I have wronged him as much he has wronged me. A greater wrong would be done by his death, seeing that he is put in my power."

Aldonza replied, "Alboazar, you are weak-hearted. I know Ramiro, and I know for sure that if you spare him from death you will never escape him, for he is a cunning avenger, as you know. And have you not heard it said that he put out the eyes of his older brother so he could inherit the kingship? And do you not recall how many battles you have fought against him, when he defeated you and killed your warriors and took spoils from you? And have you already forgotten the force he used against your sister? And how, when I was his wife and you brought me away, I endured the greatest dishonour a Christian woman could have? I can't go on living, it's not worth it, if you don't take vengeance on Ramiro.

"And if you don't kill him for the salvation of your own soul, because he is a man of another religion and against yours, and give him the death he's asking you for, you would do him a great wrong if you refused to fulfil the penance imposed on him by his confessor."

Alboazar thought about what Aldonza said, how Ramiro was a schemer and an avenger, and he was afraid of what Ramiro might do if he didn't kill him. He said to Ramiro, "You committed a great folly by coming here. I would not escape death if you had me in your power, so I will carry out what you ask for the salvation of your soul."

Then Alboazar had another thought and said to Ramiro, "If you had me in your power, what death would you give me?"

Ramiro was starving, and he replied, "I would give you a roast chicken and a loaf of fine rich bread, make you eat all of it, and give you a full wine skin and make you drink it."

Alboazar ordered Ramiro to be taken out of the closet, and he made him eat a chicken and bread and drink the wine, for which Ramiro was careful not to appear grateful. Then Alboazar took him to the corral, put him on a large stone that was there, and ordered him to play his trumpet until he ran out of breath. Ramiro asked him to first assemble Aldonza and all the ladies and all his children and relations and citizens in the corral, and Alboazar did that.

Then Ramiro blew his trumpet with all his might, so that his men could hear it, and his son Ordoño when he heard the horn gathered his vassals and brought them to the gate of the corral. Ramiro got down from the rock and went to his son and said, "Your mother is not a Moor, nor are the ladies and damsels you see with her. Keep her for later, for she deserves another death."

He drew his sword and brought it down on the top of Alboazar's head and split him to his feet. There died four sons and four daughters of Alboazar Albucadam, and all the Moors, male and female, that were in the corral. And when the slaughter was finished, there was not left one stone on another stone of Alboazar's castle.

Ramiro took his wife with the Christian ladies and maidens and put them into the galleys. Then he called Ordoño and his knights and told them how it had been with the Queen his wife, and he asked them to help him give her the hardest justice in the world. All heard this in wonder at the enormity of the evil of the woman. The tears gushed from the eyes of Ordoño, and he said to his father, "Lord, it's not suitable for me to speak about this, because she is my mother, but look to your honour."

They got into the galleys and set sail for home. When they arrived at the mouth of the River Áncora just south of the River Miño, someone told Ramiro that the Queen was crying, and he replied, "We'll see about that."

He went to her and asked her why she was crying. She said, "Because you killed that Moor, who was a better man than you." Ordoño said to his father, "The devil is in her. That could be why she ran away from you. What do you want with her?"

(People said afterwards that it was for this offence that Don Ordoño spoke against his mother that the people of Castile rebelled against him and replaced him as King of León in 955 with his brother Sancho the Stout.)

Then Ramiro ordered Aldonza tied to a millstone, and he threw it into the sea, and from that time the place is called Foz de Áncora – River-mouth of the Anchor.

Ramiro went to León, and made his courts very rich, and he spoke with his people and showed them the evil of his wife Queen Aldonza, and he told them that it would be good for him to marry Doña Ortiga, because she was of high lineage. They all with one voice applauded him and wished him good luck. He led a good life and built the Monastery of San Julián and many hospitals, and those who descended from Ortiga were very accomplished.

The Cycle of the Counts of Castile

This section is a family saga about Fernán González and his immediate descendants, and tells how the independence of the County of Castile was won and lost.

Historical Background

During the first years of the Reconquest in the 8th and early 9th centuries, the River Duero formed a natural frontier between the territory occupied by the Moorish invaders and the pocket of Christian Spanish resistance centred on Asturias. A buffer zone extending from Burgos and León south to the Duero became a strategic depopulated no man's land, which was defended by warrior bands led by the counts of Castile, local lords each with a dominion of some ten to 30 towns and villages. They were vassals of the kingdom of León, which at that time incorporated Asturias, Galicia and north Portugal, the whole region roughly corresponding to the Roman province of Galaecia formed in

AD 298. During its brief period of independence between 965 and 1029, Castile would become a democratic federation of republics headed by Fernán González and his descendants and centred on Burgos, encompassing Bizkaia, Álava, Cantabria and part of present León to the Carrión, and extending south to the Duero – "Castile, whose hair is bathed by the Bay of Biscay and whose feet are bathed by the Duero." There was also a protectorate reaching to Sepúlveda called Extremadura, which is variously taken to mean "beyond the Duero" or "extreme duress", alluding to the continual frontier conflicts. This was the new buffer zone or "strategic desert", moved further south.

During the 9th and early 10th centuries, those earlier counts gradually resettled the land under their protection, which had been depopulated after repeated Moorish attacks. Fernán refers to this repopulation in the ballad below: "Those [villas and castles] that were left by my father, I gave to men of great wealth. / Those I won I have given to men who work on the land." The counts proclaimed their territory to be independent of the kingdom of León, and the king, Ordoño II, executed them in 921 for treason. The people of Castile then elected two judges, one civil, Nuño Rasura, and the other military, Laín Calvo. Nuño Rasura's son Gonzalo Fernández, Lord of Burgos, had married Jimena, daughter of Nuño Fernández, one of the counts beheaded by Ordoño; their son was Fernán González. The eleventh-century hero El Cid was descended from Laín Calvo.

Fernán González was the most renowned Christian warrior of the tenth century. His birth date is unknown, but he is said to have fought his first battles (San Quirce and Carazo, 925) at the age of 17, and he became Count of all Castile about 930 at "an early age". His exploits, embellished in the 13th-century *Poema de Fernán González* and popular ballads based on the lost *Cantar de Fernán González* (composed within decades of his death in 970), are matched only by those of El Cid a century later. While the exiled Cid spent his career pushing the Moors back from the frontier and extending Christian control, Fernán's efforts were concentrated on defence: first thrusting the Moors from his family domain of Lara, and then frustrating their attempts to invade and occupy Castile and León, while constantly fighting off incursions from Christian Navarre. His family crest is a castle surmounted by a cross.

Alonso Zamora Vicente, in his edition of the *Poema*, notes: "History and legend are inextricably interlaced in the *Poema de Fernán*

González. ... The Fernán González of the *Poema* is a personage of indisputable epic stature. ... Legend has made him the virtual founder of Castile." A modern historian describes Fernán as "a man of great ambition, indomitable valour and a very sure political vision ... an unscrupulous politician" (Urbel, "Navarra y Castilla ..."). The epic nature of the *Poema*, in which both the well-rounded human personality and the heroic character of Fernán are artfully fused and vividly portrayed, is explained by the fact that its author was a monk at the monastery of San Pedro de Arlanza, which was founded and endowed by Fernán and supported by a *voto* (tax) imposed by him, and where he was originally buried. (He now lies with his wife, Sancha, in Covarrubias.)

The following account of the highlights of Fernán's career does not attempt to distinguish fact from fiction (but see Notes). It is mainly a close translation and paraphrasing of a combination of the *Poema*, prose chronicles that supply missing sections of the *Poema*, and various ballads and early histories, especially Mariana (1592). Anachronisms are likewise ignored. For example, the Moorish leader Almanzor (see separate chapter), who was born in 940 and only rose to prominence as a battle leader after Fernán's death, appears as Fernán's foe in battles as early as 925. Sources do not agree on chronology and dates. The most logical and best supported are followed here.

Fernán González, First Sovereign Count of Castile
(Burgos and elsewhere)

Fernán: from the Germanic *Fredenandus* – "intelligent and daring"
González: from the Germanic *Gundisalvo* – "ever-ready for battle"

"Never in the world was there such a cavalier." *Poema de Fernán González*, c. 1250

"He is the likeness of Satan, and we are his servants." Castilian warriors, tiring of constant battles.

"May Allah curse him." The Moors, whenever they mentioned him.

64

"For the glory of his strength and courage, and in particular for the great steadfastness that he showed in the events in which he took part, he was the equal of any of the ancient leaders and princes." Mariana, *Historia General de España*, 1592

Fernán's Education

The Aragoneses had designs on Castile, and they were aware that Fernán's lineage could make him an obstacle to their plans. But before they could interfere, the child Fernán was "kidnapped" by an *olenzero*. (The olenzero, a charcoal maker, is a stock folklore character common to the Basque Country and neighbouring Castile. "Olenzero" is the name of the Basque Father Christmas figure who brings presents to children.) The mysterious olenzero who took Fernán has been identified as an old knight of good lineage and wise in the ways of warfare named Martín González, but some say he was none other than Saint Eustace, patron of hunters and one of the 14 Helpers in Need, in disguise.

Fernán was reared secretly in the mountains for his safety and trained in the arts of warfare and courtly manners. As he matured and increased in ability, Martín González often told the other knights and counts that the boy would become the light and mirror of Spain. When his older brother, Rodrigo, was killed in a battle with Moors, Fernán returned to society vowing vengeance: "I'm not a wild bear to be living in the mountains. If I don't leave here, nothing is worth a fig."

Battles of San Quirce and Carazo - 925

About the time (whether before or after is uncertain) he was proclaimed Count of all Castile by the Castilians, Fernán led a small number of warriors to victory in a surprise attack against a superior force of Moors – 100 horse and 1500 foot soldiers against 7000 – on 16 July 925, the feast day of the 4th-century child martyr Saint Quirce. Sebastián, Bishop of Salamanca, accompanied the Christians. In thanksgiving and to commemorate the victory, Fernán founded a monastery on the site of the battle southeast of Burgos near his home town of Lara. He gave two-thirds of the booty collected after the battle to the monastery, and the other one-third to his warriors. Fulgencio, successor to the founding abbot, attended Fernán on his deathbed.

65

Victories followed at Muño and Castrojeriz (*xeriz* means "bloody" in Arabic), between Burgos and León, and the Moors fled from his forces after a battle at Salamanca "with loosened reins".

When Fernán easily took a well-fortified castle from the Moors at Carazo two leagues (about six miles or ten km) from Lara in a surprise night assault, Abd al-Rahman III, king of Córdoba and Miramamolin (virtual king) of Moorish Spain, ordered Almanzor, his battle leader, to deal with this new threat to his power. (Modern historians say these battles and the Battle of Lara took place before Fernán's election as Count, which they date 930 or 931.)

Battle of Lara - Saint John's Eve 925

Almanzor sent messages to the parts of Spain under his dominion and gathered seven legions of warriors at Lara, close to the sites of Fernán's two previous and several future battles. (A legion consisted of some 300 cavalry and 5000 foot soldiers.) Though full of confidence after a succession of quick and unexpected victories, Fernán's warriors were dismayed to see the overwhelming number of their opponents. Gonzalo Díaz suggested buying off the Moors with tributes, advising wise cowardice rather than honourable shame. He made a long speech that can be summed up: "Don't you see that the danger in this encounter is the threat to all Christianity, because the battle is in your territory. If we win the advantage will be small; if we lose, the province will be conquered by fear. It will be stripped of forces and fall into the power of the enemy."

Knowing that Gonzalo had expressed the fears of many of the company, Fernán rebutted his argument point by point, ending with: "Don't let their odds frighten you, for three lions can do more than 10,000 sheep, and 30 wolves can kill 30,000 lambs."

Then he mounted his horse and rode out of the encampment alone to hunt for wild boar in the mountains above the River Arlanza near Vasquebañas. He soon sighted a boar and pursued it to a wild place where it lived in a cave, but it went past the cave and hid behind the altar of a hermitage so thickly covered with ivy that it blended in with the surrounding vegetation. San Pedro was the name of this holy place, and it was inhabited by three monks who managed to scrape a poor living by hard work. They were part of a secret network of secluded

66

hermitages and monasteries that kept open a system of communication and refuge in territories occupied by the Moors.

Fernán dismounted and followed the trail into the hermitage. When he discovered that the boar had sought safety in a holy place, he took it as a sign from Heaven and began to pray: "Lord, pardon the intrusion. Holy Mary, I didn't know this was a sacred place, and I didn't come here to make an offering or as a pilgrim, but if you don't help me, Castile will be lost to the Moors."

As he finished, one of the monks, Pelayo, approached and asked who he was and what was his mission. Fernán said that he had left his army to hunt the boar, which had led him here, and he explained the predicament he and his men faced. Pelayo invited him to spend the night, and Fernán never enjoyed finer hospitality, in spite of the poor accommodation and coarse bread.

The following morning, Pelayo told Fernán that he would be victorious against Almanzor and would live to fight and win many battles, although he would be taken prisoner twice. In the coming battle, he would be in good hands. A mighty sign would appear which had never been seen before and would frighten his army, but when Fernán reassured them they would lose all fear. "And after you win the battle, don't forget us hard-working monks here in this poor hermitage. Our life here is of no account, and if God does not send us some consolation, we will have to leave this place to the snakes."

"Don Fray Pelayo," Fernán replied, "don't worry. Whatever you ask, I will give you. I won't forget the hospitality I enjoyed here. If God grants me victory, I will donate my share of the battle spoils to this place. Besides, when I die I wish to be buried here. I will build a church of stone with my tomb inside, and a hundred monks and more will live here, serving God and obeying his orders."

Fernán left the hermitage happy and satisfied and returned to Lara, where his warriors greeted him warmly. He told them all that had passed between him and Pelayo, and that he had never enjoyed such hospitality since he was born.

The following day, Fernán moved his troops into position at the Ford of Cascajares. For every Christian there were a thousand Moors, but although the Christians were very few, they were brave of heart. The Moors rejoiced to see such a small force opposing them and thought they would win easily. Their masses covered the hills and plains. They

67

advanced blowing trumpets and shouting until the hills seemed to shudder. Fernán was troubled and his people frightened at the sight.

One of Fernán's cavaliers, Pero González of Puente de Hitero, impulsively mounted his horse and spurred it to the top of a hill to launch a solo charge against the enemy. Suddenly, the ground opened in front of him, and he and his steed plunged into the gaping chasm to be swallowed by the earth as the hole closed over him.

The Christian warriors were stunned. "This is for our sins," they said. "It's a sign that God has abandoned us. We'd better turn back. It's obvious that God plans to aid the Moors. How can we fight against them?"

"I'll tell you what it means," said Fernán. "That is the sign promised by Don Pelayo. If the earth, hard and strong as it is, gives way before one of you, how can the enemy resist all of you? I see your hearts weakened before people of little worth. Have no fear. I know one thing: they will be conquered, and I will be the conqueror. Now let's see how well the Castilians can protect their lord."

Fernán ordered the banners unfurled, and he led his 300 cavaliers and hundreds of foot soldiers into the charge, shouting, "Castile!" No one who encountered him was left standing. The Castilians protected their lord, and Almanzor and his surviving troops soon fled the field, abandoning their tents and possessions. When the Christian warriors searched the Moorish camp, they found more wealth than any of them had ever seen before: silks, cups of fine gold, satchels filled with gold and silver, swords, coats of mail, and armour. Ivory chests full of jewels and other precious objects they carried to Pelayo's hermitage and laid on the altar, giving thanks to God for the victory and the bounty He had granted them. Fernán ordered that his portion, a fifth of all the spoils taken, be given to Pelayo, as he had promised. Then they all went to Burgos to rest and treat the wounded.

Some time after this and unbeknownst to Fernán, Almanzor learned of Pelayo's part in his ignominious defeat, and he came to the hermitage and ordered Pelayo and the other two monks beheaded. The martyrdom of Saint Pelayo (Pelagius) is officially dated 926.

Battle of Gollanda (or La Era Degollada) - 926

While Fernán had been serving God by defeating the Moors, Sancho I Garcés "Abarca", King of Navarre, had taken the opportunity to overrun Castile. When Fernán heard reports that Sancho's warriors had plundered Castilian towns, he sent Gustio González, the grandfather of the Seven Princes of Lara, with a message to Sancho. Fernán accused Sancho of siding with the Moors by fighting against Christians and demanded that he leave Castile in peace and make reparations for the damage he had caused. Sancho replied that Fernán was ill-advised to challenge him, that Sancho was going to come and deal with him, and that no matter where Fernán sought to escape, in towers or in the hills, Sancho would find him even if he had to pursue him as far as the sea.

Fernán gathered the greater and lesser nobility, landed gentry and other high-born gentlemen, as well as the commoners, and said: "Friends, we have done nothing against the Navarros to merit this treatment. Now they have threatened us and we must attack them."

The Castilians marched toward Navarre, meeting Sancho's army just across the Castile border in La Rioja at Valpierre, also called Gollanda and La Era Degollada, between Nájera and Bañares, where the Stone of the Count still stands to commemorate the battle. The Castilians lowered their lances and charged, Fernán in the fore. When the armies clashed, the clang of swords, the splintering of spear-shafts and the splitting of helmets echoed through the hills. The Count and the King searched the battlefield until they sighted each other and closed in single combat. So fierce were the blows they rained on each other that their armour was ineffective, and Sancho soon fell mortally wounded. Fernán also fell to the ground with a serious lance-wound in his right side. He called for his men, and they had to cut their way through the enemy to rescue him. They thought he was dead at first, and they fought to avenge his supposed death until they chased the Navarros from the field with their dead king. Then they retired and headed back toward Lara.

The Count of Piteos and Tolosa (some say Poitiers and Toulouse in France), a relative of Sancho, gathered the fleeing warriors of his counties and marched back toward Castile to avenge Sancho's death. When Fernán learned of this, though not yet recovered from his wound, he ordered his men to turn around to intercept Tolosa. His followers objected: they had been fighting day and night and had not had time to rest – the devil never rests, and he wants them to be like him – and besides, if Fernán died, Castile would be lost. Fernán should go home to recuperate for at least ten days from his serious wound and let his men go home and rest. If he didn't do this, he would surely be killed or captured.

Fernán responded: "A day lost is never recovered. Those who want to accomplish great things can't eat and sleep whenever they wish. When we speak of the great heroes of the past – Alexander, Judas Maccabeus, Charlemagne, Roland, Turpín, Solomon and others – we never count the days and nights they spent achieving their great deeds, only the deeds themselves. If they had not done those great things, they would have been forgotten. The stories of heroic exploits will be told to the end of time."

His men did not know how to respond to this, and Fernán ordered the march to begin. When they reached the Ebro they found the Tolosans in possession of the ford, but the Castilians charged and forced them back. Fernán soon killed the Count of Tolosa in single combat. He honoured his dead rival by removing his armour with his own hands as if he were his brother. He wrapped the body in a richly decorated mantle that he had won in battle with Almanzor and washed him and dressed him in fine silk. Fernán and his men fashioned a coffin with gilded nails and lined it with red cloth, and he told the Count's vassals to bear their lord home with dignity.

Battle of Hacinas - 926

Almanzor, the foremost Moorish battle leader of the 10th century, rankled at his defeats at the hands of Fernán. He sent out a call for reinforcements to Morocco and all North Africa, Turkey, the East, unnamed places and throughout Spain. Hardened warriors – 130,000 cavalry and countless foot soldiers – with their bows and ballistas, camels, forges and mills crossed the Mediterranean to assemble in Andalucía. From there they filled the roads and pathways like swarms of locusts until they descended on Fernán's home territory of Lara and set up camp at Hacinas south of Salas de los Infantes. Fernán and the Christians, numbering a mere 450 cavalry and 15,000 princes, gathered at Piedrahita de Muño north of Salas.

70

Disheartened at the sight of the overwhelming number of his enemy, Fernán stole away to visit Pelayo at his hermitage at nearby San Pedro de Arlanza. To his dismay, he learned that Pelayo had been buried eight days earlier. He went into the hermitage, where he fell to his knees and wept and prayed: "Lord, I see the Christian kings becoming vassals of the Moor Almanzor for fear of death. They threaten me when I alone stand against this sin and error. Now the Moor has come from over land and sea, hoping to get rid of me. As far as I know, I have never done anything against you. Help me now, Lord, by conquering and killing them with your power. I can't defend Castile without your aid."

Fernán then kept vigil before the altar until he fell asleep. Pelayo appeared in a robe lucent as the sun and called his name: "Are you asleep or why are you so quiet? Awake and go, for a great enemy opposes you and your people are waiting for you. The Creator has ordered what you have asked for. A great slaughter will be made against the Moors and you will win the field. I will be with you, and so will Santiago, as the Lord has commanded. Also, a troop of angels in white armour will come, each one bearing a white banner with a red cross, at the sight of which the Moors will lose heart."

A loud voice, not that of Pelayo, woke Fernán: "Arise and go, Count Fernán González. Almanzor awaits you. Divide your troops into three parts. You take the smallest group into battle from the east, and you will see me with you there. Order the next group to enter from the west, and Santiago will be in that rank. Send the third group in from the north. If you do that, you will defeat Almanzor and all his power, but don't agree a truce or make peace. The battle will last three days. If you want to know who I am, I am Saint Millán, sent by Jesus Christ."

(Millán, a 6th-century saint born in Berceo, was considered the patron of Lara. There is a carving of Millán on horseback killing Moors in the church of San Millán de Yuso.)

Fernán returned to find his camp in uproar. The men accused him of deserting them when they were most in need of his leadership and said he wasn't worth a chestnut. He told them of his visit to the hermitage and the vision he had, and reminded them that if they did not win the coming battle they and their children would live as slaves of the Moors.

"The barbarians rely on their greater numbers. We rely on justice, the strength and ability of our warriors, and most of all on the help of God."

71

They responded with one voice: "Lord, your word is our command, and let anyone who flees lie with Judas in Hell."

Fernán arranged his troops the following day. Gonzalo Díaz, who had previously questioned the wisdom of the defence of Lara, was in the front rank with Gustio González. Gustio's son, Gonzalo Gustios, father of the Seven Princes of Lara, was Fernán's captain. Two of Fernán's nephews called "the butcher wolves" gave the first blows of the battle. Don Lope de Bizkaia, great-grandson of Jaun Zuria, was there, along with the flower of Old Castile, Burgos, Treviño, Castro, Asturias, and Moorish-occupied Soria. The first day of battle was indecisive.

As they were praying that evening, the Christian warriors saw a strange and wild thing in the sky. A fiery serpent appeared in the air, red as a rose and screaming. It seemed to be wounded, and the fire that came from it illuminated the armies. They thought it had come to burn them. No one was so brave that he wasn't frightened, and they all fell to the ground in fear. They woke Fernán, but by the time he arrived the serpent had vanished. He knew that the devil was behind it to make the Christians retreat. He explained that the Moors were guided by the stars, not by God. They learned enchantments from the devil to turn the clouds and winds. Some Moor had magicked up the serpent to scare the Christians, but it had no power to harm them. Christ is the only power in the world, and He is the only one we should believe in. The troops, calmed by his words, went to sleep, and they woke at cockcrow to hear Mass and go to confession in preparation for the second day of battle.

When he wasn't standing like a castle, Fernán attacked like a lion, forcing gaps in the enemy's ranks wherever he went and bloodying the ground around him. He and a giant of a king from Africa attacked each other with lances. Both were wounded. The king fell to the ground, and Fernán's horse was killed under him. At the end of that day, neither the Christians nor the Moors had won.

On the third day, after arming themselves and praying for success, the Christians lowered their lances and charged once more against the Moors with cries of "Santiago" and "Castile". Though fatigued, all were invigorated for battle, and their swords and lances were not idle. A king of Africa cleft the helmet and head of Gustio González to the eyes. Then Fernán challenged the king and sliced through his armour, bringing him to the ground dead. But the battle was going against the Christians. A quarter of their forces had been killed, and many horses wandered with empty saddles. Fernán raised his eyes to Heaven and cried: "Lord, I don't want to leave this battle. I wouldn't if I could. I will only stop fighting if they kill me. But then Castile would be left leaderless and would be at the mercy of Almanzor, and death would be better than that. Lord, why are you angry with us? Would you destroy Spain for our sins? Why have you deserted us?"

A loud voice called out, "Fernán of Castile, I have brought you a great band of warriors."

He looked around to see who was speaking and saw Santiago in the air with a company of warriors all armed like himself and carrying white banners with red crosses. No man born had ever seen such a mighty host. Almanzor and all his retinue suddenly halted in their tracks, terrified at the spectacle. Almanzor said, "This cannot be. I thought surely I would kill or capture the Count of Castile today, and now he comes against us with these people."

The Christians, heartened by the sight of the heavenly reinforcements, lost all fear and launched a fresh attack. The Moors turned and fled from the battlefield. The Christian forces pursued them for two days and nights all the way to Almenar in Soria, slaughtering and capturing a great number before they returned to Hacinas.

The Christians prepared to carry the fallen to their home places to bury them, but Fernán suggested that it would be better to inter them at San Pedro de Arlanza rather than bring the reminder of the grief of their loss to their homes. They would never find a place of greater honour, and he had ordered that he himself be buried in the monastery when his days were done. All agreed, and the Christian dead were buried there. The Moors were buried in a mass grave at Hacinas, where the mound was still pointed out as late as the 18th century. Some say that the white banner with the red cross borne by the celestial knights in this battle was the origin of the Cross of Calatrava.

The Battle of Simancas - 939

Ramiro II, king of León and Asturias, was so impressed with Fernán's fighting prowess that he accompanied him on his next excursion to conquer the Moors of Zaragoza. To avenge this defeat, the Moorish king Abd al-Rahman III attacked the borders of Castile and León and then sent messengers to demand an annual tribute of a hundred maidens. Similar tributes had been forcibly rejected in the Battle of Clavijo in 844 and the Battle of the Fig-trees in Galicia in 791.

Fernán's response was: "You will have to seek elsewhere for the maidens, because they won't be Castilians."

Taking heart from Fernán's stance, Toda Aznar, regent for her 14-year-old son, García Sánchez, King of Navarre after his father's death, said, "You will have to seek elsewhere for the maidens, because they won't be Navarras."

Ramiro of León told them, "You will have to seek elsewhere for the maidens, because they won't be Leonesas."

But the messengers were not able to seek elsewhere, nor did they ever return to Abd al-Rahman with the replies, for they were decapitated. When the Moorish king learned of their fate, he attacked Simancas in force on 1 August 939. His "All-powerful Campaign", as he termed it, consisted of 100,000 warriors – 200 Moors for every Christian.

Ramiro said, "I truly have no advice to save us, but I commend myself to God, who guides the afflicted, and to a glorious body that lies there in my land, the lord Santiago, who is interred in Galicia [Ramiro's kingdom included Galicia], who converted that people who were then unbelievers, and who worked many miracles through our Lord."

Fernán and García (or Toda on García's behalf) responded: "There is another saint also devoted to miracles who lies in our land, Saint Millán, who helps us in battle."

Before the battle, the Moors saw the Christians kneeling in prayer and assumed that they were prepared to submit. However, the prayers were answered dramatically.

According to Mariana, "All were convinced that two angels on white horses were seen in the vanguard, and that the battle was won with their help, a thing that is not normally reported or even invented except in significant victories such as this was." A ballad in Sepúlveda's 1584 collection reports that two knights came charging on white horses, beautiful in their audacity, and together with the Christians pursued the Moors, who were put to flight with great terror, for it seemed to them that there were now a thousand Christians for each Moor. These knights were Santiago and Saint Millán.

More than 70,000 Moors were killed in the slaughter. Abd al-Rahman, leaving behind his Koran and golden coat of mail, escaped on

74

foot with 20 unhorsed cavalry. There was an eclipse of the sun the following day. The dead were piled in a cave, and 40 wolves were brought from Asturias to devour the corpses. In Córdoba, 300 cavalry officers were held responsible for the panic of the Moorish army and were crucified. Fernán gave a *voto* (a tax on the villas and towns of Castile) to the monastery of San Millán in the Mountains of Oca, earlier called San Félix, in thanksgiving for "benefits", ie, booty won in the battle, and the victory over the Moors. The significance of this battle was recognised throughout Europe.

The Convent at Silos - 954

There followed successful campaigns at Laguna, Ormaz, Osma, Sandoval, Madrid (which was a village at the time), and Silos. Washington Irving recounts this story in *Spanish Papers*.

The Moors had occupied Silos, and when Fernán attacked to retake the town he entered the chapel of the Convent of San Sebastián on horseback, thinking it had been converted into a mosque. When monks approached to thank him for ending the Moorish occupation, and he realised it was a Christian place, he removed the shoes from his horse in contrition and nailed them to the floor.

"For never," said he, "shall they tread any other ground after having trodden this holy place." From that day, we are told, it has been the custom to nail the shoes of horses on the portal of that convent – a custom which has extended to many other houses.

Near Silos on the road to Lara hoof prints of his horse can still be seen in a rock.

The Battle of San Estévan - 955
(Of Pascual Vivas and the Miracle that Befell Him)

In 955, Ordoño III, King of Asturias and León, and Fernán González, Count of Castile, combined forces to counter a Moorish incursion into their territory. The Christians were camped at San Estévan on the River Duero, and the Moors were 12 miles (20 km)

75

upriver at the fortress of Gormaz near El Burgo de Osma between Aranda de Duero and Soria.

Fernán and his knights attended first Mass in the church at San Estévan on the morning of the battle. One of their number was Pascual Vivas, a brave and especially pious man, who had made a vow that whenever he went to Mass, he would not leave the church until all the Masses for that day were finished. When the first Mass was over and all the other warriors trouped out to the battlefield, Pascual Vivas remained in the church. The battle took place at the nearby Ford of Cascajares, and he could hear the sounds of battle during the many Masses that followed. His squire stood outside the door of the church holding his master's warhorse and waiting to assist him in donning his armour, puzzled that Vivas did not join his comrades in the fighting.

By the time the Masses were finished and Vivas was about to leave the church, the battle was over and the Christian knights were returning victorious. He was afraid to leave then, thinking he would be considered a coward for missing the battle. Seeing his horse outside the church, his comrades entered and congratulated him, saying that the victory was due to the prowess of his arm. They told him that Fernán González wanted to see him to offer his own congratulations.

Vivas thought they were mocking him for having missed the battle, but he was forced to follow the other knights to the Count, who also praised his valour in the battle. He was now sure they were making fun of him, and he admitted that he had remained in the church in fulfilment of his vow and had not taken part in the fighting.

Now the other knights thought he was joking. "But of course you were there," one said. "I was next to you when you took a blow on the shoulder that pierced your armour."

The armour that Vivas had not worn and the armoured horse he had not ridden in the battle were brought to him, and dents and holes and scrapes were pointed out and the blows that had caused them were described by those who had witnessed them. Friars at the monastery explained that an angel had taken the place of Pascual Vivas so he could remain faithful to his vow.

The same story, first published by Alfonso X the Wise in his *Cantigas de Santa María* (1277), is told about Fernán Antolínez in the service of Count Garcí Fernández, son of Fernán González, in the 978 Battle of San Estévan de Gormaz. Washington Irving, in *Spanish*

Papers, explains the duplication: "Fray Antonio Agapida [Irving's composite 'source'] has no doubt that the same miracle did actually happen to both cavaliers; 'for in those days,' says he, 'there was such a demand for miracles that the same had frequently to be repeated.'"

However, local tradition gives another explanation. The battle took place on Easter Sunday, and Garcí Fernández congratulated Fernán Antolínez with the words: "Because of you we have had a happy day, Easter [*Pascual*]. May you live [*vivas*] many years." The epitaph on the tomb in the church of Nuestra Señora del Rivero, where Fernán Antolínez is buried and where he attended the Masses, reads: "Here lies 'Vivas Pascual', whose weapons fought while he was attending Mass."

Fernán Aids Sancho's Revolt - 955

Ramiro II arranged for his son and heir, Ordoño III, to marry Fernán's daughter Urraca. On Ramiro's death, Ordoño became king in 951. In 955, Ordoño's brother Sancho I the Stout led a successful revolt, aided by Fernán and García Sánchez, King of Navarre. Ordoño repudiated (divorced) Urraca, telling Fernán that if he wouldn't accept him as king, he would not have him as a son-in-law. (Urraca later married Ordoño IV the Wicked, and following his death she married Sancho II Garcés Abarca of Navarre.) Fernán's aid in bringing Sancho to the throne helps to explain Sancho's curious tolerance and respect for his headstrong and independent-minded vassal in their subsequent dealings, in the face of his queen's implacable hatred of Fernán. But Sancho's tolerance had its limits.

The Sale of the Horse and the Goshawk - 958

Sancho I the Stout was king of León and Asturias 955-958 and 960-966. (Ordoño IV usurped the throne 959-960; see below.) Fernán won the independence of Castile from the kingdom of León and Asturias in 965 by force of arms and, finally, through a trick, which began with the sale of the horse and the goshawk to Sancho in 958. The 14th-century anonymous ballad "Castilians and Leoneses", still popular and widely anthologised, describes the relationship between Fernán and Sancho, in which Fernán wasted no opportunity to insult and ridicule his liege lord.

77

Between León and Castile, a row had broken out,
The Count Fernán González and King Sancho the Stout.
They called each other whore's sons, and sons of traitors bred.
Their swords were in their hands; their cloaks were all in shreds.

A 15-day truce had been forced on them by monks. During the truce, Fernán coming from Burgos and Sancho coming from León met at opposite sides of the Ford of Carrión, the informal border between León and the not-yet-independent Castile. Sancho was riding a mule because he was so fat no horse could carry him. His men said they would cross first. Fernán's men said, no, they would go first.

While the King was smiling, his mule turned right around.
The Count spurred on his horse, which started with a bound.
The King was soaked and spattered with water and with sand.
The King spoke out with passion, the smile gone from his face,
"Good Count Fernán González, that was a disgrace.
If 'twere not for that truce the monks have made me swear,
Your head from off your shoulders I'd take without a care,
And with the blood that flowed, I'd dye this river red."
The Count said, "I can see, you're well decorated.
You ride on a fat mule, I on a graceful steed.
You wear a formal tunic, I a coat of steel.
You wear a golden cutlass, a lance is in my hand.
You bear a royal sceptre, I a sharp javelin.
You wear scented gloves, I wear gloves of mail.
You with a festive bonnet, I with a battle helm.
Your hundred men ride mules; my three hundred are knights."
The monks said, "Gentlemen, please. You promised not to fight."

Sancho returned to León to plot the destruction of the cheeky count and his insubordinate county. Fernán had pointedly been staying away from the royal court, an additional and ongoing rebuff on the part of a vassal. Sancho sent a messenger to Fernán, ordering him to attend court. To openly disobey the royal command would be more serious than mere words of insult: a declaration of disloyalty verging on rebellion. His response to the messenger is known as "Good Count Fernán González" and is frequently anthologised with "Castilians and Leoneses". In it,

78

Fernán refers to the above-mentioned repopulation of the buffer zone by the earlier Castilian counts.

"I have no fear of the king, however many his men.
I have villas and castles, all at my command.
Some were left by my father, others I won myself.
Those that were left by my father, I gave to men of great wealth.
Those I won I have given to men who work on the land.
If they had only one ox, I gave them another in hand.
When their daughters got married, I gave them a wedding trousseau.
Every morning at daybreak, they say a prayer for my soul.
They don't do that for the king; Sancho deserves it not.
He only increases their taxes, while I reduce them to naught."

Fernán prayed for guidance as usual – "Lord God, help me to gain a prize for Castile" – and it seems likely that the prayer was specifically for the success of the plan he had worked out. Suspecting that Sancho had not forgotten their past differences and fearing a trick, Fernán arrived at León with a massive escort. He was dressed in all his finery and mounted on a magnificent Arabian steed that he had captured from Almanzor, and he carried a fine goshawk the likes of which were not to be found anywhere in Spain. Sancho and his barons advanced to the edge of town to greet him with pomp and honour, and Fernán was received enthusiastically by all the people. But there was one person who considered him an enemy: Sancho's wife, Queen Teresa, who figures in the next story.

Sancho was greatly taken with the horse and the goshawk, and he asked Fernán to sell them to him. Fernán replied that they were not for sale, but if Sancho wanted them he would give them to him. This was a subtle insult. It was for a king to give such a fine gift to a vassal, not the other way around. Sancho, undoubtedly sensing the insult and not wishing to be under obligation to his vassal, persisted: he would not accept them as a gift but he insisted on buying them for a thousand silver marks.

Seemingly reluctantly, Fernán agreed, with the condition that if the thousand marks was not paid when the debt was called in, the price would double each day until payment was made. Sancho agreed to this condition, and the contract was written down and signed by both of them and by witnesses. The conclusion of this story, seven years later, will be told in the proper sequence of events.

Fernán Allied with Sancho - Campos, 958

Abd al-Rahman III invaded the district of Campos near Palencia in León. The Moors sacked towns and robbed the countryside, carrying off goods and livestock, and besieged Sahagún. Great were the laments, as fathers and sons, grandfathers, and mothers with babes in their arms were slaughtered. Sancho asked Fernán for assistance. Although Sahagún was far outside his own territory, Fernán was still a vassal of León and subject to this sort of conscription, and so he sent a call throughout Castile and brought a great army to Sancho's aid.

Without hesitation, the good Count swooped on the invaders like a starving eagle in a hunt. When the Moors heard the battle cry "Castile", they wished they were in Córdoba. Those fortunate enough to be able to flee did so, and Abd al-Rahman cried out, "Blessed be Mahomet if I escape from this." He escaped and lived for another three years.

The enemy who survived were sent back to their homes, leaving their acquisitions behind in Campos, and the Castilians returned to theirs. Sancho was well pleased with the outcome, but the devil was in his queen, Teresa, the daughter of the Navarre king, Sancho Abarca, who had been killed by Fernán 32 years earlier. She continued to plot Fernán's downfall, and to this end she sowed discontent among the Leoneses, who became convinced that they were furious with Fernán and embarrassed by his intervention and the way he had showed them up in battle. The Castilians would not be invited to court for another three years.

Payment Demanded for the Horse and the Goshawk - 958

Fernán evidently felt that this was a good time to ask for payment for the horse and the goshawk, which he had sold to Sancho the Stout for a thousand silver marks. Sancho did not pay and would procrastinate for seven years, and the matter was left in abeyance for the time being.

Fernán and Ordoño IV the Wicked in Revolt - 959-60

Sancho the Stout was so called because he was so fat no horse could be found to bear his weight. In order to be credible as a king and battle leader, and perhaps so he could ride the fine steed he had recently purchased from Fernán, he decided to reduce his bulk. His mother-in-law, Toda of Navarre, the most important mover and shaker behind the scenes at that time, was the great-aunt of the Moorish king Abd al-Rahman III. She asked him to order his personal physician, the famous Hasday ben Shaprut, to cure Sancho's obesity with a vegetarian diet. She paid her grandnephew with frontier castles. So in 958, Sancho set off for Córdoba to undergo the slimming regimen.

The magnates (wealthy landowners) of León took advantage of Sancho's absence to rise in rebellion, aided by Fernán, and they installed Ordoño IV, son of Alfonso IV the Monk, on the throne. He was described by a 20th-century historian as "not handsome nor valiant nor intelligent". This was Ordoño the Wicked, also called the Hunchback, who figures anachronistically in the story of Jaun Zuria a century earlier. Fernán's daughter Urraca, divorced by the now deceased Ordoño III, married Ordoño IV. When word of the usurpation reached Sancho in Córdoba, he appealed to Abd al-Rahman for help. The Moorish king "felt honoured to have in his hands the ability to make peace or war, to make and unmake kings", according to Mariana, and he sent his battle leader Almanzor to sort out the problem.

Ordoño quickly fled to Asturias without trying to defend himself, was expelled by the Asturians, and ended up eventually in Córdoba, where he died in 962. Fernán (imprisoned at this time in Navarre; see next episode) and the magnates capitulated, and the now-slimmed Sancho regained his throne in 960.

Fernán and Sancha of Navarre - 960

Sancho's wife, Teresa, was the daughter of Toda Aznar and Sancho Abarca of Navarre, whom Fernán had killed in the Battle of Era Degollada in 926. Her brother was García Sánchez, Sancho Abarca's successor to the throne of Navarre. García had a daughter named Sancha. Teresa, "a woman of fierce spirit", according to Mariana, hatched a plot to avenge her father's death. Fernán's first wife, Urraca, being dead, Teresa invited him to marry Sancha. García, who knew nothing of Teresa's machinations at this time, was harrying Castile. Fernán warned him, then attacked and defeated him with the aid of Lope of Bizkaia, great-grandson of Jaun Zuria. Peace was made, and Fernán announced his coming wedding with Sancha. The Castilians welcomed the news as a way to assure a lasting peace with Navarre. Meanwhile, Teresa sent a letter to García:

"To my honoured brother Don García of Navarre from your sad and loving sister Doña Teresa. You well remember the death at the hands of Count Fernán González of our beloved father, Don Sancho King of Navarre, a true, honoured, noble and virtuous king whom I loved above all. If I were king, as you are, I would avenge our father's death. Now you have the opportunity, for I have invited the Count to marry your daughter, Sancha. He will come to Navarre unsuspecting and unguarded. You can capture and kill him, and thus will our injury be set right."

García was delighted to cooperate. He put on a friendly face and arranged with Fernán to meet him just inside the Navarre border at Cirueña, not far from Valpierre, where Sancho Abarca had been killed. They agreed that each was to be accompanied by five unarmed men. When Fernán arrived like a lamb to the slaughter, he was confronted with García and forty men better prepared to give battle than to celebrate a wedding.

Seeing himself entrapped, Fernán prayed, "Holy Mary, save me, for I have been betrayed." Then he cried out, "It's the end of the world for me. This is what Pelayo warned me would happened." Defenceless with no shield or lance, Fernán took refuge in the church of San Andrés and sent his men home. At nightfall, García, unwilling to attack a holy place, offered to spare Fernán's life if he would give homage to him. Fernán agreed, but such an unreasonable deed weighed heavily on God, and a loud voice like a peacock was heard, and the altar split from top to bottom. The result can still be seen today, and well it should, for such a despicable action should never be forgotten.

Fernán was put in chains and imprisoned in Castroviejo, some 12 miles (20 km) away, to the southeast of Nájera. All Castile mourned and dressed in black when they learned that their Count lay in solitary confinement in Navarre. The Moors took advantage of Fernán's imprisonment by attacking Gormaz, San Estéban and Osma, and they reinstalled the no longer stout Sancho on the throne of León.

A count from Lombardy (some say Normandy) on a pilgrimage to Santiago de Compostela stopped in Castile to call on Fernán, who he knew by reputation but had never met. When he heard about the Count's imprisonment, he went to Castroviejo, bribed the guards, and visited him in his cell to hear the story from his own lips. Then the Lombardian asked to see Sancha, who he discovered was a lovely young woman.

"My lady," he said, "there is no malice or evil in your nature, but the Castilians hold you responsible for the misfortune of their lord, Fernán González, because it is for love of you that he finds himself in this predicament. Without his leadership against the Moors, the Christians will be defeated, and your name will be cursed like that of the Cava. It is in your power to save his life, and if you don't it will be your fault that he is lost. In that way you are the most powerful woman in Spain. If you decide to marry him, you will also be the most fortunate, for he is a fine man."

The Lombardian continued on his pilgrimage to Compostela, and Sancha sent a trusted messenger in secret to Fernán, who she had never met before. The messenger returned to report: "The Count tells me that he is in deep distress and that you are the only one who can help him escape, if you so wish." And she added: "I beg you, Princess, go to the Count and help him. Don't abandon such a man. You will have committed a great sin if he dies."

"Well, I tell you," said the Princess, "I am unfortunate for so many evil things happening to me at once, but that will soon change. I'll go to the Count and do something. His strong love has conquered me. I'll risk going to see him and baring my heart."

Fernán was moved frequently so that the Castilians would not be able to find and rescue him, and the 12th-century *Crónica Najerense* says he was being held in Tubía when Sancha visited him. Having bribed the guards, she arrived at the prison cell, which was like the den of a wild animal. Fernán said, "What are you doing here?"

She said, "Good Count, this is a good love. A woman will forget her family to go with a lover who is the most important thing in the world to her. You have suffered much for my love, but I beg you not to worry anymore, for I will get you out of here, but you must promise that you will pledge yourself to me and never leave me for another woman. If

83

you don't do that, I will leave you here and you will never escape, and it will be your own fault."

Fernán said to himself, "If only this could happen," and he promised the princess that they would be husband and wife forever if she did what she said she would do.

"Let's go, then," said Sancha. "Everything is prepared."

Easing their way with the Princess's money and authority, they stole away at night, avoiding the nearby Camino de Santiago, and went by way of an evergreen oak forest. Fernán, dragging his chains, was barely able to walk, and she had to assist him up the slopes. At dawn, they hid in a thick copse on a hilltop to await darkness.

Meanwhile, an evil archpriest – an inspector-general priest with wide-ranging powers – was hunting nearby with goshawk and hounds, an activity prohibited by canon law. The hounds picked up the scent of Fernán and the Princess and burst into the copse, surprising the pair. When the archpriest discovered them, he was as pleased as if he had taken Acre and Damiata single-handed. (These were Christian victories over the Saracens in 1249, about the time of the composition of the *Poema de Fernán González*.)

"So, traitors, here you are," said the archpriest. "You can't get away. You'll never escape King Don García. You will both have an evil death to die."

"For the love of God," said Fernán, "if you keep our secret, I'll give you one of my richest cities in Castile for you and your descendants forever."

The evil archpriest, full of cruelty, had no mercy.

"If you wish to keep this a secret, leave me alone with the Princess so I can have my will of her."

This wounded Fernán more than a spear-thrust, and he said, "You demand great pay for a little work."

But the Princess, being clever and artful, went to the archpriest and said, "I'll do what you want, so that we don't lose our lives and Castile. But not here where the Count can see us. Take off your clothes and leave them here with the Count, and we'll go out of his sight."

The shameless archpriest was delighted to hear this. He stripped, and when they had moved away from Fernán, the archpriest opened his arms to embrace the princess. Such a strong and resourceful woman had never been seen before. She grabbed him with a head-hold and threw him to the ground, saying, "Now, traitor, I'll get even with you." Fernán took a knife from the archpriest's clothes and, dragging his chains, crawled to the evil archpriest and stabbed him, and so they both killed him.

They took the archpriest's mule and clothes and his goshawk and struck the main road for Castile, the Camino de Santiago that runs from France to Compostela by way of Burgos. Meanwhile, Nuño Laínez and other loyal followers of Fernán had been searching for him and had vowed not to return home until they found him. They had made a stone statue of their lord and were carrying it with them in a wagon, giving homage to it and kissing its hands as if it were Fernán in the flesh. Setting off from Burgos, they arrived at Arlanzón on the first day. The next day they crossed the wild Mountains of Oca and reached Belorado on the Camino de Santiago, where they stopped for the night.

The following morning, the Castilians had just travelled a league from the town when Fernán and Sancha, approaching from the opposite direction, saw the strange procession in the distance. They left the road and took cover.

"What will we do, lord?" said Sancha. "Those are either my father's men or Almanzor's."

But when the company came closer they could see by the men's standards that they were Christians, and not from Navarre but Castile.

"Don't worry, lady. They are my people bearing my escutcheon. You will be their countess, and they will kiss your hand."

They came out of hiding, and when the Castilians recognised their lord, they were overjoyed, and they ran to him and embraced him and kissed Sancha's hand.

"Princess Doña Sancha," they said when they heard what had happened. "You were born in a good hour, and we welcome you as our lady. We don't know how to thank you for what you have done for us. We were dead, and now we are alive again thanks to you. We Castilians are your happy captives."

They returned to Belorado and found a blacksmith to remove Fernán's chains, and then went on to Burgos, where Fernán and Sancha were married. The wedding feast was not yet over – it had started only eight days previously – when news came to Fernán that his new father-in-law, García Sánchez of Navarre, had attacked Castile.

85

Fernán called up his warriors, and after a short but fierce battle, from which many horses departed with empty saddles, Fernán saw García in the middle of the battlefield. He called on him to meet in single combat. They charged with lowered lances, and Fernán gave García such a blow that the blade of his lance broke through García's shield and armour and pierced his flesh, and he fell to the ground. Fernán took him prisoner and ordered him to be put in chains, and he refused offers from the Navarros to exchange him for hostages.

After a year (Mariana says three months), the Countess Sancha pleaded with the Castilians: "You know how I rescued your lord, Fernán González, from the prison in which my father, King Don García, had placed him. Now the Count seems like a villain to me, for he refuses to release my father, and the Navarros are angry with me because of this. I ask you to beg the Count to give my father to me, and I will be forever grateful. This is the first favour I have ever asked of you. Ask the Count – no, demand of him – that he release my father."

The barons were won over, and with one heart they went to their lord and petitioned for García's release. Fernán replied that although it was a serious matter, if it was their wish he would be happy to grant it. He ordered the king's chains to be struck off, and he sent him back to Navarre.

When García arrived back in Estella, his capital, he called a meeting of his barons and said, "You know how I have been dishonoured by Fernán González and all his county. My dishonour is yours. I will be avenged or die." Once again the Castilians and Navarros met in battle in Valpierre, and as before Navarre was defeated.

Fernán Imprisoned by Sancho - 961

Queen Teresa continued to plot vengeance against Fernán. She told Sancho to order Fernán to attend court in León to discuss weighty matters pertaining to the realm, of which Fernán and Castile were still vassals. Perhaps mindful of the unresolved debt for the horse and the goshawk, Sancho was happy to cooperate, and to this command was added the threat that if Fernán did not come, Castile would be confiscated. Fernán told the Castilians of his suspicions and commended the care of his son, Garcí Fernández, to their care if he was killed or imprisoned by Sancho, but he obeyed the command, taking with him only seven knights.

This time Sancho did not come to the city limits to greet him, and there was no friendly welcome as before, which Fernán took as a bad sign. When Fernán knelt to kiss the royal hand, Sancho withdrew his hand and accused him of insulting him by avoiding the court for three years. Fernán replied that since the battle in Campos the Leoneses had taken against him, and it was for that reason, not out of disloyalty, that he stayed away. Then he reminded Sancho of the debt he owed for the horse and the goshawk. Sancho ordered him thrown into prison in chains.

When the Castilians learned that their lord was a prisoner, they grieved as if they were faced with death. The Countess Doña Sancha, when she heard the news, fell to the ground in a faint and lay as if dead for the rest of the day. When she came round, they said to her, "Don't worry about the Count or about yourself. We'll rescue him, whether by force or by art or some other way."

However, after much discussion they could not hit upon a strategy that seemed feasible. But because the human heart is constantly stirring and planning until it accomplishes its desire, and so makes light of difficulty, for great love conquers all things, the Castilians had such a strong desire to release their lord from prison that their hearts told them what was best to do. (All sources strongly imply that credit for the scheme and its implementation should go to Sancha.) It came to this.

Five hundred well-armed knights swore by the Holy Evangelists that they would accompany the Countess to try to rescue him. They left Castile by night, and, avoiding the main roads, they took to the mountains and out-of-the-way valleys so that they would not be discovered. When they arrived at Mansilla near León, where Fernán was imprisoned, they prudently parted from the Countess and hid on a high mountain above Somosa. The Countess Doña Sancha, wearing a pilgrim's food pouch at her neck and carrying a pilgrim's staff, went to León with only two knights.

She sent a message to her uncle, King Sancho, saying that as she happened to be passing by on pilgrimage to Santiago de Compostela, she would like to take the opportunity to visit her husband. Sancho was delighted to receive her, and he came with a large retinue a league out of the city to greet and welcome her as an honoured lady and his niece.

They proceeded into the city, and Sancho went to his palace and she to the prison to see the Count.

When she met her husband, she embraced him with tears streaming from her eyes. Fernán told her not to worry, as suffering was all God wanted for all mankind, kings and nobles alike. Sancha sent a message to the king, saying that she knew that she was asking a lot, but would he be so kind as to order her husband freed from his chains for the night, as a fettered stallion could never make foals. Sancho said, "By God, that's true," and he ordered the chains to be struck off.

And so the Count and the Countess spent the night happily together. They arose before daylight the next morning, and, following Sancha's plan, they exchanged clothes. When they arrived at the prison gate, with Fernán dressed in Sancha's clothes and Sancha hiding behind him in the darkness, Sancha told the porter to open it. The porter, having been warned by Sancho of the Countess's talent for jail-breaking, said, "Lady, the king told us to make sure all was well with you." She said, "For God's sake, porter, you won't get any reward if you keep me here talking so that I can't continue my pilgrimage."

When the porter heard the voice of the Countess, thinking it was coming from the figure dressed in her clothes, he opened the gate. Fernán went out, and Sancha stayed inside behind the gate, hidden in the shadows so the porter couldn't see her. Fernán followed his wife's instructions and soon met her two knights with her horse. He mounted, and the knights led him to Somosa, where the rest of the company greeted their lord's safe arrival with great cheer.

When Sancho learned that Fernán had escaped and by what trickery his niece had got him out, he thought he had lost his kingdom, but he did not wish to do wrong against the Countess. He went to see what she had to say.

"Lord," said Sancha, "I arranged to let my husband out of prison because I could see that he was miserable. I did it because I had to. And after taking such advantage of your civility, I had to do it well. Because I have done the right thing, nothing bad should befall me. Now you, lord, must act as a good lord and king and treat me as the daughter of a king and the wife of a high-born noble, and you don't want to do anything bad to me, because I am a member of your family, and anything you do to dishonour me will be a dishonour to you."

Mariana, who calls Sancha "a manly female of resourceful genius", reports that she went on to say that Sancho should pardon her as a person of royal blood, that she couldn't be held to blame for doing what was necessary to free her husband, that what she had done was just, even praiseworthy, or at least pardonable, and that the main virtue of kings is to raise the unfortunate and fallen.

Once Sancho recovered from his chagrin and Sancha's torrent of argument, he said, "Countess, you have done a good thing like a good lady, which will be recounted to your advantage forever. I will order my servants to take you to where the Count is, so that you will not have to spend another night away from him."

This was done, and when Fernán saw Sancha he rejoiced and realised that God had had mercy on him, and they returned to Castile.

Independence for Castile - 965

Fernán sent a message to Sancho to bring to his attention that payment for the horse and the goshawk was now long overdue. Sancho ignored him, and Fernán harried the lands of León and appropriated livestock. He also withheld the tribute payable by a vassal to his liege lord, and he ordered the landowners of Castile to do the same. When word of Fernán's depredations and Castile's withholding of tribute reached Sancho, he demanded payment. Fernán said he and Castile would pay the tribute when Sancho paid for the horse and the goshawk. The debt was now seven years old.

Sancho sent his steward with a thousand silver marks, but Fernán reminded him of the terms of the sale: the price was to double each day that payment was in arrears. When the steward returned without a receipt, Sancho's financial experts began to work out the amount accumulated over seven years. They soon ran out of paper and calculated that there was not enough money in all Europe to satisfy the debt. Sancho was dismayed. He regretted his impulsive purchase and feared he would lose his kingdom. He consulted with his counsellors, and they advised him to grant independence to Castile in exchange for the cancellation of the debt, "for the Castilians are such good and strong men and such fine upholders of justice."

Fernán was well pleased with the bargain, for it meant that he never again would have to pay tribute or kiss the hand of any man in the world. However, the independence of Castile ended with the assassination of his great-grandson, Count García Sánchez, in 1029, which is related in the chapter "Widowed Before She Was Wed".

Fernán After Death

The Battle of Las Navas de Tolosa in Jaén Province, 16 July 1212, was a turning point in the Reconquest, when a Christian coalition headed by Alfonso VIII of Castile and including Pedro II of Aragón and Sancho VII of Navarre broke the power of the Moors, though outnumbered nearly two to one (100-150,000 to 60-80,000). Before assembling his army in Toledo, Alfonso visited Santiago de Compostela to pray for success, and he heard a blind man sing:

> He who visits Santiago
> and not the Saviour
> venerates the servant
> and not the Lord.

By this he understood that he was to go to Oviedo and pray at the Cathedral of the Holy Saviour. After he had done that and retired for the night, two mysterious hooded visitors demanded to see him. They identified themselves as Fernán González and Rodrigo Díaz El Cid, and they promised him victory in the coming battle. It was reported that during the battle two unknown warriors dressed in black, who refused to give their names, were seen in the midst of the Christian army causing great slaughter among the Moors. They disappeared when the fighting was over.

Citing his source as Bishop Sandoval, Washington Irving tells the following story in *Spanish Papers*. When King Fernando III the Saint attacked Seville, he took with him some bones of Fernán. As Fernando entered the city on 23 November 1248, "great blows were heard to resound within the sepulchre of the count at Arlanza, as if veritably his bones which remained behind exulted in the victory gained by those which had been carried to the wars." There is a tradition that his bones stir on the eve of great national events.

Garcí Fernández and the Traitor Countess

In an evil day and an hour of woe
Did Garci Ferrandez wed!
One wicked wife he has sent to her grave,
He hath taken a worse to his bed.
(from "Garci Ferrandez", Robert Southey, 1801)

Some modern commentators attribute the achievements of Fernán González not so much to fighting prowess and divine aid as to personal charm, political astuteness and pure luck, especially in his choice of wives. His son Garcí Fernández, second sovereign Count and self-styled Emperor of Castile, failed to inherit any of these virtues except that of personal charm. His tenure as Count saw the weakening of the unity and resolve of the Castilian counts, his son in revolt, civil war, and the loss of territory to the Moors, and he died through the treachery of his (perhaps second) wife. He was especially unfortunate in his dealings with women in spite of, or perhaps because of, his physical attractiveness. He was known as Garcí of the White (or Beautiful) Hands, and he had to constantly wear gloves to avoid having women fall helplessly in love with him when they saw his hands, which were evidently quite unsuitable for the wielding of weapons.

Modern historical accounts report that Garcí Fernández (938-995) was married only once, to Ava de Pallars y Ribagorza, from whom he had two children, Sancho and Elvira. The wedding took place some time between 958 and 961, and among Ava's dowry were a sword of pure gold worth 5000 sueldos and a gold cup worth 5100 sueldos. (Compensation for a man's death was 500 sueldos.)

The most dramatic – and perhaps legendary – events of Garcí's life are recounted in ballads from as early as the 12th century under the title of "The Traitor Countess", in which only the form of treason leading to his death agrees with dry modern history. Mariana's 1592 *Historia General de España* follows the narrative line of the ballads, which were generally taken as fact by earlier historians, including Alfonso the Wise in his 13th-century *Estoria de España*. The following account is based on the ballads and Mariana, who cautions: "Many take all this for false ... The truth – who can know?"

Shortly after Garcí succeeded his father as Count in 970, a French woman named Argentina passed through Castile with her parents on pilgrimage to Santiago de Compostela. Garcí met her and was instantly enchanted by her elegance. He bared not only his beautiful hands, but also his enamoured heart, and he asked her parents for her hand in marriage. After six years of a childless union, Garcí fell ill and was confined to bed for some time. Mariana says that "because Garcí was ill in bed, or for the loathing she had for him, or because she was homesick, she went back to France with a French count who was returning from Compostela; so say our stories."

When Garcí recovered from his illness, he vowed to avenge his honour. He and a squire, disguised as pilgrims, travelled on foot to the sanctuary of Our Lady of Rocamadour in France near where his wife and her lover were living. Garcí made cautious inquiries and learned that the French count had an exceedingly beautiful daughter named Sancha by a previous wife, and he looked for a way to meet and speak with her.

Meanwhile, Sancha, who hated Argentina and felt rebellious towards her father, said to her servant: "I can't bear this anymore. You have seen the beggars who stand at our gate for the food we give them. Go and watch carefully and see if there are any gentlemen among them, and if you find a suitable one bring him to me, because I want to talk to him."

The servant watched the beggars for several days until she noticed Garcí Fernández and saw that although he was poorly dressed he had a noble bearing. When she saw his white hands, which were the most beautiful she had ever seen, she knew in her heart that he was a gentleman. She took him aside and asked if he was of noble blood.

"My blood is more noble than that of the lord whom you serve," he replied.

The servant reported this to Sancha, who ordered him to be brought to her. When he arrived in her room, she said, "I beg you to tell me why you have said that you are of greater nobility than the lord of this land, who is my father."

"I am in your power," said Garcí. "You hold my life and death in your hands. I'll tell you who I am if you promise that it will never be known through you."

She promised, and he went on: "I'll tell you the truth and I won't lie. I am Count Garcí Fernández of Castile. Your father has done me great wrong by taking my wife from me and bringing her here. I have made a vow not to return to my land until I have killed them both. To fulfil that vow, I have dressed as you see me so that no one will recognise me and prevent my revenge."

Doña Sancha was delighted to hear this, for she had been seeking a way to achieve the same result.

"Lord," she said, "what reward would you give to the person who provided you with a way to accomplish what you have said?"

"I'll marry you and take you to Castile, where you will be Countess and lady of my land."

They spent two nights together in her room. Some say they were married then, while others report that they married later in Burgos. Sancha laid out her plan to Garcí. She gave him a knife, tied a string to his foot, and concealed him under the bed of her father and Argentina. She told them she loved them so much that she couldn't bear to be apart from them even for one night, and she begged to be allowed to spend the night with them in a separate bed in their room. This was agreed. When she saw that they were asleep, she tugged on the string to alert Garcí. He crawled out from under the bed and cut off the heads of the guilty couple.

Garcí and Sancha returned to Castile, where Garcí announced to his people that he had fulfilled his vow of vengeance, and he triumphantly brandished the heads as proof. Sancha was welcomed as the new Countess of Castile. They had two children, Sancho García and Elvira.

However, establishing a power base south of the Pyrenees was only the first step in Sancha's wider scheme: to realise a childhood dream and marry Almanzor, who was the virtual king of Moorish Spain at this time.

To further her ambition, Sancha set about weakening the defences of Castile. When her son, Sancho, came of age, she instigated a revolt with him at the head, which led to civil war. Then she opened secret negotiations (and perhaps more personal relations) with Almanzor and told him to expect a signal from her when the time was ripe for him to attack. He was to wait in the castle at Gormaz until he saw heaps of straw floating down the river Duero. For several weeks, Sancha fed Garcí's warhorse with bran instead of barley, with the result that the horse looked fit and sleek but would be unable to bear his master in battle. Sancha persuaded Garcí to allow his troops to go home for a rest (to spend Christmas with their families, according to versions that place his death in December). Then she gave the signal.

The battle took place at Piedrasalada between Langa and Alcozar east of Aranda de Duero on 18 May 995. With a disabled horse and facing impossible odds, Garcí was seriously wounded and captured, and he died on 25 May in Medinaceli, where Almanzor himself would end his days seven years later.

The Traitor Countess and her Son

Garcí Fernández's son, Sancho I García, succeeded as Count of Castile. This was an obstacle to Sancha's plan to marry Almanzor, because she felt she needed to own substantial property in order to bring a suitable dowry to the marriage. Presenting Castile to her intended would suffice. She prepared a poison to rid herself of her son. One of her servants observed this and told her lover, who was Sancho's steward, who in turn warned his master. When Sancha offered her son a drink, he suggested, with feigned gallantry, that she sample it first. This she refused to do. Sancho insisted, putting a dagger to his mother's throat. She drank the poisoned beverage and fell down dead.

Sancho later repented of his action, and he built the Monastery of Oña in honour of his mother. The *Crónica de Veinte Reyes* explains that *mioña* was the word used in Castile for "lady", and since the Castilians had taken Sancha as their lady, that was the name, minus the "mi", the Count put on the monastery.

The steward who gave Sancho timely warning of the poison was Sancho Espinosa Peláez. The Count appointed him and his relatives as his household guard, and that family, the Monteros of Espinosa, continued to perform that office for succeeding counts and later for the kings of Castile.

The daughter of Garcí Fernández, Elvira, married Bermudo II the Gouty, king of León. Ironically, in view of Elvira's mother's (perhaps legendary) childhood ambition, Elvira and Bermudo's daughter, Teresa, was given in marriage to Almanzor to safeguard León from attack. One of Elvira and Bermudo's two sons was Alfonso V, king of León.

94

"Widowed before she was wed"

García Sánchez, great-grandson of Fernán González, was the fourth and last Count of an independent Castile. In 1017 at the age of one, he succeeded his father, Sancho García son of Garcí Fernández. In 1029, the Castilian nobles arranged a politically motivated marriage for him with Doña Sancha, the beautiful sister of Bermudo III, King of León. Bermudo was married to García's sister Teresa at the time.

The 13-year-old García travelled with a great entourage from Burgos to León for the wedding, accompanied by his brother-in-law King Sancho Garcés III of Navarre and his retinue. (Sancho Garcés was married to García's sister Munia.) Along the way, they attacked the castle of Fernán Gutiérrez at Monzón de Campos near Palencia, which was surrendered to them by its infirm owner after a brief struggle. They made camp in Barrio de Trobajo near León while they waited for Bermudo to arrive from Oviedo. Doña Sancha was already in León, along with García's sister Teresa. Eager to meet his bride-to-be, García took an unarmed escort of 40 men and continued on to León, leaving Sancho and the Navarros behind.

Many years previously, Fernán González (some say it was García's father) had dispossessed Count Vela of his lands in Álava, and from that time the Vela family had been enemies of Castile. The Vela brothers, Rodrigo and Íñigo, had been watching for an opportunity to avenge their family's misfortune. When they got word of García's journey, they set off for León, where they knew he would be accessible and vulnerable. When García arrived, they went out to greet him and kiss his hands and ask that their family's lands be returned to them, saying that they would gladly become his vassals. García was pleased to grant their request, and they kissed his hands again.

García then went to meet his intended bride, and they spent the day together taking such great pleasure in each other's company that they found it painful to part. Doña Sancha said to García, "It was not wise of you to come to León unarmed. You never know who is your friend and who is your enemy."

"I have done no wrong to anyone," said García. "No one has any reason to wish me evil."

"There are those in León who would do you wrong," said Doña Sancha.

Meanwhile, the Vela brothers discussed how to kill García. "The Castilians are fond of the sport of *tablados* [throwing javelins at a target]," said Íñigo. "We'll erect a tablado in the street, and when García's escort gather to compete, we can kill them all."

They set up the tablado, and when the competition started they closed the gates of the city so that the Castilians would not be able to escape and no aid could reach them, and they ordered their followers to kill them. When the slaughter began, García heard the commotion and went into the street to see what was happening. The Velas' men seized him and brought him to the brothers. García pleaded for his life and promised land and wealth to the Velas if they would release him. Rodrigo considered this a fair bargain, and he suggested they accept the offer and later eject García from Castile. But Íñigo objected:

"You should have said that before we killed all those knights. We can't leave things the way they are."

Doña Sancha learned that the Count was in the hands of the Velas, and she went to them and begged them to let him go and kill her instead. One of the conspirators, Count Fernán Laínez, gave her a blow with his fist. Powerless, García could do nothing but call them dogs and traitors, and the Velas stabbed him to death with javelins. Doña Sancha flung herself weeping on his body. Fernán Laínez grabbed her by the hair and threw her down the stairs.

Word came to Sancho Garcés of Navarre of these events, and he marched to León with his army, but they were unable to enter the closed gates. He demanded that the Velas deliver García's body to him, and they threw it from the top of the wall. Sancho took the body to the Monastery of Oña, where García's father and grandmother were buried.

The Velas then besieged the castle of Monzón. Fernán Gutiérrez surrendered without a fight and invited the brothers to dinner. The brothers assumed that Fernán would be on their side against García's people because García had taken his castle, but Fernán secretly sent an appeal for help to Sancho Garcés. Sancho arrived and quickly defeated the Velas, burning them alive as traitors to their lord. Fernán Gutiérrez surrendered his castle to Sancho. Fernán Laínez, however, managed to escape disguised as a page and fled to the mountains of León. Sancho then married his son Fernando to Doña Sancha. But Sancha – "widowed before she was wed" (Mariana) – said that she would not allow the marriage to be consummated until she had been avenged on Fernán Laínez, who had participated in the assassination of her husband-to-be and had struck her and thrown her down the stairs.

Sancho initiated a search, and Fernán Laínez was seized and brought before Doña Sancha so she could exact justice with her own hands. She took a knife and cut off the hands that had helped to kill García and had struck her, the feet that had enabled him to commit such crimes, the tongue that had plotted treachery, and finally she cut out the eyes that had seen his lord die. Then she ordered that he be dragged on a sledge through all the cities and towns of Castile and León accompanied by a crier to announce who he was, so that all could see what punishment was meted out to the man who had killed the Count of Castile.

The Seven Princes of Lara (or Salas)

A minor challenge between boastful young men, compounded by injured female pride, leads to violence resulting in death, revenge, treachery, and counter-revenge. Based on real people and historical events between 974 and 995, this legend is a restrained epic in miniature in which the staples of tragedy are woven together in a character-driven headlong dash to the inevitable conclusion. Anonymous ballads, probably fragments of a lost epic that have been honed by countless singers over the centuries, relate the most dramatic episodes with colourful details and subtle touches that are so artlessly depicted and true to human nature that they lend an air of authenticity. The moving scene in which Gonzalo Gustios speaks to the severed heads of his sons and his old friend, their tutor, is one of the gems of Spanish literature. The account below closely follows the content and style of the ballads and the 14th-century *Crónica de Veinte Reyes* (Chronicle of Twenty Kings), with additions from other sources.

The Wedding

Ruy (Rodrigo) Velázquez was lord of Vilviestre, southeast of Salas in the district of Lara near Burgos, part of what was then the independent county of Castile. With only 300, he killed 5000 Moors. If he had died then, what great fame he would have left behind him. He would not have killed his nephews, the seven princes of Lara, nor sold their heads to the Moor.

He led an attack deep into Moorish territory at Calatrava near the River Guadiana, and among the booty he collected was a finely carved bench with gold inlay, which he presented to Garcí Fernández, Count of Castile, when he went to ask for the hand of the Count's first cousin, Lambra, in marriage. Lambra was from Briviesca in the district of Bureba, northeast of Burgos. Her deceased father, Gonzalo, lord of Bureba and Aza, had been an older brother of Fernán González, father of Garcí Fernández.

The wedding was held in Burgos, the reception in Salas, and the celebrations lasted for seven weeks. Invitations were sent to friends and relatives as far as Galicia and Portugal, and there were so many guests that the inns were not able to hold them all.

A merchant sent by Almanzor arrived with gifts for the ladies: a dining room suite for Garcí Fernández's wife "Ava" and an ivory tumbler trimmed with gold for Lambra. Garcí noticed this and said to Ruy, "I don't know why, but I don't like these gifts." Ruy went to the merchant and thanked him on behalf of the ladies. "It's nothing," said the merchant. "Don't forget that the chests of my master, lord of Córdoba – keep this to yourself – are inexhaustible. Remember that, for a wedding like this could ruin anyone."

Doña Sancha, sister of Ruy Velázquez, and Gonzalo Gustios the Good, Lord of Salas, had seven young sons. The boys had been raised by a fine knight named Nuño Salido, who taught them battle skills and good manners, and all had been knighted on the same day by Garcí Fernández, with Nuño Salido as their sponsor. The eldest, Diego, was the lieutenant and standard-bearer for Garcí Fernández at the Battle of San Estéban.

When the boys arrived in Salas for the wedding reception, Sancha sent them to the accommodation she had arranged, and she warned them not to venture out after dinner, for with so many people in the streets brawls were bound to occur. When they finished eating, they obediently stayed in and played board games.

The Challenge

Meanwhile, on a whim, Doña Lambra had set up targets in the plaza for the young horsemen to test their skill at *tablados* (javelin-throwing) and Ruy had promised a magnificent prize to the winner. But the targets were placed so high that none succeeded until one of her cousins from Bureba, Álvar Sánchez, managed to hit the mark, though he didn't move it. He shouted, "Love me, ladies, love me, one at a time, for one knight from magnificent Bureba is worth twenty or thirty of the flower of Lara."

When she heard this, Doña Lambra said for sport, "Oh, damned be the woman who denies you her body. If I weren't married, I'd give you my own."

Doña Sancha was annoyed at this. "Lambra, be quiet. Don't say such things. You've just been married to Don Rodrigo. If my sons heard what you said there'd be a row."

"Be quiet yourself, Doña Sancha, you who spawned a litter of seven sons like a sow in a dung heap."

The boys' tutor, Nuño Salido, was there, and when he heard this insult he wept with anguish and helpless fury. He left and went to the place where the boys were staying. When he entered, he found them playing their board games. The youngest, Gonzalo González, or Gonzalvico as he was often called, noticed Nuño leaning sadly against a railing.

"Why are you so sad, master?"

Nuño said nothing, but Gonzalo persisted: "Tell me who has made you angry."

Nuño explained what had happened and added, "I beg you, my son, don't go to the plaza."

But nothing could stop Gonzalo. He called for his horse and set off at a gallop for the plaza, taking with him only his squire, who carried a goshawk on his hand. When he arrived, he saw the target that only Álvar Sánchez had been able to hit. He asked for a javelin and, rising in his stirrups, he threw it so hard that it hit the target in the centre and broke it, and it fell to the ground.

"Love me, whores, love me," Gonzalo shouted, "one at a time, for one knight of the house of Lara is worth more than forty or fifty from magnificent Bureba."

The Response and the Outcome

By this time, the rest of the brothers had arrived, and they were pleased with Gonzalo's success. Not so Doña Lambra, and Álvar abused Gonzalo with foul language. Gonzalo's response was to give him such a great blow with his fist that he knocked out his teeth and broke his jaw. Álvar fell from his horse and died. Some say it was the fall that killed him and not the blow, and so his death was accidental.

Doña Lambra screamed and ran at Gonzalo and scratched his face, saying, "Never has a woman been so insulted at her wedding as to have this sort of thing happen."

Ruy Velázquez arrived, and when he heard what had happened he grabbed a spear and went to Gonzalo and hit him so hard over the head with the shaft that blood poured forth from five places.

"I've never done anything to you to deserve this," said Gonzalo. "I think I'm going to die from it, but I ask my brothers now that if I die they should take no revenge. And I beg you not to hit me again, because I don't think I can take any more."

These words angered Ruy Velázquez so much that he tried to hit Gonzalo on the head again, but Gonzalo dodged the blow, and it struck his shoulder instead so that the spear shaft broke in two. Gonzalo, who had no weapons, took the goshawk from his squire's hand and threw it into the face of Ruy Velázquez. The goshawk's talons raked his nose and mouth, causing a torrent of blood. Ruy Velázquez ordered his weapons to be brought to him, and he called for his 200 knights. The princes gathered their relations, and the two factions faced each other.

But Count Garcí Fernández and Gonzalo Gustios made peace between them. Then Gonzalo Gustios said to Ruy Velázquez, "You are an esteemed knight, and there is no one among the Christians or the Moors who does not fear to have you as an enemy, and so they envy you. For your own protection and as a favour to me, I ask you to accept my sons as your household guard."

Ruy Velázquez replied, "I will be content with that, honoured brother-in-law. I will honour them and love them as my nephews, and they will be well treated as the sons of my sister, whom I love so much."

Doña Lambra Escalates the Dispute

Ruy Velázquez went away with Garcí Fernández and Gonzalo Gustios into the country. Doña Sancha with her seven sons and their tutor, Nuño Salido, accompanied Doña Lambra to her estate at Barbadillo del Mercado on the River Arlanza. One day after hunting with their birds, the princes returned to Barbadillo and went into a garden near Lambra's rooms to relax while they waited for dinner to be served. This was August and the weather was hot. Gonzalvico stripped down to a minimum of clothing and, with his goshawk on his hand, went swimming in the river to cool himself and the bird. When Lambra saw this, she was incensed, and she said to her ladies, "Do you see the way Don Gonzalo is dressed? I think he's doing that to make me fall in love with him. I assure you that I'll avenge this insult." She called a manservant and told him:

"Get a cucumber and fill it with blood and go into the garden and throw it at Gonzalo González. He's that man with the goshawk on his hand. After you do that, come to me and don't be afraid, for I'll protect you. In this way I'll avenge the death of my cousin Álvar Sánchez."

(Throwing a blood-filled cucumber at a man was a multi-layered insult, "the most serious affront one could inflict on a gentleman", according to Mariana. Isabel Muñiz, a medical doctor, has explained [*La Leyenda...*] that it symbolised the venereal disease of blennorrhoea, a gonorrhoeal infection which was the cause of 90% of male sterility. The disease was usually contracted in ghettos, and the implication was that the sufferer had had sex with Jews, "the most unpardonable offence for a gentleman". So serious was the insult that it was repayable only with a life.)

When the princes saw the man coming toward them, they assumed he was bringing them something to eat because dinner was delayed. But the servant did what his mistress ordered: he threw the cucumber at Gonzalo and left him covered in blood. The servant ran back into the house. When the brothers saw what had happened, they were angry, and they discussed what they should do.

101

"We'll hide our swords under our cloaks and go up to the servant. If he doesn't show any fear, we'll know it was meant as an ignorant joke, and we won't do anything. But if he runs to Doña Lambra and she protects him, we'll know that it was at her instigation and was meant as an insult. If that's the way it is, he won't escape with his life."

They went into the palace, and when the servant saw them he ran to hide behind Doña Lambra.

"Auntie," said the princes, "don't get in the way just because you want to protect this man."

"Why not? He is my servant, and if he has done something wrong I will punish him. I warn you not to harm him while he is under my protection."

The princes dragged the servant out from behind her skirts and killed him in front of her, splattering blood over her clothes and even her headdress.

The seven princes left with their mother and went to Salas. Doña Lambra ordered a bed placed in a corral. She draped it in black to make it look like a funeral bier, and with her maidservants made such a great wailing and mourning as had never been heard before, and she called herself a widow forgotten by her husband.

The Complaint of Doña Lambra

When Ruy Velázquez returned home, Lambra ran to him with her face scratched and hair dishevelled and delivered herself of this complaint:

"Those who are supposed to protect me don't like me. The sons of Doña Sancha have reviled me. They have twisted my belt so that I had to mend it. They have threatened to cut my skirts to shame me like a prostitute, and to put their falcons among my pigeons and rape my ladies both married and unmarried. They have killed my cook under my petticoat. If you don't avenge me of this, I'll go to Córdoba and become a Muslim and let the Moors enjoy me, and I'll ask Almanzor to avenge me."

"Calm yourself, my lady," said Ruy Velázquez. "I have plans to take vengeance on the princes of Lara with a trick that those born and yet to be born will talk about forever."

102

(In one version of the incident at the wedding reception, young Gonzalo heard Lambra's insult to his mother, and he said to Lambra, "I'll cut your skirts to a hand's breadth and more above your knees to shame you," a punishment associated with prostitutes. However, this is missing in most versions, the implication being that Lambra invented the threat to incite her husband's revenge.)

Ruy Velázquez Betrays Gonzalo Gustios

Ruy Velázquez met with Gonzalo Gustios and his seven sons and assured them that there were no hard feelings about the incident with Doña Lambra, and that they had no need to fear him. Then he said to Gonzalo Gustios:

"Brother-in-law, these wedding celebrations have cost me a lot of money, and Count Garcí Fernández didn't help me with the expenses as much as I had expected. However, Almanzor has promised financial help. So if it is convenient for you, I would be grateful if you would go to Córdoba with a letter for Almanzor. He will be pleased to meet you, and he will give you a lot of money, which I will then share with you."

"I will be happy to do as you ask," said Gonzalo Gustios.

Ruy Velázquez went to his palace and hired a Moor to write a letter in Arabic to Almanzor. He then cut off the scribe's head so he could not reveal the treachery. This is what the letter said:

"The sons of the bearer of this letter, Gonzalo Gustios, have gravely dishonoured me and my wife. Because I am not able to avenge myself on them here in Christian territory, I am sending their father to you so that you can immediately behead him. I will gather my army and take his seven sons with me and go to Almenar. Send your captains Viara and Galve there with a large army, and I will place my nephews, the seven princes of Lara, in their power. Have them beheaded, and when they are dead you will have the Christian lands at your will, because these men are more contrary than any others, and they give the greatest support to Count Garcí Fernández."

When Gonzalo Gustios arrived in Córdoba, he gave the letter to Almanzor and said, "Your friend Ruy Velázquez sends greetings and he asks that you reply to this letter."

Almanzor opened the letter, and when he read the horrific deed requested of him, he tore it up.

"Gonzalo Gustios, do you know what this letter says?"

"No."

"Ruy Velázquez wants me to cut your head off immediately. I'm not going to do such a villainous thing. I'll put you in prison instead."

Almanzor placed him under house arrest in his own residence in Córdoba. This was probably more a protective custody intended to keep Gonzalo from returning home to be assassinated at the order of Ruy Velázquez. Almanzor said nothing to Gonzalo Gustios about the plot mentioned by Ruy Velázquez in the letter to ambush his sons. Mariana coyly reports: "The prison was rather free, so that a certain sister [Zenla] of the king [Almanzor] was able to enter to communicate with Gonzalo. From this conversation was born Mudarra González, founder of the noble line of the Manriques." Mudarra would later avenge his seven half-brothers.

According to the *Crónica de 1344*, Almanzor asked his sister to go to Gonzalo and "make him comfortable", saying, "I will appreciate it very much and it will please me." To which she responded bitterly, "That's how all the Christians of Spain get their pleasure." Pressing home his point, Almanzor continued, "Make him comfortable in every way if you want to please me. If you don't do this, it will not be to your advantage. In other words, if he dies, I'll have your head cut off." Zenla then entered into the arrangement with more enthusiasm.

Ruy Velázquez Betrays the Princes

Mariana says that the letter from Ruy Velázquez only asked Almanzor to behead Gonzalo Gustios, with no mention of killing the seven princes, and that Ruy Velázquez organised the ambush separately with the Moorish captains without Almanzor's knowledge, after he learned that Gonzalo was still alive.

Ruy Velázquez went to his nephews and said, "While your father is away to see Almanzor, I think it's a good idea to make an incursion to Almenar in Arabiana [east of Soria in the foothills of Moncayo] in Moorish territory. You're welcome to come along with me if you like; otherwise, you can stay here and guard our land."

The princes replied, "Don Rodrigo, we would look like cowards if you were to go with your army and risk your life while we stayed here."

"Then get ready. I'll assemble my army, you come behind, and we'll meet at the vega of Hebros [Vega-Ebrillos]."

Ruy Velázquez mustered an army of volunteers eager to go with him because of his reputation as a good leader. The army set off, the seven princes of Lara and Nuño Salido following with their own troop of 200 warriors. Their mother, Doña Sancha, accompanied them as far as Canicosa, nearly to the border of Lara.

The princes had just taken leave of their mother and reached a pine grove near a small river, when they heard an owl screeching. They looked up and saw an omen that could not be ignored: at the top of a withered pine tree a young red-tailed eagle was being killed by a treacherous sparrowhawk. Nuño Salido, who was wise in the ways of omens, felt that this boded ill for their venture. He turned to the princes and said, "We should return home and not proceed in the face of these omens. I'm not going any further. Let's stop and eat, and perhaps the signs will improve."

The youngest of the brothers, Gonzalo González, said, "Don Nuño Salido, don't say anything, because you well know that what we do here is not on our own account. The signs are not meant for us but for our leader, Ruy Velázquez. But you're old and no longer fit for battle, so you go back, because we still intend to follow our uncle."

"Boys, it weighs heavily on my heart that you wish to follow this road, because the omens tell me that whoever crosses that river will not see Salas again."

"Be quiet," said Gonzalo. "Don't say any more, because we don't believe anything you say."

"It makes me sad that you don't believe me and you dismiss me like this, because I know well that we will never see one another again."

The princes spurred their horses across the river and continued on their way, and Don Nuño Salido turned back towards Salas. But he began thinking that he wasn't performing his duty to those he had raised. "Why should I fear death at my age, being so close to it, while those boys, who have a long life ahead of them, are not afraid? And if the princes are killed and Ruy Velázquez survives, he will surely kill me anyway. And won't people suspect that it was I who led the boys into a trap?" Then he turned again to follow the road the princes had taken to the meeting place at Hebros.

105

Meanwhile, Ruy Velázquez was waiting there impatiently. He took a great oath by the cross of his sword that he would rip the soul out of anyone who detained the princes of Lara. When the seven brothers arrived, their uncle came out to greet them and asked why Nuño Salido was missing. They explained about the bad omens.

"Nephews, those were good omens. They mean that we will win great spoils from the enemy and that our side won't lose anything. Nuño Salido has done a bad thing by not coming with you, and may God make him regret it."

While he was saying this, Nuño Salido arrived, and when the princes saw him they welcomed him with joy. But Ruy Velázquez said, "Don Nuño, you have always opposed me at every opportunity, and you are doing it yet. I will be very unhappy if I don't get even with you for this."

"Don Rodrigo," said Nuño Salido, "I have never gone with falsehood and trickery but always with truth. Anyone who says that those omens that we saw are good and for gain lies like a traitor, and he says it because he is preparing treachery."

When Ruy Velázquez heard that, he called out to his vassals: "Damned be the day I paid your wages, for you see Nuño Salido dishonour me in front of you and you do nothing to punish him."

One of his vassals, Gonzalo Sánchez, shouted, "Give me the right to do it."

He mounted his horse and, drawing his sword, went for Nuño Salido. But young Gonzalo González got in front of him and gave him such a punch with his fist that he fell dead at the feet of Ruy Velázquez. Greedy to avenge himself with the deaths of his nephews, Ruy Velázquez called for his weapons, and the seven brothers with their 200 followers faced their uncle and his army ready for battle.

Gonzalo González said to Ruy Velázquez, "What is this, uncle? You have taken us from our land to fight against the Moors. Now you want to kill us. People will speak badly of you if you continue this quarrel. We will pay the legal blood fine of 500 sueldos for the death of this knight so that the matter will end here."

Ruy Velázquez realised that he would not be able to fulfil his heart's desire at that time, so he told Gonzalo that this would satisfy him.

The Ambush

With peace restored, the combined forces set off for Almenar the following morning and reached it later in the day. Ruy Velázquez ordered the seven brothers to range through the countryside to collect spoils. He had previously sent a message to the Moors to let their herds out to tempt the brothers.

"Boys," said Nuño Salido, "you don't want to take herds that will be of little profit. It would be better to wait a while for more Moors with more booty."

As he said this, they suddenly saw more than ten thousand Moors on horseback.

> Many flags and banners streaming.
> many lances honed and shined,
> many weapons brightly gleaming,
> many shields of rare design,
> many limber battle steeds.

"Who are those?" Gonzalo González asked his uncle.

"Have no fear," said Ruy Velázquez. "I've been over this land three times and taken spoils, and I've never met a Moor who stood in my way. Go out and raid as far as you like, and if it becomes necessary, which I know it won't, I'll come to your aid."

Ruy Velázquez then went in secret to speak with the Moors. Nuño Salido followed him unobserved and listened to him tell them that now was the time to attack the seven princes, because they had only 200 men, and the Moors would surely be able to kill them all.

When he heard this, Nuño Salido shouted, "Traitor! You have betrayed your nephews. May God punish you for this. As long as the world endures, people will speak of your treachery against your own blood."

Then he ran toward the seven princes and said, "Arm yourselves, boys, for Ruy Velázquez and the Moors have conspired to kill you."

The brothers quickly armed themselves. The Moors were so numerous that they separated into fifteen squadrons and completely surrounded the princes. Then Nuño Salido said:

"Take courage, boys. Don't be afraid, for the omens that I told you were against us are not. They are really good, because they tell us that we will be victorious and gain great booty from our enemies. I want to fight in the first battle rank. From now on, I commend myself to God."

As the Moors approached, he embraced each of the brothers in turn, and when he came to the youngest he kissed him on the face and said, "Gonzalo González, son, what saddens me most is what your mother will feel. You are the mirror of her and the one she loved most."

With that, he charged into battle and killed many Moors, but they came and surrounded him and killed him. The princes attacked with the battle cry "Santiago!" The Moors fell on the Christians like rain, while Ruy Velázquez stood apart with his troops.

Fernán González, namesake of the father of Count Garcí Fernández, was the first of the brothers to fall. Their 200 knights fought bravely, but they were soon slain, and the remaining six princes withdrew to a hilltop to rest. The eldest, Diego González, approached the Moors to ask for a temporary truce. Almanzor's captains, Galve and Viara, granted the truce, but Ruy Velázquez countermanded them.

"Don Rodrigo," said Diego, "you have neglected to keep your word that your troops would come to help us. My brother Fernán González and our company of 200 lie dead on the battlefield. For God's sake help us. For His holy mother, remember that we are Christians and the sons of your sister and Castilians to whom you are obligated."

Ruy Velázquez said, "You go on a fine adventure where I won't accompany you. Remember the dishonour you brought on me at the wedding in Burgos, when you killed my relative Álvar Sánchez, and what you did to my wife, Doña Lambra, when you killed a man in front of her that she was protecting, and the fine knight that was killed with a punch in front of me. You are good knights from Lara, and you fight valiantly. Will I help you? Don't depend on it. You will all die by the sword."

Don Diego returned to his five brothers and told them of the bad help he had found in their uncle. A thousand Christians from the troops of Ruy Velázquez moved out to aid the brothers, but the traitor called them back, saying, "Stay here, friends, and let's see how they fight. If they need help, I'll give it to them."

But 300 of them went over to the side of the princes anyway. When the brothers saw them coming, they thought they were attacking on their uncle's orders, but the knights shouted, "We are from Lara and we're coming to help you. Your evil uncle wants you dead. If we survive, we ask for no other pay but to be freed from vassalage to him if he returns to Castile."

The princes gave their word, and they entered once more into battle. A thousand Moors were killed, but at the end no Christians were left alive but the six brothers, who were too exhausted to lift a sword. The Moorish captains, Viara and Galve, took pity on them and called a truce and brought them into their own tent and gave them food and drinks. When Ruy Velázquez saw what the captains were doing, he told them that he had instructions from Almanzor that the brothers were to be killed. This was a lie. When Almanzor discovered it he wrote a letter to Ruy accusing him of treachery, and it motivated Almanzor later to help Mudarra avenge his half-brothers. But the captains believed the lie, and when Ruy threatened to have them beheaded for disobeying Almanzor they sent the princes back to the battlefield.

The Moorish warriors pressed in heavily while Ruy Velázquez looked on, but the princes were determined to sell their lives dearly and they made the enemy pay in blood. Finally the Moors killed their horses from under them, and then killed the brothers and decapitated them in the order of their birth. When the youngest, Gonzalo González, saw his brothers dead, he let go at the Moor who had decapitated them and gave him such a punch in the throat that he fell down dead. Then he snatched the sword from his hand and killed twenty nearby Moors before he was surrounded and beheaded.

Ruy Velázquez then returned to Vilviestre satisfied that he had exacted the best vengeance he could, and the Moors went to Córdoba with the heads of the seven princes and Nuño Salido.

Almanzor Presents the Heads to Gonzalo Gustios

Not all sources agree that Almanzor had prior knowledge of the ambush, and most imply that he only learned of the deaths of the princes when the heads were delivered to him. He was greatly saddened, and he broke the news to Gonzalo Gustios as gently as possible. He ordered the heads washed with wine and placed on a white linen sheet in the order in which they were born, and he went to where Gonzalo Gustios was imprisoned.

109

"How are you doing, Gonzalo Gustios?" he said with forced gaiety.

"Very well, sir, and I'm happy to see you, for I know that it's the custom of a great lord to visit a prisoner when he is about to set him free."

"That's correct, but first I want you to do something for me. My armies have just returned from Almenar, where they defeated a Christian host from Castile. They have brought eight heads, one of an old man and the others of youths and all high born. Since you're from Castile, I'd like you to come and identify them for me."

He said this as if he didn't know whose heads they were.

"Show them to me, and I'll tell you who they are and their family history, for there isn't a noble in Castile that I wouldn't recognise."

Almanzor took him to where the heads were, and when Gonzalo Gustios saw them he fell to the floor as if he were dead. When he came to, he cried out, "I recognise these heads to my sorrow. The seven princes. My seven beloved sons. And this one is their tutor, my dear friend the good Nuño Salido."

He raised a great and sorrowful lament, and no one who heard him could have failed to be moved to tears. One by one he picked up the heads with a groan and spoke of their deeds and courage. First he took the head of Nuño Salido and spoke to it as if it were alive.

"God save you, Nuño Salido, my loyal comrade. Where are my sons that I left in your care? But pardon me, comrade. I shouldn't ask that of you. You are dead like a good teacher, like a worthy man."

He replaced the head and took that of his eldest son in his arms, smoothing the hair and beard with his hand.

"Oh, my son Diego González, man of great goodness, I loved you the most, you who were to be my heir. You were the principal lieutenant of Count Garcí Fernández, who loved you well. You carried his banner at the Ford of Cascajares [Battle of San Estévan 978] and came out with great honour. Three times the banner fell, and three times you raised it again and killed two kings and a governor with it. Ruy Velázquez would have been a great man if he had died in that battle."

Washing it with his tears, he kissed the head and returned it to its place and picked up the others in the order of their birth. The next was his second son, Martín González.

"May God have mercy on you, my valued son Martín. You were the best games player in Spain. A refined gentleman, you spoke well in the

110

plaza. I don't care whether I live or die, but I fear that your mother will suffer much."

Setting that one down, he lifted the third head.

"Son Suero González, the whole world honoured you. You were a master with birds of the hunt. You knew how to help your birds when they moulted by gently plucking out the dead feathers. Any king would have been happy to have your company in the chase. Your uncle Ruy Velázquez afforded you a bad wedding – he sent you to death and left me in captivity."

And taking up the head of the fourth son, he looked at it sadly.

"Oh, son Fernán González – namesake of the best in Spain, the Count of Castile who christened you – slayer of bears and boars, friend of companions, never were you seen associated with those of little worth."

He picked up the head of Ruy González and held it to his heart.

"My son, my son, there was never anyone like you, a fine brave knight and reliable right-hand man. A king would have been proud to have your abilities. Your uncle Ruy Velázquez arranged a sad wedding for you."

And taking up the next head, he brushed the hair away from the face with his hand.

"Oh, son Gustios González, you had good skills. You would never lie for gold or silver. Courageous, fine warrior, great sword wielder – whoever you attacked was left dead or taken captive. Sad the report of your fate that will come to Lara."

As he lifted the head of his youngest son, his sorrow doubled.

"Son Gonzalo González with the eyes of Doña Sancha. What news will come to her, who loved you most of all. What an elegant person you were, a sweet talker with the ladies and the maidens, generous giver of gifts, dextrous with the spear. One needed to be sharp-witted to argue with you. Although I return to Lara, I will never be worth a crumb of bread. I have no relative or friend to avenge me. Better that I were dead than to see such a sad day's work."

At the sound of the old man's grief, all Córdoba wept. Then, for the great sorrow he had in his heart, Gonzalo Gustios grabbed a sword that was hanging on the wall and attacked and wounded seven Moors who were standing nearby, until he was overpowered. Then Almanzor's sister, Zenla, who had been comforting Gonzalo Gustios in his captivity, came to him and said:

"Take courage, lord Don Gonzalo, and leave off weeping and feeling sorry for yourself. My twelve sons were all killed in battle on the same day, fighting against you and your sons at the Ford of Cascajares, but I never lost my dignity and courage over it. And if I, a woman, can keep up my courage and not let it get me down, the more so should you, a knight. Crying will not bring your sons back."

(The *Crónica* says her story about losing all her sons was untrue, made up only to comfort Gonzalo. In *Bienandanzas*, Zenla says at this point, "Lie with me, and perhaps if God is willing we will have a son, for now we have none." The *Crónica* adds, "Maybe you can still make sons who will avenge the others." This source says that she did not know she was pregnant until after Gonzalo left.)

Almanzor said to him, "Gonzalo Gustios, I am sorry for what has happened to you. I am releasing you from prison and sending you home with the heads of your sons and whatever else you need."

Gonzalo Gustios said, "Almanzor, may God reward you for the fine things you have said and the mercy you have shown me."

Zenla then took Gonzalo Gustios aside and said to him, "Don Gonzalo, I am pregnant by you. What do you want me to do about it?"

"If it's a boy, raise him until he is old enough to know right from wrong, and then tell him he is my son and send him to me in Salas."

He took a gold ring from his hand and broke it in two and gave one half to her, saying, "Keep this half-ring, and when the boy is grown give it to him to bring with him so that I will know him by it."

Don Gonzalo took his leave of Almanzor and Zenla and the others and went to Salas, accompanied by Almanzor's guards to assure his safe passage. A short time later, Zenla gave birth to a son and named him Mudarra González.

When Gonzalo Gustios returned to Salas, he interred the heads of his sons in the church of Santa María, and he and his wife, Doña Sancha, retired to Burgos, where they lived a wretched life, continually persecuted by the powerful Ruy Velázquez and Doña Lambra. Gonzalo went blind from weeping. Isabel Muñiz says this was a psychosomatic blindness that excused Gonzalo from attending court, where he would have to encounter Ruy and Lambra. In the words of a ballad:

El Cid   Burgos

Clockwise from top left: El Cid, Doña Jimena, Martín Antolínez (with chest), church of Santa Gadea.

Plaque: "In this church of Santa Gadea, King Alfonso VI made his famous vow in front of El Cid."

Santiago

Clockwise from upper left: Santiago Matamoros (Moorslayer), Compostela; Santiago Matamoros, Mezquita in Córdoba; Santiago Peregrino (Pilgrim), Cathedral in Astorga; Santiago Peregrino, Compostela.

Santiago's body miraculously arrives in Padrón.
Impressed by the wonders worked by his followers,
the pagan Queen Lupa is baptised.
Fuente del Carmen, Padrón.

Along the Camino de Santiago

Above: the bridge at Hospital de Órbigo, León, scene of the Paso Honroso of Don Suero de Quiñones (see pillar on the title page and story on page 172).

Below: the Camino between Órbigo and Astorga, and the Ave Fenix albergue at Villafranca del Bierzo.

Above: left, the imposition of the chasuble on San Ildefonso, Jaén; right, Puerta del Sol, Toledo, with the same scene above the arch.

Below: Mezquita del Cristo de la Luz, Toledo.

The Seven Princes of Lara

Calle de las Cabezas, Córdoba

Almanzor's house where
Gonzalo Gustios was held.
Calleja de los Arquillos is
next to the plaque, which
summarises the story.

Calleja de los Arquillos
(Lane of the Arches),
where the heads of
Gonzalo's sons were
displayed.

Salas de los Infantes

Seal of Salas: Doña Sancha welcomes Mudarra into the family, surrounded by the heads of the Seven Princes of Lara.

The church of Santa María in Salas de los Infantes, where Gonzalo Gustios interred the severed heads of his sons.

The Hand and the Key of the Alhambra. The hand is over the outer entrance of the Gate of Justice, the key over the inner, below the statue of Mary Mother of Jesus. (Photo enhanced.)

Fermín Leizaola Calvo next to a stone circle in the Gipuzkoa hills, above, who told me the story about the Bridge of Oiartzun, below.

Santo Domingo de la Calzada

Above: Shrine to the Pilgrim

Right: Inscription: "In the midst of the forest he forged a way and made a road for the pilgrim."

Below: On the town seal: sickle with which Domingo felled trees, chickens that crowed after being roasted, bridge representing his road-building activities.

EN MEDIO DE BOSQUES
ROTURO CAMINO Y EL
MISMO SE HIZO CALZADA
PARA EL PEREGRINO

Church of Santa María, Ondarroa, where **Leokadi** was turned to stone.

O que non vai de vivo unha vez vai de morto tres

The souvenir T-shirt: "If you don't visit once alive, you must visit three times dead."

San Andrés de Teixido

Jaun **Zuria**

Jaun Zuria's coat of arms – two wolves carrying sheep – on the former escutcheon of Bizkaia.

Fernán González and his escutcheon, a castle and a
cross, above a cloister doorway at the ruins of the
monastery of San Pedro de Arlanza, which he founded
and endowed in thanksgiving for victory in the AD 925
Battle of Lara and where he was originally interred.

Above: Iron Age Celtic castro (city) c. 6th century BC, Asturias, abandoned when Celts left Spain.

Below: Sala de Justicia, Alcázar, Seville, showing "bloodstains" where Pedro the Cruel's half-brother Fadrique was killed.

Guzmán el Bueno

Tarifa

MUY NOBLE MUY LEAL
y HEROICA CIUDAD DE TARIFA
GANADA A LOS MOROS REINANDO SANCHO IV
EL BRAVO EN 21 DE Septiembre DE 1292

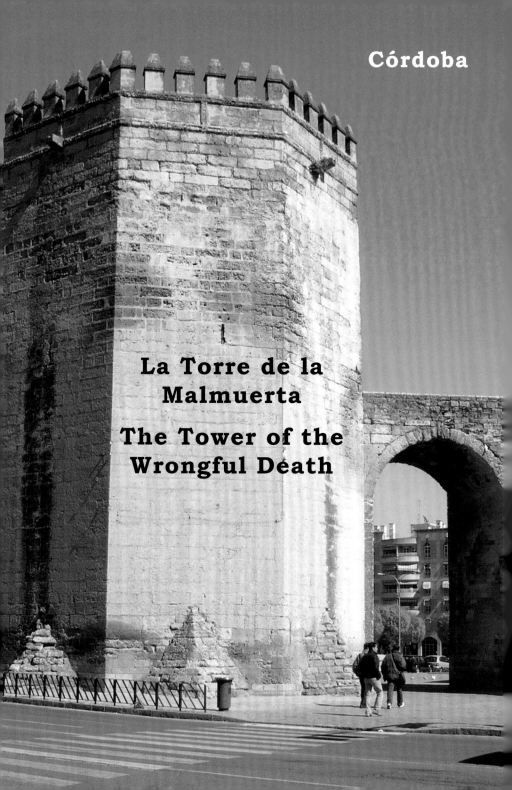

Córdoba

La Torre de la Malmuerta

The Tower of the Wrongful Death

Sad am I who live in Burgos,
blind from constant weeping,
never knowing when the sun sets
or when night comes creeping.

Doña Lambra my oppressor
keeps alive my sorrow:
every day her servants throw
seven stones at my windows.

Mudarra's Revenge

Mudarra was born 24 September 976, according to Muñiz. Almanzor had no children, and he treated the son of his sister as if he were his own son. He was happy that he had in Mudarra the means to avenge the insult to him – the lie Ruy Velázquez told about his orders to kill the princes – and the treachery against Gonzalo. He chose wet-nurses who produced the best milk to raise the boy. At the age of five, Mudarra was the size of a seven-year-old, and he closely resembled the youngest of his murdered half-brothers, Gonzalvico González. When he was ten, Almanzor had him trained in the arts and skills of a warrior and a gentleman. On being knighted at the age of 18, Mudarra was given 200 warriors related to him on his mother's side to serve him as lord, and there was not a Moorish warrior to equal him for valour. He was aware of the treachery done to his father and the death of his brothers, and he knew that his father had given the half-ring to his mother to be used as a token of recognition.

He told his mother that he wanted to meet his father if he was still alive, and he asked her to give him the half-ring, which she did. She also told him that she had never been with a man before or after his father. He then announced his intention to Almanzor, who gave him his blessing and wished him good luck and sent with him a troop of 300 armed and mounted knights selected from 5000 highborn Christian captives, with five years of future service paid.

As Mudarra set off on his way to Castile, Doña Sancha had a dream that she told to Gonzalo the following day.

"I dreamed that I saw you and me standing on a hilltop in Córdoba, and a goshawk came and landed on my hand. Then the goshawk saw

Ruy Velázquez nearby and attacked him and tore off his arm, making rivers of blood. I knelt down and drank his blood."

"I wish that your dream would come true," said Gonzalo.

Mudarra stopped at the church of Santa María in Salas to view the chest that contained the heads of his half-brothers, and there he learned that his father and Doña Sancha had moved to Burgos. When he arrived in Burgos and announced himself to Sancha and Gonzalo and explained the circumstances of his birth, Gonzalo denied being his father, saying, "Since I married Doña Sancha I have never married a Moor or a Christian."

Mudarra replied angrily, "If you don't want me for a son, I don't want you for a father. But may God allow me to avenge the princes, for they are my brothers, and let me be baptised to save my soul, and I care nothing for any other form of inheritance."

Doña Sancha said to Gonzalo Gustios, "If you could see as you used to see, and you could see his head and face, you would say he was your son Gonzalvico. Don't deny that he is your son for fear of me, for that he surely is. You didn't do anything wrong, for a man who is a captive is not subject to the law. Don't be ashamed to recognise your own flesh and blood."

And so Don Gonzalo told her all. Then he said, "If he is the son of the princess, he will give me a sign."

Mudarra said, "I don't have to give you proof, but here is the half-ring that you gave to my mother the princess."

Don Gonzalo took it and held it against the half-ring that he had, and the two halves miraculously stuck together so that they could not be separated. And then a second miracle occurred. Don Gonzalo saw the ring with his eyes, and he praised God that he could see as well and clearly as before, and he embraced Mudarra as his son and wept and said, "Son Gonzalo González, this image is your own self."

According to *Crónica de Veinte Reyes*, Gonzalo Gustios and Mudarra set off and went to where Count Garcí Fernández was in Burgos, and Ruy Velázquez was there with him. Mudarra challenged Ruy Velázquez, who was about 50 or 60 years old by then, in front of Garcí Fernández, but Ruy Velázquez laughed off the challenge. This angered Mudarra, and he went for him with his sword. But Garcí Fernández grabbed him by the hand and stopped him, and he made him agree to a truce for three days.

114

Mudarra kept track of Ruy's movements for the next three days, and when the truce period had expired, he waylaid him on the road. Shouting, "Die, false traitor," he ran at him and with one blow of his sword laid him dead on the ground. He also killed 30 of Ruy's followers.

The ballads depict a more colourful version of the encounter. Ruy Velázquez was aware of Mudarra's arrival in Burgos, but the two had not met. Ruy had been hunting, but he had caught nothing and had lost his falcon and was out of sorts. He was leaning against a beech tree and cursing Mudarra as the son of a renegade, saying that if he got his hands on him he would rip the soul from his body. Mudarra, who had been stalking him, approached, taking him by surprise, and greeted him courteously.

"God save you, good sir, there beneath the beech tree."

"And the same to you, gentleman. Your arrival is welcome."

"Tell me your name, sir, and I will tell you mine."

"I am Don Rodrigo of Lara, brother-in-law of Don Gonzalo and brother of Doña Sancha. My nephews were the seven princes of Lara. I curse little Mudarra, the son of the renegade, and if I had him here before me I would tear the soul from his body."

"If you are Don Rodrigo of Lara, I am Mudarra González, son of the renegade Gonzalo Gustios and stepson of Doña Sancha. The seven princes of Lara were my brothers. You sold them, traitor, in the Vale of Arabiana. With the help of God, I will here quit you of your soul."

"Wait, Don Mudarra, while I go and get my weapons."

"I'll give you the 'wait' that you gave to the princes of Lara. Die now, traitor, enemy of Doña Sancha."

According to the *Crónica de 1344*, as Ruy Velázquez lay dying, his sister, Doña Sancha, knelt beside him and scooped his blood into her hand and said, "Praised be God and thanks to Him for the mercy He has shown, for now I can realise the dream I have dreamed, which is to drink the blood of the traitor."

But Mudarra took her by the arm and lifted her up, saying, "Lady Mother, God does not wish this to happen, that the blood of a traitor should enter a good and loyal body such as yours."

Sancha then said, "If God and Mudarra are willing, this is the justice I wish to see done. Let two poles be erected and the traitor hung by the arms and feet between them, and all the relatives of those who died in battle with my sons, along with anyone else who wishes to do so, let them come and throw javelins or spears or any other weapons at his body until it is broken in pieces, and when his body has fallen to the ground, let them throw stones at it."

Estoria de los Godos (c. 1460), a sensationalised variant of the *Crónica de 1344*, adds that boys threw the body to the dogs, and what the dogs refused to eat was burned and covered with stones.

In that place where the lifeless body of Ruy Velázquez fell, the Castilians piled more than ten cartloads of stones. And even today, whoever passes that huge cairn, instead of reciting an "Our Father" they throw another stone on the heap, saying, "An evil rest to the soul of the traitor. Amen."

Mudarra waited until Count Garcí Fernández had died (995) before taking his revenge on Doña Lambra, because the Count and she were first cousins and Mudarra did not wish to do it while the Count was still alive. He seized her and had her stoned and burned – some say burned alive. After reporting that Mudarra meted out the same justice to Lambra as he had to Ruy Velázquez, *Estoria de los Godos* ends the episode with the pious prayer: "May God do the same to her damned soul, in His holy and eternal kingdom, amen."

Alternatively, Lambra fled to Garcí, imploring his protecton against Mudarra, claiming that she was not responsible for Ruy's actions. Garcí refused to help her: "I will order Mudarra to burn you alive, and may the dogs shred your flesh and may your soul be damned for what you have done."

At the end of the detailed narrative in *Crónica de Veinte Reyes*, we are told: "Now you who are listening to this story should know that when Mudarra came from Córdoba to Salas his father baptised him and made him Christian who had been a Moor." However, it is believed that Mudarra put off being baptised until after he killed Ruy. Vengeance is meritorious in Islamic law, but a sin for a Christian.

Mariana finishes his bare-bones account with a charming domestic scene.

"[By his vengeance on Ruy Velázquez and Doña Lambra, Mudarra] thus gained the goodwill of his stepmother, Doña Sancha, and his relatives and inherited his father's property. Sancha adopted him, and she did it in this manner, crude but memorable. On the day he was baptised and knighted by Garcí Fernández, Sancha put a wide shirt on

116

him through the sleeve, pulled his head out through the head hole, and gave him a kiss on the face, by which she brought him into the family and accepted him as her son. From this custom comes the saying, 'enter through the sleeve and leave through the head hole.' This means that when one has been received into a family, their relationship stretches more every day."

Almanzor

This king Don Pelayo, serving the Creator,
guarded well the land, there was no one greater.
Because of him the Christians never sorrowed more,
but they never lost their fear of the general Almanzor.
(Poema de Fernán González, stanza 121)

"Mortuus est Almanzor, et sepultus est in inferno – Almanzor is dead and buried in Hell."
(Cronicón Burgense)

Almanzor was born about 940 with the name Ibn Abi Amir and some 40 years later adopted the title *al-Mansur*, "the Victorious". An astute politician, he was the foremost Moorish military leader of the 10th century, leading 56 battles, although he only rose to prominence in 977. He is unlikely to have ever met his legendary nemesis, Fernán González, who died in 970. Almanzor died of an unidentified illness in 1002.

Almanzor looms large throughout legendary events of the 10th century, even appearing in a 925 battle against Fernán González 15 years before his birth, and one account has him being defeated by Charlemagne in the previous century. But most stories about him are basically factual. His conquest of Barcelona on 6 July 985 is still remembered as "the day the city died".

In a 997 raid on Santiago de Compostela he sacked the city and made Christian captives carry the bells of the cathedral on their shoulders to Córdoba, where they were upturned and used for lamps in the Mezquita. Almanzor had overseen the final stage of its construction in 988 to make it the largest mosque in Europe (23,400 sq m) then and

117

now. When Fernando III the Saint took Córdoba on 29 July 1236 and recovered the bells, he made Moorish captives carry them back to Santiago, where they miraculously rang for several days under their own power. In 1526, the Cathedral of Córdoba was installed inside the Mezquita, with the triumphant mounted figure of Santiago Matamoros above the high altar. Santiago de Compostela and Córdoba were declared sister cities on 5 July 2004.

Almanzor married a number of Christian kings' sisters and daughters for political purposes. His incitement of the treachery of the wife of Garcí Fernández is dealt with in the "Garcí Fernández and the Traitor Countess" chapter. This is said to have come about because of Garcí's support of Almanzor's supposed son, Abdallah. (The Arabian historian Aben Ayvan said that Abdallah was probably not his son, and Almanzor himself seemed to have had doubts.) Abdallah was caught plotting against Almanzor and fled to Garcí, who gave him asylum. As part of a truce and on Almanzor's promise not to harm Abdallah, the young man was handed over to him, but Almanzor killed him.

Mariana reports on the 997 raid on Santiago de Compostela: "The tomb of Santiago was not touched, no one knows why, but it is only stated that Santiago returned to his seat and church and severely punished the disrespect. A great sickness broke out among the Moorish army, and a large part of them died in great pain. Almanzor asked a local man what was the cause, and the man replied that a disciple of the Son of Mary was buried in the church. Almanzor immediately abandoned the enterprise, but he did not arrive home. He died of the sickness in Medinaceli."

A Moorish historian reported that the inhabitants of Compostela fled at Almanzor's approach, and he encountered only one person, a monk sitting beside the tomb of Santiago. On being asked why he was there, the monk replied, "To honour Santiago." Almanzor ordered that the monk be left in peace.

Almanzor evidently had caught the "sickness" and recovered, but then suffered a relapse at Calatañazor in Soria near the Castile border in 1002. "On that day," says Mariana, "a figure dressed as a fisherman was seen from a distance at the river bank, singing in a sad voice, 'In Calatañazor Almanzor lost his tambour.'" Other sources report that the sorrowing figure was seen near Córdoba on the day Almanzor suffered a fatal wound in the Battle of Calatañazor in July 1002, from which he died in Medinaceli on the night of August 10-11. When the "fisherman" was approached, he faded from sight. One commentator claimed it was the devil, lamenting the losses suffered by the Moors.

Recalling a line from the Koran that God would preserve from hell those whose feet were covered with the dust from the road of the Lord, Almanzor had collected the dust from his clothes after each battle, and it was used to fill his coffin.

The Cave of the Sleepers
(Loja, Granada)

The story of the Seven Sleepers of Ephesus, dating from as early as the sixth century, is one of the most widely known legends of Christianity. According to *The Golden Legend*, a 13th-century collection of legends of saints by Jacobus de Voragine, seven young Christian noblemen of Ephesus hid in a cave to escape persecution by Emperor Decius in AD 270. When they were discovered, Decius ordered the cave walled up so that they would die of starvation. In 478, God put the idea in the mind of a man of Ephesus to build a stable, and his workmen dismantled the blocked entrance of the cave for building material. The Seven Sleepers awoke, thinking they had only been asleep one night, and when they told their story they were regarded as saints and as living proof of the truth of the resurrection. They died shortly after meeting the Christian emperor Theodosius.

The story is recounted in the Koran, Sura 18, where variants of the number of the Sleepers are mentioned: three, five, seven, in addition to a dog. According to tradition, the number remains vague because when Mohammed was asked how many there were, he replied, "I'll tell you tomorrow." But because he didn't add "God willing," God didn't hear him when he asked, and so he never got the answer.

In the 11th century, descriptions of the Cave of the Sleepers on a north-facing slope near Loja began to appear in Arab writings. The number of the mummified bodies found there varies: three, four, five, but most frequently seven plus a dog. Several writers over the following centuries reported that the Muslim inhabitants of Loja kept the bodies covered with clothes, and, when asked who the Sleepers might be, they said they had no idea, and that the Christians they had replaced hadn't

119

known either, nor had the Goths who the Christians had replaced. Rosal and Rosal, in *Noticias Históricas de la Ciudad de Loja*, conclude that the bodies were a primitive collective burial.

One 12th-century writer recorded this story. There was a group of depraved libertines who offered a prize to whoever would go to the Cave at night and bring back an object to prove he had been there. A man from Granada accepted the challenge. He cut off the ear of one of the Sleepers, and when he brought it to the group's house in Loja, the whole town was awakened by a loud voice saying, "They have torn off the ear of Yamlija, one of the men of the Cave."

A group of townspeople marched to the house and broke down the door, demanding to know where the ear was. The offender was pointed out, the ear recovered, and the malefactors were whipped to death. At dawn, a local lord, accompanied by friends and people of the town, took the ear to the Cave and sewed it back on the head of Yamlija.

Late Middle Ages (11-16th centuries)

El Cid

The History

Rodrigo (Ruy) Díaz de Vivar, El Cid Campeador, was born in the village of Vivar near Burgos about 1040 and died in Valencia in 1099. Much of the story of his life as a battle leader (*campeador*) and governor (*cid*, from the Arabic *al-Said*) is legend, in spite of, or more likely because of, the fact that the first of numerous ballads celebrating his heroic adventures was composed five years before his death, and the first written account appeared as early as 1105. The 3730-verse 12th-century *Cantar* (Song) *de Mio Cid* has inspired many derivative ballads, poems, plays and other art forms, including a 16th-century epic poem of 8000 verses and the 1961 film starring Charlton Heston. The historical facts in brief:

Rodrigo was raised and educated with Sancho II, son of Fernando I, king of Castile and León. When Fernando died in 1065, the kingdom was divided among his four children. Sancho as the eldest inherited Castile, Alfonso VI was given León, García got Galicia and Portugal, and Zamora went to Urraca. Alfonso wanted to annex Castile and attacked Sancho. Rodrigo, Sancho's battle leader with the title Campeador, helped him defeat Alfonso. In the siege of Zamora in 1072, Sancho was assassinated by a traitor, probably at the instigation of Alfonso, who now added the crown of Castile to that of León and effectively became king of Christian Spain. As a supporter of Sancho, Rodrigo was exiled from Christian territories and hired himself out to Moorish leaders, eventually becoming the self-made warrior-governor of Valencia, while paying at least lip service to Alfonso as king. That is the factual framework around which are constructed the following stories.

Rodrigo Marries Jimena

Jimena Gómez was the niece of Alfonso VI and the great-granddaughter of Alfonso V of León. She was so beautiful that when she ventured out of doors the sun would pause in its course in order to see her better, according to a ballad recited by an old woman in Vivar to the author of a guidebook in the mid-20th century. In 1074, Jimena's father, the Count of Oviedo, insulted Rodrigo's father, Diego Laínez. Diego presented his sword, which he could no longer lift, to his son and said, "A man who lives without honour is not worthy to live. Such an outrage can only be avenged by blood. Prove that you are a son worthy of a father like me. Avenge me and avenge yourself. Kill him or die trying."

Rodrigo challenged the Count to a duel and killed him. He then cut off his head and presented it to his father, who said, "The one who has brought me that head will now be the head of my house."

After Sancho was killed, there was an uneasy truce between Rodrigo and Alfonso for a time, while Rodrigo nominally served the king as battle leader. According to what is probably history, in order to mend fences between Castile and León after the murder of Sancho and the usurpation of his crown, Alfonso urged Rodrigo to ask Jimena to marry him, and she accepted.

> "I killed your father, Jimena
> To avenge a serious wrong.
> I killed a man, and I give you a man;
> I'm here at your command.
> In place of a father who's dead,
> You now have an honoured husband."

The 16th-century ballad "Romance de Jimena Gómez" has a more pro-active feminist version. Jimena came to Alfonso and demanded justice:

> "The king who doesn't give justice no longer deserves to be king,
> Nor to parade on a horse, or wear golden spurs on his heel,
> Nor eat his bread on linen, or make his home with the queen,
> Nor assist at holy Mass; he no longer merits these things."

The king, on hearing her words, said aloud to himself:
"Oh, help me, God in Heaven, tell me what to say.
If I kill or imprison El Cid, my court will surely rebel,
And if I don't give justice, my immortal soul will pay."

Jimena assured him that his court would not rebel because what she meant by justice was that the king should order Rodrigo to marry her, so that the man who had done her such wrong by killing her father would at least do her some good.

"I have heard it said, and now I see that it is true," commented Alfonso: "the wisdom of women is unnatural."

The De-bearding of Count García Ordóñez

A man's beard was so potent a symbol of his virility and so intimately connected to his honour that the penalty for plucking or cutting it off was the same as for castration and more severe than for an injury leading to the amputation of a limb. Even for a minor plucking, the assailant was fined one sueldo for each hair pulled out. Compensation for a man's death was 500 sueldos. Rodrigo partially de-bearded the powerful Count García Ordóñez and got away with it, literally and legally.

In 1079, Rodrigo was sent by Alfonso to collect tribute from his vassal, Almutamiz, the Moorish king of Seville. While Rodrigo was enjoying Sevillan hospitality, the Moorish king of Granada attacked Almutamiz's territory and penetrated as far as Cabra with the aid of Christian knights from Aragón and Navarre led by García Ordóñez. Rodrigo defeated them, took Ordóñez prisoner and grabbed him by the beard and tore out part of it, which he kept for many years in a pouch hanging at his neck as a souvenir of the encounter and a constant reminder to Ordóñez of his dishonour. The incident is recorded briefly at the beginning of *Cantar de Mio Cid*, where we are told: "From then on, the Moors and Christians called Ruy Díaz de Vivar el Cid Campeador, which means 'the Battler'." Near the end of the *Cantar*, Rodrigo taunts Ordóñez that the part of the beard that he tore out never grew back. The fact that Ordóñez never demanded compensation for the affront added to his dishonour.

De Mena's *Tradiciones y Leyendas Sevillanas* adds a colourful, though anachronistic, detail to the story. The 18-year-old Rodrigo (he was actually about 38 at the time) rode out at the head of 100 cavalry to confront Ordóñez and his army of 1500. He sent an emissary to tell him to go away and leave Seville alone. Ordóñez laughed at the emissary and said, "Advise that boy from Vivar that before he plays at war he should wait until his beard starts to grow."

When this was reported to Rodrigo, he ground his teeth and said to his knights, "I swear that without growing my own beard I'll tear out that of Count Ordóñez."

De Mena's account says that this was the first time Rodrigo used a cavalry manoeuvre of his own invention called "the Castilian turn", which remained part of Spanish cavalry tactics until the 19th century. It consisted of a frontal charge that carried through the enemy lines, with a quick reverse charge that caught them from behind by surprise.

The Oath at Santa Gadea

In the ever-shifting political alliances of the time, Rodrigo was soon replaced as Alfonso's battle leader by García Ordóñez, who was now Rodrigo's implacable enemy. Rodrigo strongly suspected Alfonso of complicity in the murder of his friend Sancho, Alfonso's brother, and he embarrassed the king by making him publicly swear an oath that he had had "neither part nor art" in it. This was performed at the church of Santa Gadea (now Águeda) in Burgos in a ceremony that unashamedly merged pagan and Christian traditions. Alfonso was made to swear on an iron lock, a wooden crossbow, and the four Evangelists, while holding a Crucifix in his hand. Humiliated by what was in effect a public accusation of murder and forced to (probably) lie on a sacred oath to deny it, and convinced by the scheming García Ordóñez that Rodrigo was a traitor, Alfonso exiled him.

The Exile

Given nine days to remove himself from the king's territories, Rodrigo gathered 300 knights and left Vivar, weeping and sighing to see the houses of the village thus deserted. The company arrived in Burgos expecting to be offered accommodation by the townspeople, but they had been forbidden by Alfonso to give them anything. Seeing all the doors and windows closed and shuttered, Rodrigo kicked at a locked door. A nine-year-old girl looked at him and said: "Campeador, you girded on your sword in a good hour. The king has ordered us not to open our doors to you or help you in any way, or we will lose our lands and houses and even the eyes out of our faces. Cid, you can gain nothing from our misfortune, but may God favour you with all His holy powers."

The Money-lenders and the Chests

Rodrigo and his men camped on the edge of Burgos that night. Rodrigo's nephew Martín Antolínez was the only one who provided food and drink for the company, but this meant that he would have to leave with them in the morning. Between them, Martín and Rodrigo hatched a plan. They prepared two locked chests filled with sand and stones and decorated with leather and gilded nails. Martín went to two Jewish money-lenders in Burgos, made them swear not to reveal anything of the enterprise to either Christians or Moors, and told them that the chests were filled with gold and jewels. Rodrigo needed money to support his band of warriors in their campaigns against the Moors, from which, of course, they expected to win booty, but the chests were too heavy to carry with them. If the money-lenders would accept the chests as collateral for a loan of 600 marks, Rodrigo would pay them back with interest in a year. They had to promise not to open the chests on pain of voiding the agreement.

Having confidence in the famous warrior's abilities, they accepted the conditions and gave Martín 300 gold and 300 silver marks and a finder's fee of 30 marks for himself as well. On his return, Rodrigo opened the chests and revealed (as the Jews may have suspected) that they contained nothing but sand and stones, but he said that the true treasure in the chests was his word, which was worth more than the money they had loaned him.

As proof that this legend is true, in the cathedral in Burgos, where Rodrigo is interred, one of the chests is displayed bearing the label "Cofre [Chest] de El Cid".

The Bat and the Drum and the Flag of Valencia

History tells us that El Cid fought two battles at Valencia. One was the 19-month siege ending in June 1094 in which he took the city, and the other came later that year when he was in turn besieged.

According to *Cantar de Mio Cid*, Búcar, King of Morocco, crossed the Straits of Gibraltar with 50,000 (other sources say 150,000) warriors to besiege Valencia. The incessant loud drumming from the camp of the Moors frightened El Cid's wife, Jimena, and their daughters, but the hero light-heartedly assured them that the dowry for the girls' forthcoming weddings would be provided by booty taken from the Moors when they were defeated, that now the women would have the opportunity to see how their warrior-husbands made their living, and when the battle was over he would bring them the drums so they could see what they were.

This may be the inspiration of a story told to me by a Valencian woman named Julia, which explains why a bat appears on the coat of arms of the city. The night before the battle for Valencia (she did not say which one), a bat became trapped in a drum. As it flapped about in an attempt to escape, the beating of its wings on the drumheads attracted the people's attention. They told El Cid, who said it was a sign that they would be victorious in the battle. They won, but El Cid got his mortal wound. He placed his hand on the wound and drew his fingers across the yellow flag of Valencia, making four red stripes. That is why the escutcheon of Valencia City bears a red-striped yellow lozenge and a bat. (See the more usual version of the red stripes in the chapter "Guifré the Hairy and Charles the Bald: The Blood-striped Flag of Cataluña".)

Cantar de Mio Cid agrees with history that El Cid did not die in that battle. In the *Cantar*, he killed Búcar with his famous sword Colada, which he had taken from García Ordóñez, and thus acquired Búcar's sword, the more famous Tizona, which the *Cantar* says was valued at more than a thousand gold marks.

126

In the spectacular climax of the 1961 film *El Cid*, the dead body of Rodrigo is tied to the saddle of his renowned steed, Babieca, to lead the charge that routed the Moors besieging the city of Valencia. This is a firmly entrenched part of his legendary career and widely believed to be true. History says that he died peacefully in his bed in 1099. The exact date most frequently given is 10 July.

Babieca

El Cid's long-lived horse was with him from his youth. Rodrigo's godfather gave him his choice of colts, and he selected one that was rough and unruly. His godfather called him an idiot – *babieca* – for his decision, and Rodrigo transferred the name to the horse. In one version of the story of Alfonso's discovery of the Mezquita del Cristo de la Luz in Toledo (see that chapter below), it is Babieca, bearing Rodrigo, who genuflects at the white stone. Babieca died in 1102 at the age of about 45 and is buried in the grounds of the monastery of San Pedro de Cardeña, where Rodrigo was originally interred. The inscription on the horse's tombstone refers to the time Alfonso asked Rodrigo to give a demonstration of Babieca's speed, and, the king having admired the horse, Rodrigo evidently felt obligated to offer Babieca to him:

"King, I give you Babieca, my swift horse."
Then the king answered, "I do not wish that.
If I take the horse he will not have such a fine master.
A horse like that is for someone such as you
To conquer the Moors and be their pursuer,
For because of you and the horse we are well honoured."

El Cid After Death

As a demonstration of his (at least nominal) loyalty to Alfonso, even though he was exiled, Rodrigo had sworn not to cut his beard until they were reconciled. This never happened, and by the end of his life the beard had flourished magnificently. *Cantar de Mio Cid* refers to it 23 times and frequently mentions its elegance: "Oh Campeador fair-bearded", "the Cid, the nobly bearded", "that victory gave much honour to his beard." A beard symbolises a man's dignity and honour, and to

127

pluck or cut it is a deadly insult. When he swore by his beard, El Cid often boasted that no one had ever done him this dishonour:

"By this beard that no one ever plucked ..."

In an encounter with his long-time adversary Count García Ordóñez, El Cid reminds him: "No son of woman ever plucked this beard, as I did to yours at Cabra, Count, when I took both your castle and your bit of beard, which hasn't even grown back yet to what little it was then. I keep it here in my wallet as a souvenir."

The body of El Cid was taken from Valencia in 1102 and displayed for ten years in the church at San Pedro de Cardeña near Burgos. According to Alfonso the Wise's *Estoria de España*, the body had been on display for seven years when a Jew approached it while the abbot was giving a sermon in the plaza and the church was deserted.

"So this is the body of the famous Rodrigo Díaz El Cid," he said to himself. "They say that never in his life did any man pluck his beard. I wonder what he can do to me if I pluck it now."

The sheathed sword Tizona was in Rodrigo's left hand, and his right hand was tucked inside his cloak. As the man reached his hand out toward the body, the right hand of El Cid suddenly emerged and fell to the hilt of the sword and drew it a hand's breadth out of the scabbard. The man cried out and fell backwards onto the floor in a faint. The abbot and others heard his shouts and came running in to revive him by splashing water in his face. When they heard his account of what occurred and saw the right hand of El Cid out of his cloak and gripping the hilt of his sword, they praised God for this demonstration of the power of the hero.

From that day until it was interred next to Jimena in front of the altar three years later because of decomposition, the body of El Cid remained in that posture, because they could not remove his hand from the sword or return the sword fully into the scabbard. The body was moved to Burgos for security in 1835 and has rested in the Cathedral since 1921. The subsequent chapter in *Estoria de España* says that the Jew converted to Christianity as a result of the incident and was baptised with the name Diego Gil.

The Burnt Hand
(Toledo)

When Fernando I died, leaving Castile to his eldest son, Sancho II, and León to Alfonso VI, Alfonso tried to annex Castile, but Sancho defeated him with the help of El Cid and exiled him in 1072. Alfonso found refuge in Toledo, the former Christian capital, which was then in Moorish hands. The governor of the city, Al Mamún, saw an advantage in befriending the opponent of the present king of Castile and León, and placing the possible next king in a debt of honour could serve as insurance for the future.

Although officially the Moor's enemy, Alfonso was treated more as an honoured guest than a prisoner. He was accommodated in a modest palace with a sumptuous garden and servants and other personnel to look after his every need and desire. However, it was tacitly understood that if he left without permission, he would be pursued and killed.

One day, Alfonso was resting on a couch in the garden when he overheard Al Mamún and his advisors discussing the defences of the city: which points were weakest, whether it was better to station some defenders on the surrounding hills or concentrate them all within the walls, and so on. Al Mamún asked how such a strong city could be taken. One of the advisors said, "If all the bread, wine and fruits were taken from around the city for seven consecutive years, Toledo could well be taken in the eighth year for lack of food." This information was of great interest to Alfonso, who might in future attack the city as the Reconquest rolled southward. One of the advisors suddenly noticed Alfonso.

"The Christian is spying on us. He must have heard what we were saying about the defences."

Alfonso closed his eyes and pretended to be asleep as Al Mamún and the others approached.

"He is sleeping," said Al Mamún. "He didn't hear anything."

"We can't be sure of that," said a suspicious advisor.

"I suggest a test," said another, and he called loudly to a servant to bring a pot of molten lead. Alfonso passed this first test: although he suspected the purpose of the lead, not a muscle twitched. When the pot was brought to him, Al Mamún took Alfonso's hand and opened it and poured a few drops of the molten lead into his palm. Alfonso leapt up.

129

"What is this? Is this your idea of hospitality, to torture a sleeping man?"

The Moors were convinced that Alfonso had not heard their discussion of the defence plans. They expressed their deepest apologies and summoned a doctor to treat the injured hand.

When Sancho was assassinated in the siege of Zamora later in 1072, Alfonso was declared king of Castile and León. The scar left by the molten lead helped him to remember clearly all that he had overheard. He did not attack Toledo while Al Mamún was governor, but he used the knowledge to his advantage when he captured the city from his benefactor's successor in 1085. However, it only took four years of deprivation for the occupants to capitulate.

Mezquita del Cristo de la Luz
(Toledo)

Next to the magnificent 14th-century mudéjar (Christian-Islamic art style) Puerta del Sol in Toledo is a smaller, older gate, the Puerta de Valmardón. Next to this gate on Calle del Cristo de la Luz (Street of Christ of the Light) stands the 10th-century former Muslim sanctuary now called the Mezquita del Cristo de la Luz.

When El Cid liberated Toledo in 1085 after nearly four centuries of Moorish occupation, King Alfonso VI ceremoniously entered the city through the Puerta de Valmardón. His horse stopped suddenly in front of the mezquita, knelt down reverently on a white stone in the pavement, and refused to move on. Respecting his horse's instinct, Alfonso ordered that the wall of the mezquita be breached. When this was done and a hidden chamber revealed, the king entered and found a lamp burning in front of a crucifix. Some accounts say an ancient monk greeted the king with relief that he could now die in peace after his centuries-long vigil. Others say there was no sign of human presence, but it is agreed that the chamber appeared to have been sealed and that the lamp had been burning miraculously since Toledo was taken at the beginning of the Moorish Conquest in 711. Alfonso ordered all the Muslim inscriptions removed from the sanctuary, had a Mass celebrated immediately, and converted the mezquita into a Christian chapel.

A variant of this story has El Cid entering the city, and it is his horse, Babieca, who kneels.

Santo Domingo de la Calzada
(La Rioja)

Santo Domingo de la Calzada
donde cantó la gallina después de asada

Santo Domingo of the Roadway
where the chicken crowed after being roasted

Of the many pilgrim roads – Caminos – to Santiago de Compostela, the most popular one is the French Camino. It begins as two roads crossing the Pyrenees from France to Spain at the passes of Somport and Roncesvalles, becomes one Camino at Puente la Reina in Navarre, and continues through Logroño, Burgos, León and Ponferrada to Galicia, to name only the major cities and towns and ignoring several alternative routes. This main Camino passes through Santo Domingo de la Calzada.

Early in the 11th century, a pious and unassuming young man named Domingo García (1019-1109) from Viloria de Rioja applied for admission to the monasteries of Valbanera and San Millán and was rejected for his uncouth appearance and lack of education. (Not to be confused with the Spanish Domingo de Guzmán, who founded the Dominicans in France in 1216.) So he set about the self-imposed vocation of serving pilgrims bound for Santiago de Compostela.

He built himself a hut along the stretch of the French Camino between Nájera and Redecilla, where the route passed through a wilderness that was dangerous because of the poor condition of the road and the bandits who preyed on travellers. He built and maintained paths and bridges and established restaurants and *albergues* (hostels) for the pilgrims, and he also constructed a causeway across a bog. Under Domingo's civilising influence, a settlement sprang up around his homestead to become the present Santo Domingo de la Calzada, which at one time had grown to such importance that it had a bishop.

The casual visitor who is not aware of the Miracle might be surprised to find a live white cock and hen roosting in the Cathedral of

131

the Holy Trinity in a special chicken coop installed in the 15th century. The tradition of keeping the birds here originated at some time between the 12th and 14th centuries, and it is explained by this story.

A German couple and their 18-year-old son, Hugonell, were travelling the French Camino on their way to Santiago de Compostela, when they stopped at Santo Domingo de la Calzada to spend the night at the inn and to venerate the relics of Santo Domingo. A waitress at the inn became infatuated with Hugonell and sneaked into his room at night. She jumped into his bed, hopeful, as one account coyly puts it, of "amorous communication", but he rejected her advances.

The scorned and angry woman planted a valuable antique silver cup in Hugonell's bag and then accused him of theft. He was quickly arrested, found guilty and hanged. His distraught parents continued on their pilgrimage to Santiago de Compostela.

On their return to Santo Domingo de la Calzada a month later, they decided to pay their respects to their dead son, whose decomposing body they expected to find left hanging on the gallows, with the eyes plucked out and skin flayed by carrion birds as a warning to would-be thieves, which was the custom of the time. To their astonishment, they saw that his body was uncorrupted, and he appeared to be sleeping rather than dead. When they approached, he opened his eyes and smiled at them. He explained that Santo Domingo, invisible to all other eyes, had stood by him from the moment of his execution and supported his body so that the noose would not tighten around his neck.

The parents rushed to the judge to tell him what had happened and to ask him to take their son down from the scaffold. The judge, who had just seated himself before a dinner of a roasted cock and a roasted hen, listened politely to their story. When they finished, he said, "Your son has been hanged, and he is no more alive than this cock and this hen on the platter in front of me." At that, the roasted, headless birds leapt from the table and ran out the door, crowing loudly as they went. The waitress was hanged for her false accusation. As a reminder of their predecessor's miscarriage of justice, judges of the town were formerly required to wear a rope around their necks. This was later changed to a symbolic ribbon.

In recognition of that miracle, a council of 180 bishops in 1350 granted indulgences "to the Cathedral of La Calzada, where are kept a white cock and hen, and to whoever walks around the tomb reciting the

Our Father, Hail Mary and Glory Be". The current practice is to walk around the tomb of Santo Domingo 12 times on 12 consecutive days, saying the prayers each time.

Many pilgrims take a white feather shed by the resident cock or hen as proof that they have passed through the town on their pilgrimage to Compostela. To hear one of the birds crow is regarded as a good omen for their journey.

The miracle of the cock and hen may be the most famous story on the Camino and is certainly the main reason most Spanish people are aware of Santo Domingo de la Calzada, but two other events in Domingo's life are also worthy of notice.

Between the obvious white cock and hen on the town's coat of arms there appears a tree with a sickle. A silver sickle is displayed in a glass case in the cathedral along with the reliquary that used to protect it. A sickle is also carved into a stone next to the cathedral in the Plaza de España with the inscription: "In the midst of the forest he forged a way and made a road for the pilgrim."

Domingo went to the neighbouring town of Grañón to ask if he could fell some evergreen (holm) oaks for his construction work. They refused permission, so he asked if he could take as many trees as his sickle would cut. They laughed at the tool that was obviously suitable only for cutting grass or crops and said yes. Miraculously, the sickle was able to fell as many trees as Domingo needed.

The other event is not unique. Dido used a similar trick to delineate the desired extent of her citadel in Carthage. Domingo asked a local lord to give him some property to construct buildings to house and care for the pilgrims. The lord agreed jokingly to let him have as much land as a bull hide would cover, whereupon Domingo cut a bull hide into strips and used them to mark out the boundaries of the space he needed. Perhaps he had to resort to this minor deception in the early days, but in 1076 King Alfonso VI visited the town and met Domingo, approved of his good works, and gave him all the land he needed to expand.

Domingo was named Patron of Public Works Services by a ministerial order in 1939. Plaques in his honour have been placed next to his tomb in the cathedral by the College of Engineers of Roads, Canals and Bridges ("patron and precursor") and by the College of Technical Engineers of Public Works. He is recognised as the "grandfather saint" by the Spanish Society of Gerontology for his long life.

Domingo's feast day is 12 May, the date of his death in 1109, and is celebrated by a week of festivities.

San Andrés de Teixido
(Galicia)

On the north coast of Galicia at the base of Cabo Ortegal is the shrine of San Andrés de Teixido. Andrés (the Apostle Andrew, brother of Peter) was martyred by being crucified on an X-shaped cross, which is reflected in the Saint Andrew's Cross of Scotland, of which he is the patron saint, and integrated into the British Union Flag. It is also part of the *ikurrin*, the Basque flag. (See "Jaun Zuria" notes.)

A relic of the saint was taken from Rome to the city of Estella in Navarre in the year 1270, and some time afterwards a relic was brought to the present sanctuary at Teixido. Galicians are familiar with this site, but it is little known outside the region. From the nearest town, Cedeira, it is six miles (ten km) uphill to 628m above sea level, then one kilometre down to an exposed, windy cliff overlooking the Atlantic Ocean. In spite of its remote location and the treacherous tracks leading to it before the construction of modern roads, an old verse in Galician says:

> A San Andrés de Teixido
> vai de morto o que non vai de vivo.

> Anyone who does not visit San Andrés de Teixido
> when he is alive must visit after he is dead.

The T-shirt that I bought at a souvenir shop near the little church says that if you don't visit once alive, you must visit three times dead:

> O que non vai de vivo unha vez
> vai de morto tres.

This story explains why the pilgrimage is necessary.

134

San Andrés was depressed because his own sanctuary was neglected while pilgrims flocked from all over the world to the shrine of his fellow apostle Santiago (Saint James the Greater) at Santiago de Compostela in the south of Galicia, which is regarded as the third most holy site in Christendom. One day, as he was walking the roads alone, he came upon Jesus Christ, who asked him why he looked so sad.

"Master," San Andrés said, "I am sad because people go to Santiago from the farthest corners of the world, and my sanctuary is empty, as if I were a less faithful disciple of yours and less caring about the well-being of mankind."

Christ replied, "I promise you this, that no one will enter heaven unless he has visited your shrine at least once, alive or dead."

When the pilgrim is leaving the shrine, he will encounter snakes, toads, frogs, beetles and other insects and vermin. He must be careful not to step on them or damage them, because these are people who did not make the pilgrimage when they were alive, and they are doing so under different forms.

A Galician woman, Amparo Ordóñez, told me that her mother says if you haven't gone to the shrine before you die, a member of your family can do it for you after your death. However, if he stops to eat lunch or take a rest, when he is ready to resume the journey he must remember to say, "Now, let's all of us go," or the spirit of the dead person might stay behind at the resting place.

Christian pilgrims carry a heavy stone on the way to the sanctuary and leave it at the side of the road as a symbol of the forgiveness of their sins, resulting in heaps of stones. There is evidence of pre-Christian activity at the sanctuary, and it was also a custom in honour of Hermes, protector of travellers, to carry a stone on the journey up the hill and deposit it. The Galician word for a small cairn of this nature is *milladoiro*, which a popular Galician traditional music group has borrowed for its name.

The Vow of Muño Sancho
(Soria)

In the time of Alfonso VI, in the late 11th century, Don Muño Sancho of Hinojosa, a powerful but chivalrous warrior with 70 knights at his command, held recently reconquered and repopulated frontier lands to the east of the city of Soria. One day he and his knights were hunting along the border when they came across a festive party of unarmed and richly dressed Moorish men and women bearing jewellery and objects of gold and silver. Seizing the opportunity for booty and ransom, he and his men quickly surrounded the Moors, much to their captives' consternation.

One of the young Moors asked for the name of the leader of the knights, and when he was told it was Muño Sancho, he identified himself as Abadil and said, "I have heard that Don Muño is a valiant warrior with a fine sense of courtesy. We are willing to pay a ransom for our release, but I beg you to allow us to continue on our way without delay to celebrate my wedding with my bride, Alifra."

When Don Muño learned this and saw the beauty and stateliness of the young couple, he replied, "I have captured you and you will remain my prisoners for fifteen days. During that time you will be guests in my castle and celebrate your wedding there."

He sent word to his wife, Doña María Palacín, to prepare a banquet for the wedding party, and during the following two weeks he spared no effort in making their wedding and reception more lavish than they could have ever hoped to provide for themselves. At the end of the celebrations, he showered them with gifts and escorted the party safely into their own territory.

Many years later, King Alfonso organised a campaign against the Moors, and he called on the aged Don Muño and his 70 knights for assistance. There was a battle that some say was near Uclés in Cuenca and others say was in Don Muño's territory between Almenar and Hinojosa del Campo, close to where the Seven Princes of Lara had met their doom more than a century earlier. Don Muño lost an arm in the encounter but refused to retire from the battlefield, saying, "I would rather die as Muño Sancho than live as Muño Manco ['one-armed']."

One of the Moorish warriors singled out Don Muño, and their fierce combat resulted in Don Muño falling to the ground with a mortal wound. He and his warriors had long before taken a solemn vow that they would make a pilgrimage to the Holy Sepulchre in Jerusalem, but the continued demands of borderland vigilance had made it impossible to fulfil the promise. With his dying breath, Don Muño begged pardon of God for failing to visit Jerusalem.

When the Moorish warrior removed the helmet of his fallen opponent, he was horrified to discover who it was. For this Moor was Abadil, whom Don Muño had so chivalrously befriended years before. Abadil and his victorious army, along with the defeated Christians, joined in a grieving funeral procession to Don Muño's castle to break the sad news to his widow, Doña María, and to beg her forgiveness. Abadil paid for the tomb where Don Muño is buried in the cloisters of the convent of Santo Domingo de Silos. On one side of it is carved a scene of a festive party of Moorish men and women, and on the other a group of knights is seen kneeling in front of an altar. This is the explanation for the second picture.

On the day of Don Muño's final battle, the Spanish chaplain of the Patriarch of Jerusalem was notified that a troop of Spanish knights was approaching the Holy Sepulchre, and he went out to welcome them. To his pleasant surprise, he recognised his old friend and neighbour, Don Muño of Hinojosa, as their leader. The chaplain greeted him but received no response. The knights looked neither to the left nor right but continued straight for the shrine, where they dismounted and entered to kneel before the altar.

As the puzzled chaplain looked on, the men suddenly vanished before his eyes. He wrote to Spain to report the incident, and was informed that Don Muño and his 70 knights had all perished on the battlefield on the very day they had journeyed to Jerusalem, to honour after death the vow they had been unable to fulfil in life.

María Pérez the Manly
(Soria)

The historical basis of this legend is the 1127 Peace of Támara, a treaty in which Alfonso VII of Castile and León (1105-1157) and Alfonso I of Aragón (1074-1134) agreed on the borders of their territories.

María, Álvar and Gómez Pérez, reputedly descended from Fernán González, Count of Castile, were famous warriors of their time, but only María Pérez "la Varona (Manly)" is still celebrated today.

On the death of Alfonso VI in 1109, his daughter, Urraca, widow of Raimundo of Galicia, became queen of Castile and León, which included Asturias and Galicia. Her and Raimundo's son was Alfonso VII, who was later named Emperor of All Spain. Urraca married the overbearing Alfonso I "the Battler" of Aragón for political reasons, probably to prevent him from taking her kingdom by force. She nicknamed him "the Celt-Iberian" for his barbarous and cruel nature. Their marital relationship eventually deteriorated to such a degree that he imprisoned her in Soria, but she escaped and divorced him in 1113.

When Alfonso VII succeeded to the throne of Castile and León on the death of his mother in 1126, Alfonso of Aragón boasted that he could beat anyone in his step-son's realm in single combat. The Castilian accepted the challenge, set a date, and nominated Álvar Pérez as his champion. Álvar arrived openly at the camp set up at Barahona, south of Soria City, for the encounter. Alfonso VII also summoned María Pérez, but she arrived in secret. Brother and sister agreed to the plan the Castilian king proposed: that María would wear Álvar's armour and fight in his place. Even if she lost, she would give a good account of herself, and Alfonso of Aragón would be humiliated.

The following day, Alfonso of Aragón and his opponent, faces obscured by helmets, broke several lances against each other on horseback, then proceeded to swordplay on foot. The spectators noticed that Álvar Pérez seemed to have changed his fighting style. He was more agile than usual, and he danced around Alfonso giving him no rest. By late morning, the Aragón king had tired, and at midday the Castilian champion managed to disarm him and lay him on his back. Alfonso was forced to yield.

Then María dramatically removed her helmet to the astonishment of the crowd and the acute embarrassment of the Battler.

For her accomplishment, Alfonso VII conferred on her the title "la Varona". The chastened Alfonso of Aragón was sport enough to award her the right to add the four red bars of Aragón to her coat of arms – diagonally to designate a trophy. He ceased his predatory attitude toward Castile and León, which was undoubtedly the result Alfonso VII had hoped for, and turned his warlike attention to the east against the Moors. They agreed their territorial limits in the Peace of Támara, and from then on, we are told, they acted like brothers or like father and son.

María later married Don Vela of Aragón, brother of Alfonso I, and when he died she joined a convent. Her family, beginning with her son Rodrigo, substituted Varona for Pérez as their surname. Some say the four red bars on the family's coat of arms come from her marriage to Don Vela, not from defeating Alfonso.

Other versions of the legend say that it was Alfonso VI of Castile and León who named El Cid as his champion in response to Alfonso I's challenge, substituting María secretly; or that María was a warrior in a battle between Aragoneses and Castilians, and in the confusion of the fighting she came up against Alfonso the Battler and took him prisoner; alternatively, that La Varona was Elvira, daughter of the Count of Barahona.

Local tradition holds that Barahona takes its name from Varona, but others say it derives from the Basque meaning "good mountain".

The Lagarto of La Malena
(Jaén)

A *lagarto* (lizard) has been the official symbol of the city of Jaén since 1249, so it was well before that time that a resident of Jaén brought a "lizard" – probably a baby crocodile – back from a journey as a present for his daughter. It eventually escaped and found refuge in a cave near a spring in the old quarter of the city called La Magdalena, or La Malena for short. As it grew larger over the years, so did its appetite, and it progressed from eating small beasts of the wild to chickens and

139

other domestic animals. When it started eating children and then adults, the residents of La Malena were afraid to leave their houses. They demanded that something be done.

All attempts to kill the lagarto failed. Either the would-be saviour could not catch it or it killed him when he confronted it. Finally, a prisoner condemned to death offered to rid the city of the menace in exchange for his freedom and a pardon. This was accepted, and he asked for and received a horse, a lance and a sack of gunpowder.

He bought some freshly baked loaves of bread and filled one of them with the powder, leaving a fuse trailing from it. He rode the horse to the monster's lair, and when the lagarto was tempted out by the aroma of the bread, the prisoner threw a loaf to it. The lagarto swallowed the bread with one gulp. From the safety of the horse's back and with the lance for protection, the prisoner continued to throw one loaf after another and thus led the lagarto further from the cave until it was in front of the church of San Ildefonso. Then he threw the loaf filled with powder. When the lagarto swallowed it, he lit the fuse, and the explosion killed the monster.

The story goes on to state that the lagarto's hide was mounted on a wall inside the church. A friend of a friend has said that he thinks he saw the hide in the church some years ago, though I searched recently and couldn't find it. The shopkeeper I spoke with in the shop facing the 18th-century neo-classical main entrance to the church of San Ildefonso denied that the monster's hide had ever been in that or any other church in Jaén.

"It's just a legend," he said emphatically.

The event has given rise to a local curse: "May you explode like the lagarto of La Malena."

The Lagarto of Seville

According to what is probably history, as related in de Mena's *Tradiciones y Leyendas Sevillanas* and on a Seville website, the Sultan of Egypt sent gifts to Alfonso the Wise about the year 1260, along with a request to marry his daughter. Alfonso rejected the request but kept the gifts, which included a crocodile from the Nile. When the crocodile died, its hide was stuffed with straw and hung in the Patio de los

Naranjos of the cathedral in Seville, where it remains to this day to amaze the tourists and delight the children.

However, Lauriño's *Historias y Leyendas de Andalucía* has another explanation for the lagarto's presence in the cathedral. The same crocodile given to Alfonso ate a canon (an official of the cathedral). This version says that the crocodile in the cathedral is made of wood and was placed there as a warning of what will happen to anyone who attacks a member of the clergy.

The Lovers of Teruel
(Teruel)

Heaven, which kept us apart in life, will unite us in the tomb.
(from Los Amantes de Teruel*, Juan Eugenio de Hartzenbusch, 1837)*

You are a continual hope, consolation and example,
For where there is an Isabel, there will always be a Diego.
(from Himno a los Amantes de Teruel*, Carlos Luis de la Vega, 1977)*

The visitor who arrives in Teruel by train, upon leaving the station to climb the neomudéjar (1921) Escalinata to the old part of the town, is confronted by a large relief sculpture (also 1921) depicting a young woman bending over a dead youth. These are the Lovers of Teruel, whose tragic story has been in oral tradition since shortly after their deaths in 1217 and has frequently been retold since the 16th century in music, art, drama, dance and poetry.

The ancient escutcheon of the de Marcillas had long been respected, but the family had fallen on hard times. The de Seguras were newly rich landowners. Isabel de Segura and Diego Martínez de Marcilla played together as children, and as they grew older their friendship gradually turned to love. To them it seemed as natural as breathing that they would some day marry, but their romantic plans were socially improbable at best. Not only was the Marcilla family impoverished, Diego was the younger son, and any inheritance would go to his brother.

141

Isabel's father strenuously opposed their relationship, and he forbade her to see Diego. His daughter's marriage should increase his family's wealth, not diminish it.

The lovers met in secret and discussed what was to be done. The only way for Diego to make enough money to qualify as a suitor was to go away and seek his fortune. In those days, a worthy warrior could quickly acquire wealth and position through plunder and captured property. They came to an agreement: Diego would join the Christian army then assembling in Barcelona to fight against the Moors. If he failed to return in five years, Isabel was to give him up for dead and marry another. This coincided with a vow Isabel had made: to keep her virginity until she reached the age of twenty, five years and a day from then. They parted with heavy hearts, relieved only by the fact that Isabel's father had reluctantly agreed to wait for five years before he would force her to marry a man of his choice.

Diego joined the army of Pedro II of Aragón and distinguished himself in the famous battle of Las Navas de Tolosa in 1212. After Pedro's death the following year, Diego took part in an invasion of North Africa. He proved to be a fine soldier and quickly won the respect of his comrades and the approval of the officers. Success followed success, until eventually he won his officer's insignia and was awarded a knighthood for his valour. He was also granted extensive properties as spoils of war, and he inherited the estate of a French comrade whose life he had saved. Diego was suddenly a wealthy man with a title.

Meanwhile, Isabel waited in vain for some word from him. Some say he never wrote, wishing to surprise her with a triumphal return. But more say his letters, which might have offered her some hope with confirmation that he was still alive and reports of his steady advancement, were intercepted by Isabel's parents, who planned to marry her to a wealthy friend for financial benefit as soon as the five-year period expired. This was Don Rodrigo de Azagra, a retired knight who had recently moved into neighbouring Albarracín. They also told Isabel falsely that they had received news that Diego had been killed in battle.

As soon as he was confirmed in his new fortune Diego set off for home to bring Isabel the good news. He began his journey in good time, though with a close margin, to arrive less than five years after he had left Teruel, but his ship was delayed by a storm. After landing in

142

Valencia, he received word along the road that Isabel was to be married on the day that the agreed waiting period expired, and he made the greatest haste, never resting, and pausing only to change horses. But when he arrived in the city late in the evening, he was greeted by the sight of public festivities in honour of the wedding that had taken place that morning.

Diego went into Isabel's house and mingled unrecognised with the invited guests. Eventually the newly married couple took their leave in preparation to withdraw upstairs to the wedding chamber. Diego made his way secretly to the chamber and concealed himself under the bed, determined to prevent the consummation of the marriage.

As Isabel got into bed to join Rodrigo, Diego caught her by the hand. Gasping with surprise, she immediately recognised the hand as Diego's. Rodrigo asked her why she had gasped.

"I suddenly remembered a vow I made when I was fifteen – to remain a virgin until I had reached the age of twenty. I won't be twenty until tomorrow, so I beg you not to ask me to do what a man expects of his bride on their wedding night."

Rodrigo reluctantly granted her request, and he soon fell asleep. Then Isabel cautiously got out of bed, Diego slid out from under it, and they moved into an alcove to talk. Diego explained about the letters he had written and why he had arrived late, and she told him that the letters had been kept from her and how her father had told her that Diego was dead and insisted that she marry as soon as the five-year period had ended.

"I accept that it is God's will that we not be united in this life," Diego said, "but at least give me a kiss or I will die."

"I wish that things were otherwise, my love. I understand your grief and pain because I feel the same emotions. But now that I am married, I no longer belong to myself, and I cannot give to you what belongs to my husband, not even a kiss."

For the love he had for her, Diego would not force her to do what she felt was improper. He turned to leave, stopped suddenly, and fell dead to the floor. Isabel threw herself onto his body and wept so loudly that Rodrigo woke up, asking what was wrong.

Isabel went to him before he could see Diego's corpse and related the events of her and Diego's relationship, only changing the names.

"I dreamed that a young friend of mine had agreed to marry her lover ..." she began, and when she reached the present "... he arrived too late to prevent the marriage. He asked her to at least give him a kiss so that he would not die of grief, but she refused because she felt it would not be right, and then he died. That's why I was crying. Tell me, do you think she did the right thing?"

Rodrigo laughed and said, "She was very silly and prudish and overly cruel to one she loved, not to give him one kiss when he was alive to save his life, when she would kiss him a thousand times in her mind after he died."

She then showed him Diego's body, saying, "I am that silly and prudish woman, but I have kept my honour."

When Rodrigo recovered from his astonishment, they discussed what they should do. They realised that it would be legally awkward and socially scandalous for the body to be found in the bedroom, and Diego's family might want revenge, so they decided to take the corpse out and leave it in the doorway of Diego's family's house.

Came the morning, and the discovery of the dead youth caused grief in his family and consternation among the townspeople. The funeral was set for the following day.

At the Mass in the church of San Pedro, Isabel's family, the de Seguras, as one of the leading families in the town, were seated in the front pew near the open casket. Isabel, her head covered with a black veil of mourning, sat through the ceremony with her pale face buried in her hands. Then, before anyone realised what she was doing, she stood and walked to the casket, threw back her veil, and placed a kiss on Diego's bloodless lips so forcefully that the sound could be heard throughout the church, and she fell onto his body with her arms around him. Her shocked parents rushed to her side to pull her away, only to discover that she was dead.

Most versions of the story imply or state that she died of grief, but one, the Papel de San Pedro, which was discovered in the archives of the church of San Pedro in 1806, suggests suicide. During the procession to the church, Isabel speaks to Diego in her mind:

"I will live no longer. I will follow your example and die, husband, for you deserve that name more than the second one. I consider the devotion you showed me to be a pact until your death, and I want to repay that with my death, so that fame will make us one in the tomb, and

144

the story of our love will immortalise us. Wait, Diego, until I can come and give you what I ungratefully denied you, for if poison and dagger fail me, grief will suffice to give me a sure death. You will see me within an hour, and I will be very happy if one gravestone will cover us both, for our souls burn with a pure and chaste love."

All agreed – both families, the townspeople, local officials, even Rodrigo – that Isabel and Diego should be buried together as husband and wife. Their alabaster figures now lie on separate coffins in the church of San Pedro, their hands stretched toward each other without quite touching.

Each February 14, Teruel celebrates its best-known story with a spectacular re-enactment of the dramatic events in the streets of the town. Any engaged couple named Isabel and Diego may be married during the festival.

Diego Machacha and the Unforgiven Offence
(Jerez)

Diego Pérez de Vargas was a fierce warrior famous for saving the castle of Martos, owned by his liege lord, Don Álvar Pérez de Castro, in 1240. Don Álvar and most of his troops were away with King Fernando III the Saint's army, leaving his nephew, Don Tello, and 45 warriors to hold the castle and defend Álvar's wife and the women of the household. Don Tello and the warriors had ridden out to raid nearby Moors when a large force of Moors stormed the castle. Álvar's wife cleverly had the women disguise themselves as soldiers and parade around the battlements carrying weapons to make the Moors think the castle was well defended, but the attackers were on the point of breaking in when Diego bravely led the apparently suicidal charge that scattered and demoralised them. His horse's hoof prints can still be seen at the top of the castle hill.

During one battle Diego broke his sword and lance and ripped a branch from an olive tree to use as a club. Don Álvar saw this and called out encouragement: "Así! así! Diego; machacha! machacha! – So, so, Diego, smash them, smash them." He thus earned the sobriquet "Machacha" (the Smasher), and several generations of his descendants took Machacha or the variant Machuca as their surname.

Diego and his brother-in-law, Pero Miguel, had never got on well together, and there had been a running dispute over an offence that Diego had committed against Pero. On the day before the battle at Jerez led by Prince Alfonso, Diego asked Pero to forgive him for the duration of the battle, so that they could concentrate on fighting as comrades. Pero refused.

During the engagement the following day, Pero, a strong and accomplished warrior, was seen frequently in the thick of combat. But when the battle was over, his tent was empty and his horse riderless. He was never seen again. No other Christian soldiers were lost. Ever afterwards, this incident was given as a warning to warriors never to go into battle without pardoning those who asked forgiveness.

Tentudía
(Badajoz Province)

Don Pelayo Pérez Correa, Master of the Order of Santiago 1242-1275, was fighting a battle against the Moors in the Sierra Morena in the south of Badajoz near the Huelva border during the campaign of King Fernando III the Saint. He was winning the battle, but daylight was fading, and he knew that the battle would be lost if it had to be continued on the following day. He prayed, "Holy Mary, detain your day – *detén tu día.*" Daylight was miraculously prolonged and the battle was won. He built the church called Nuestra Señora de Tentudía in thanksgiving, and he is buried there.

The Valour of Garcí Pérez
(Seville)

The courage of Garcí Pérez de Vargas of Toledo and his coolness in the face of danger were the subject of many a tale told round the campfires of knights, both Christian and Moor. This incident took place at the beginning of the siege of Seville, mounted by King Fernando III the Saint in the summer of 1247. Fernando observed the encounter from start to finish from the top of a hill. A ballad version of the story appears in the *Libro del Repartimiento*, and a prose account is in *Estoria de*

146

España, both of which were written at the order of Fernando's son, Alfonso X the Wise. It has been speculated that Alfonso wrote the ballad himself, having heard the story from his father.

A party of foragers had set out from the Christian camp to forcibly requisition provisions from the countryside, with an escort of knights to ensure compliance and guard against interference by Moorish warriors. Garcí Pérez and another knight, with their accompanying squires, were late leaving the camp, and the main party had advanced some distance ahead of them and was out of sight.

Suddenly they came across seven armed and mounted Moorish warriors ahead of them on the road. Garcí's companion said they should retreat, as knights were not required to fight against such odds.

"Even though I may die," replied Garcí, "I wouldn't think of turning back, lest such an awkward withdrawal should give the appearance of cowardice."

The other knight turned around and went back to the camp. Seeing this, Fernando ordered horsemen to ride to Garcí's rescue immediately.

Don Lorenzo Juárez, who was standing by the king's side, said, "If those Moors know who Don Garcí Pérez is, they will not meddle with him. If they don't know, you will have an opportunity to see why he has made such a name for himself."

Garcí ordered his squire to hand him his helmet and mailed hood and undercap and his arms. As he laced up the hood, he failed to notice that the undercap that protected his bald head from the roughness of the hood had fallen to the ground. He placed his helmet on his head, closed the visor and set his lance in the socket. He warned his squire not to make any rash moves, and they proceeded calmly on their way. Knowing by his escutcheon who he was and familiar with his reputation, the Moorish knights moved to the side of the road to let him pass.

After he had gone a little way past them, Garcí noticed that the undercap was missing and realised that he must have dropped it while he was lacing up the hood. He explained to the squire that they were going to have to retrace their steps to look for it.

"But, sir," began the terrified squire.

"That cap was embroidered for me by a fair lady," said Garcí. "And besides, this bald head of mine needs it for a cushion."

147

As Garcí and the squire turned and moved step by step towards the Moors once again, Fernando said, "He's going to attack them single-handed."

"We'll see," said Lorenzo.

The Moors had not stirred the first time Garcí passed them, and they did not move now as he and the squire made their way past them again. Garcí found the undercap, ordered his squire to pick it up, and turned around once more to pass the Moors a third time and continue on his original course to follow the foragers.

Such was the honour and glory that this deed brought to Garcí – much to his embarrassment, for he was a modest man – that many times afterwards he was asked who was the companion knight who had left him on the road to face seven enemy warriors alone. And as often as he was asked, even by the king himself, he would appear confused and swear that he was not acquainted with the man. This was not true, for he knew the coward well and often saw him in the camp.

But as Mariana comments at the end of his account of the incident, what advantage would there be to Garcí if he advertised the cowardice of another, and made an enemy of him and caused him to be scorned? On the other hand, his silence on the matter following his own show of valour made the perfect ending to the story.

Don Quijote places Garcí Pérez among Caesar, Alexander, Hannibal, Fernán González and El Cid who performed deeds "as true as they were valiant" (*Don Quijote I*, 49).

Three Miracles of Our Lady

My sources for these three legends are:

Milagros de Nuestra Señora, Gonzalo de Berceo (c. 1198 - c. 1265): 26 verse stories composed in Castilian between 1246 and 1252. Berceo, a secular priest at Santo Domingo de Silos and San Millán de Cogolla, was the first author known by name to write in the major vernacular language of Spain.

Cantigas de Santa María: songs written in Galician-Portuguese, the literary language at the time. Of the 420 canticles in the final edition, 356 relate miracles and the rest are praise hymns with melodies. They were commissioned and collected between 1270 and 1282 under the close supervision of the scholar-king Alfonso X the Wise (1221-1284), who is believed to have written a small number of them himself. During a serious illness in 1277, he asked for a copy of the first edition of 100 cantigas to be placed in his hands. Cantiga 209 uses the first person ("I will tell you what happened to me") to relate how the book cured him.

Miracula Beate Marie Virginis, according to an online edition of MS Thott 128 in the Royal Library of Copenhagen. This early 13th-century collection of 28 prose stories in Latin was probably one of Berceo's and Alfonso's sources.

Berceo makes it clear that these stories are meant to be inspirational and devotional and are not to be taken as fact, when he says in stanza 16, line 4 of his introduction, "Let us keep what is inside and leave the outside."

The story of San Ildefonso, which was known in the eighth century, comes first in all of my sources. The second story does not mention which of the nine Marian feasts the priest celebrated every day. As his source for The Pilgrim Tricked, Berceo cites Saint Hugo, Abbot of Cluny 1049-1109, who wrote the now lost *Vita Beatae Virginis*.

My versions of these stories are close translations based mainly on Berceo, with explanatory or background information from other sources woven into the text.

The Chasuble of San Ildefonso

In fair Toledo, that royal city beside the great River Tajo, there lived an archbishop who was a sincere friend of the Glorious Mother of God. He was called Ildefonso, according to the history books, a shepherd who nourished his flock, a moderate and serious man who lived a holy life and used great common sense. Among his many good works, two services to the Blessed Mother stand out. He wrote an elegant book in defence of the doctrine of her perpetual virginity, challenging the arguments of three renegade authors. At the Tenth Council of Toledo in AD 656 he sponsored the change of the Feast of the Annunciation – the message brought by the Angel Gabriel that Mary had been chosen to be the mother of the Messiah – from 25 March to 18 December. The feast had frequently fallen within Lent, when hymns in her praise were not allowed, and celebrating it a week before the Nativity of her Son was felt to be more appropriate. (This change was temporary and evidently

149

only valid in Spain.) The members of the Council also gave Ildefonso the task of composing the Mass for the feast. For these services he was awarded a great honour.

On the next Feast of the Annunciation (in 657, the year Ildefonso became archbishop), there were very few Toledans who stayed at home and did not go to the Cathedral. Ildefonso was about to enter the sanctuary in advance of the arrival of King Recesvinto to celebrate the Mass, when he saw sitting in the ornate episcopal chair the Mother of the King of Majesty herself, and in her hand was a copy of the book he had written about her virginity. This made him very happy. Then she did something no one had ever heard of before. She presented him with a chasuble not sewn with a needle or woven by human hand, but worked by angels.

"My friend," she said, "this is your reward for the double honour you have paid me. You have written a book in my praise, and you have moved my feast from a useless date. For your new Mass of this Feast, I bring you a gift of great splendour: a chasuble to wear to celebrate the Holy Sacrifice. But this is certain: no one but you is permitted to wear this chasuble or to sit in this chair. God will not hesitate to severely punish anyone else who presumes to put on this vestment, and this chair where you normally sit is for you alone."

And then she took herself away from human sight. Ildefonso continued to grow daily in the exercise of good works in honour of God and His Blessed Mother, and when he died he was received into heaven by Our Lord.

The next archbishop was a proud, arrogant and frivolous-minded man named Siagrio, who held his predecessor in little regard. He thought himself the equal of Ildefonso, but he was in fact a worthless boor despised by the Toledans. He was deceived by his own pride and the Old Enemy into seating himself in the chair reserved by the Blessed Mother for Ildefonso alone, from where he demanded that the angel-fashioned chasuble be brought to him. The mad words spoken so lightly by the stupid wretch brought great sorrow to Our Lady.

"Ildefonso was never worth much," he said. "I'm as consecrated as he was, and we are all equal anyway, so why should I not wear his chasuble?"

If Siagrio had not put himself forward in that way, and if he had held his tongue a bit, he would not have fallen under the anger of God, for

150

which serious sin we suppose he is damned. He ordered his ministers to bring the chasuble as he was about to go to the altar to begin the Mass, but he was not allowed to do it, nor did he have the power, for what God does not want, cannot be.

Although the holy vestment was wide enough, when Siagrio put it on it suddenly shrank and grasped him round the throat like a strong chain, and so he was strangled for his great madness.

The Simple Priest

A poor and simple priest of little education celebrated the Mass of Holy Mary every day, instead of saying the specific Mass designated for each day, because it was the only one he knew. The Mass he said was one of several in which the Introit begins "Salve Sancta Parens" (Hail, Holy Mother) and which contain frequent references to Our Lady's intercession on behalf of her devotees. Another priest reported this to the Bishop, and the Bishop said, "Tell that son of the wicked whore (*fijo de la mala putanna*) to come to me without delay."

The wretched priest appeared before the Bishop, pale and trembling and full of shame. The Bishop asked him if it was true what the other priest had said, that he celebrated the same Mass regardless of the day, and the poor simple priest admitted that it was so. The Bishop said, "Because you don't know how to say any other Mass, and you have no sense or ability, I order you to stop saying Masses altogether. Find some other way to make a living."

The poor priest went into the church and fell to his knees in front of the statue of the Blessed Virgin and prayed. He explained what had happened and asked her to help him.

The Blessed Virgin appeared to the Bishop in a vision and preached him a sermon in strong words: "I have never done anything against you, proud bishop, so why have you done such a serious and wicked thing to me? I have never taken as much as one grain from you, and yet you have taken my priest from me. Because he was celebrating the Mass in honour of me every day you have accused him of heresy. You have treated him like a beast and taken away his permission to say Mass. If you don't allow him to say my Mass every day as he has been doing, there is going to be serious trouble, and you will come to a bad end 30 days from now. You will see what it means to make me angry."

These threats frightened the Bishop, and he sent for the priest immediately. He apologised, admitted that he had been wrong, and he asked the priest's forgiveness. He then told the priest to continue saying Our Lady's Mass as he had been doing, and if he ever needed clothes or shoes or anything else, all he had to do was ask and the Bishop would give it to him.

The priest continued to serve the glorious Holy Mother Mary, and when his life on earth was finished, his soul went to glory, to the happy fellowship.

The Pilgrim Tricked by the Wicked Enemy

Giraldus was a man of little prudence, and he followed a life of folly and sin like an unconstrained bachelor. The idea came to him one day to go on pilgrimage to Santiago de Compostela in honour of the patron saint of Spain. He set his affairs in order and assembled some companions.

On the night before he set out on the Camino de Santiago, he committed a serious sin. He lay with his mistress instead of keeping vigil. He didn't confess or receive absolution, and contrary to religious law he went on his pilgrimage in the state of mortal sin.

On the third day of his journey, he was walking some distance ahead of his companions when he saw a man dressed as a pilgrim and wearing the scallop shell, the emblem of pilgrims to Compostela. The man stood in the road and barred his way. It was the Old Enemy, Satan himself, disguised as Santiago. He hailed Giraldus and said: "You're as foolish as a lamb. You left your house to come to mine without receiving absolution for the sin you committed."

"Who are you?" asked Giraldus.

"I am Santiago," said Satan. "You should know that you can't complete the pilgrimage successfully without doing penance. You will not please Holy Mary, and you will not receive the salvation you seek unless you do what I tell you."

"What do you want me to do?" asked Giraldus.

"First, cut off your genitals and then kill yourself. You will receive your eternal reward for making a sacrifice to God with your own flesh."

Giraldus, believing that it was indeed Santiago who was speaking, grabbed his genitals and cut them off with a sharp knife, and then drew

152

the knife across his throat. He fell down mortally wounded and excommunicated. When his companions arrived and saw his body, they were greatly shocked and couldn't imagine how it had happened. It was obvious that he had not been killed by a robber, as nothing had been taken from him. They ran away, afraid that they would be arrested and charged with his murder and hanged.

When they had left, the Old Enemy, with his attendants great and small, began to carry Giraldus's soul to hell in a not too gentle manner. Just as they were going past the church of Saint Peter, at a signal from God, Santiago with Saint Peter by his side came and said to the demonic cohort, "Why are you taking my pilgrim? You have no right to do that."

One of the devils said stubbornly: "Iago, you are arguing against all reason. Giraldus committed a sin by killing himself by his own hand. He must be judged as a brother of Judas. He is a member of our parish in every way. You're a mean man to go against us."

Santiago replied, "You are certainly not going to rejoice in this death. If you had not told him that you were Santiago, and if you had not taken on my appearance and displayed the scallop shell that is my symbol, he would not have mutilated his body with his own hands, and he would not be lying by the side of the road. He did it because he thought he was acting in obedience to me. You killed my pilgrim with your clever lies. Now, since you continue to argue, we will take the matter to the judgement of Holy Mary, the Mother of God."

They placed their arguments before the Glorious Mother of God, each stating his case strongly. She carefully considered both sides and then concluded the proceedings with a wise decision. She reasoned that Giraldus had innocently taken Satan for Santiago, and since he had to obey Santiago, he was not guilty of sin, and so she denied the petition of the Trickster. She said to him, "I hereby order that the soul of Giraldus be returned to its body so he can perform penance. He will be judged on what he does after that."

God ratified the decision and ordered that the poor soul be returned to its body, and the devil and his followers were disappointed to lose their case. The limp body arose, confused and irritated like a man who had just awakened, and Giraldus washed his face. The wound from the throat-slitting quickly healed leaving only a thin thread, and the pain disappeared. Everyone said, "This man was very fortunate."

However, the parts that he had cut off never grew back. Nothing remained but a scar and a hole through which he could pass water when nature demanded. He called for his travelling pack and put it on his shoulders, and he continued on his way to Compostela happy and relieved. He gave thanks to God and Holy Mary and to Santiago to whom he was going on pilgrimage. His companions sang as they walked with him, for this miracle was a joy for them every day.

When they arrived in Compostela, Giraldus's story was heard throughout the city, and everyone came to look. They said, "Such a thing must be written down so that people in the future can hear of it and rejoice."

When he arrived back in his own land with his pilgrimage completed, the people heard what had happened. There was great excitement, and they were impressed to see this Lazarus brought back to life.

Thinking about how God had taken away his wicked appetites, Giraldus left his family and friends and entered the monastery of Cluny dressed in penitential clothing. Brother Giraldus told his true story to Hugo, Abbot of Cluny, who put it in writing.

The Chest of Relics and the Chasuble of San Ildefonso

A Chest of Relics, dating from the time of the Apostles, was removed from Jerusalem when the Persians conquered the city in 614 and was taken to Africa, then to Seville for safekeeping. When San Isidoro of Seville was appointed bishop of Toledo, he took it there with him.

Alfonso the Wise's *Primera Crónica General* (Chapter 614) lists the contents of the Chest, which included a glass vial containing the blood that came from the side of Jesus on the Cross, a piece of the Cross, part of the Crown of Thorns, some of the bread miraculously multiplied for 5000 people, bread from the Last Supper, manna that rained on the Israelites in the desert, one of the utensils used in the converting of water to wine at the wedding feast at Cana, milk from the breast of the Mother of Jesus, the hands of Saint Stephen, the right sandal of Saint Peter, hair of the Holy Innocents, hair of Mary Magdalene that she used to wash the feet of Jesus, and bones of prophets and saints too numerous to mention.

The same chapter says that King Don Pelayo and Archbishop Urbán took the Chest from Toledo to Asturias when the Moors invaded, and deposited it in the Cathedral of Oviedo; the Chasuble of San Ildefonso was also in the Cathedral at this time. Other documents between the 11th and 18th centuries state that the Chasuble was – or was said to be – in the Cathedral, but when the list of contents of the Chest was read out in a speech in 1993 on the occasion of the Feast of Our Lady the Virgin of Covadonga near Oviedo, the Chasuble was not mentioned.

A letter written by Father Sebastián Sarmiento, preserved in an archive in Toledo, describes the opening of the Chest by four bishops in the late 16th century as described to him by one of those present:

"After opening the first chest, which is large, they found another small one, then another and more small ones, until they came upon a very small coffer about the size of the palm of a large man's hand. This bore an inscription that said 'The Chasuble that Our Lady Gave to San Ildefonso'. They were amazed, because it seemed to them impossible that it could contain a chasuble. They opened the coffer with great difficulty, so much so that they nearly despaired of being able to open it. Inside they found a sky-blue light silk cloth in the form of a Portuguese cloak big enough to cover the tallest man in Spain, seamless and with no trace of weaving, like an onion-skin, so light and delicate that the men's breath made it swell like a sail in a strong wind. Folding it the way it had been, they returned it to the coffer, swearing that they would say nothing to anyone until they were 60 miles [100 km] from Oviedo."

Since that reported 16th-century inspection of the Chasuble, no one has claimed to have seen it. Several likely locations in the Cathedral of Oviedo have been searched to no avail. The Chest of Relics remains in the Cámara Santa of the Cathedral, but the Chasuble seems to have disappeared.

Guzmán the Good – of the Heroic Deed of Tarifa
(Tarifa)

Don Alonso Pérez de Guzmán, governor of Tarifa, stood on the wall of his encircled city and watched a party of the besieging Moors approach with their hostage, Don Alonso's young son, named Alfonso, mounted on a horse and bound hand and foot. Some say the son had been kidnapped from the city, possibly with the connivance of spies within. Alternatively, he had bravely but rashly sneaked out of the city on a self-assigned solo mission to assassinate the Moorish leader and was captured.

"Don Alonso," said the leader of the Moorish party. "Surrender the city or we will kill your son."

Don Alonso drew his dagger from its sheath and threw it to the Moors, saying, "Use my dagger to kill him, if that is your wish, but I refuse to surrender." The Moors lifted the siege and departed, leaving behind the dead body of the governor's son.

To honour him for his display of loyalty and to consol him for the sacrifice of his son, King Fernando IV ordered that "the Good" be added to Don Alonso's name.

That is the well-known legendary version of the incident. A storyteller normally does not let facts get in the way of a good story, but in this case legend obscures the more intriguing historical account.

Alonso Pérez de Guzmán el Bueno (1256-1309) was the progenitor of a noble line that included his namesake who was the commander of the ill-fated Invincible Armada of 1588, as well as many leading military and political figures. On either side of the Pérez de Guzmán coat of arms are two towers, the Pillars of Hercules (the Straits of Gibraltar), symbolising Don Alonso's governorship of the strategically significant city of Tarifa. Tarifa is situated on the southernmost tip of Spain, 15 miles (24 km) across the Straits of Gibraltar from Morocco. A banner wrapped around the Pillars reads: "Non Plus Ultra – No Further". This is interpreted as a warning to would-be invaders from Africa. The crest is a crenellated castle tower from which the figure of a man, representing Don Alonso, brandishes a long dagger. From the tower waves a banner with the motto: "Preferre Patriam Liberis

Parentem Decet – The Freedom of the State Is Worth the Death of the Subject."

Don Alonso was the illegitimate son of Pedro Nuñez de Guzmán. Insulted in the court by allusions to his birth, he took service in Fez with Sultán Ben Yusef of the powerful Benimerines clan, on condition that he not be required to fight against Christians. The dragon at the base of the Pérez de Guzmán coat of arms is a reminder that Don Alonso killed a man-eating dragon while he was in the sultan's service. He was summoned to Spain by Alfonso X the Wise to deal with the king's rebellious son, Sancho; he returned to Africa, then was called back to Spain to serve Sancho on the King's death. He was based in Seville.

Ben Yusef and his Benimerines, flexing their increasing political and military might, had crossed the Straits and taken Tarifa from the Christians in 1275. After Ben Yusef's death in 1286, the Christians reconquered the city from his son, Aben Yacub.

Don Alonso's wife, Doña María Coronel, persuaded the king to post her husband to Tarifa as its *alcaide* or governor in order to extract him from the machinations of his mistress in Seville. This was done in 1293, and the family moved to Tarifa with the exception of the oldest son, Alfonso, who had previously left for Portugal with his foster father, Prince Juan, King Sancho's traitorous brother. Nursing grievances against the Castilian king, the son then accompanied the Prince to Morocco, where they joined with Aben Yacub and the king of Granada to mount a massive attack against Tarifa in 1294. Unable to breach the defences, they encircled the city.

History and legend are in accord on the incident of the dagger, more or less as recounted above: that Don Alonso agreed to "sacrifice" his son to save Tarifa, whence the motto, "The Freedom of the State Is Worth the Death of the Subject." But all legendary and most historical sources omit to mention that young Alfonso was a willing participant in the attack on the city. More important, to enhance the horror and poignancy of a father choosing patriotic duty over his son's life, they ignore the fact that Alfonso was not killed by the Moors. He survived to become a supporter of the usurper Enrique II against Pedro the Cruel, and his wife, Doña Urraca Osorio, was burned at the stake as a rebel by Pedro. (See the following chapter.)

However, history and legend agree that "the Good" was added to Don Alonso's name as a reward for his loyalty. A plaque mounted on a tower of the castle in 1850 by a descendant of Don Alonso describes him as "padre del segundo Isac – father of the second Isaac".

Pedro the Cruel and Enrique the Bastard
(Seville and Montiel)

Alfonso XI, King of Castile and León, was succeeded on his death in 1350 by his legitimate son, Pedro I the Cruel, who has been described as a psychopath by one modern historian. The usually calm and dispassionate Mariana (*Historia General de España*, 1592) was uncharacteristically exercised by the resulting upheavals:

Alfonso's death was followed by turmoil, storms, cruel and bloody wars, deceits, treasons, exiles, innumerable deaths, many great lords killed violently, many civil wars, disregard for both sacred and profane things. It is impossible to say whether all these disorders were due to the king or to the nobles. Popular opinion blames the king, so much so that he was called "the Cruel". But good authors blame the waywardness of the nobles, who so followed their unchecked appetites, greed and ambition in all things good and bad, that the king was obliged to punish their excesses.

Pedro had a running dispute with the nobles, who wanted a greater share of political power. Indicating a loaf of bread one day, he commented that it would be enough to feed all those who were loyal to him. History and legend supply an abundance of stories to illustrate the reason for his evil reputation. Here are a few.

Although Pedro was married to Doña Blanca de Borbón, niece of Charles V of France, he was living openly with the famously beautiful Doña María de Padilla, who later was posthumously awarded wifely status by the Church at Pedro's insistence. This situation scandalised society and "resulted in the total destruction of the King and the kingdom" (Mariana). Pedro took no notice of his mother's and aunt's warnings that the glaring affront to his wife could bring about war with France. He eventually had Doña Blanca poisoned, "abominable madness, an atrocious, inhuman and savage deed" (Mariana).

158

Pedro's illegitimate half-brother Fadrique held the prestigious position of Master of the Order of Santiago. According to Mariana, Pedro had Fadrique killed in 1358 so the post could go to María's brother, but legend gives a more romantic version. Pedro discovered that Fadrique was having an affair with María, and he sequestered her in the Alcázar in Seville. The lovers hatched an escape plan with the aid of a confidant. María left the Alcázar disguised as a peasant, and she was to join Fadrique, who was dressed as a mule-driver. However, their confidant was an agent of Pedro, and Fadrique was soon captured. He was killed on Pedro's orders and in his presence in the antechamber of the Alcázar called the Sala de Justicia (Hall of Justice), where the bloodstains on the floor tiles used to be pointed out to the visitor. (The tiles were cleaned during a recent renovation, and most of the current Alcázar guides know nothing about the supposed bloodstains. However, stains that look as if they *could* be of blood remain on the tiles.) Some sources say the murder took place in the Plaza de las Muñecas, also called the Alfajía de los Azulejos.

After Fadrique's murder, Pedro ordered a cousin, Don Juan de Aragón, killed in Bilbao and his body thrown out the window into the plaza. One author, according to Mariana, says Pedro wielded the javelin himself. Refusing to allow funeral services, he ordered the body taken to Burgos and thrown into the river, from where it was never recovered.

Doña Urraca Osorio, the wife of Alfonso, the rebel son of Don Alonso Pérez de Guzmán the Good, was one of the leading adherents to the cause of Enrique the Bastard, Count of Trastámara, Pedro's illegitimate half-brother and challenger for the throne. Pedro arranged to have her convicted of treason, for which the penalty was burning at the stake. As the flames rose and began to burn off her light clothes, her loyal servant, Leonor Dávalos, leapt into the fire and embraced Doña Urraca to preserve her mistress's modesty with her own body, and so both died.

Pedro directed his harsh treatment at the nobles, including the clergy, but the common people celebrated the fairness and common sense he displayed in his dealings with them (probably to thwart the nobles and remind them of his power), whence comes his less well-known alternative sobriquet "the Just". Examples of this aspect of the king's character are few and generally unsubstantiated, but here are two.

A shoemaker had been gratuitously killed in the street in Seville by a deacon of the Church. The victim's son complained to the Church authorities and insisted that the murderer be punished. They did nothing more than suspend the deacon's power to say Mass for one year. A short time later, Pedro was holding public audiences on one of his frequent visits to his favourite city, and he was approached by the son of the shoemaker. The boy presented his grievance: that the punishment given by the Church authorities was too lenient. Pedro agreed with the boy and asked him if he thought he could kill the man who had killed his father. The boy said he could, and Pedro told him to do it. The boy did so and was immediately arrested. Pedro intervened and made the Churchmen listen to the boy's explanation. Overriding their objections that their punishment of the deacon had been sufficient and that the boy should be executed, Pedro ordered that the boy be set free and allowed to remain free, and he imposed as sentence that the boy not make shoes for one year, to mock the Church's light sentence on the deacon.

A poor man died, and the parish priest refused to bury him in sacred ground, the Church's property, unless his relatives paid for the plot, the sepulchre and the funeral service. They protested that they could not afford to pay, and the priest laughed and told them that they could bury him in a field for free. Pedro heard about this, and he was scandalised that a man of the Church would refuse to perform this basic corporal work of mercy. He ordered that the priest be buried alive in the cemetery where now stands the Basilica of Our Lady of Hope of Macarena.

During the 1360s, an offshoot of the Hundred Years War between England and France was a civil war in Spain between Pedro and his half-brother Enrique. Enrique hired the French mercenary Bertrand du Guesclin, leader of the White Companies, in an attempt to seize the throne from Pedro. Pedro defeated Enrique at Nájera in 1367 with English support led by the Black Prince, Edward son of King Edward III of England.

The Black Prince's Ruby (the size of a hen's egg, 170 carats, five centimetres long) in the Imperial State Crown of England was given to Edward by Pedro in payment for his support at Nájera. Pedro had acquired it from the usurper King of Granada, Abu Said, who was known as the Red King for his red hair and beard. Abu Said brought the great uncut stone with him when he was a guest in Pedro's palace in

Seville. Pedro coveted the ruby, so he seized the king, had him stripped and mounted on an ass and led around a field while his knights used him for target practice with their lances until he was dead.

The Black Prince's health and finances were broken by his victory at Nájera, and he and Pedro had a falling out over a delay in payments to the English mercenaries. So when Enrique rose again in 1369 he was able to defeat Pedro's army at Montiel in La Mancha. Pedro was killed "in the course of negotiations" or while he was attempting to flee, and many say Enrique personally assassinated him. That much is reported as fact by modern historians. The proverbial expression "I neither break kings nor make kings" is said to originate in this incident, and it may have been inserted by a ballad maker into the following widely accepted though unsubstantiated detailed description of Pedro's death.

After his army's defeat at Montiel, Pedro found himself trapped and unable to flee, so he tried to bribe Bertrand du Guesclin into helping him escape. Bertrand led him to his tent, where Enrique was waiting, and the half-brothers began to fight. Enrique stabbed Pedro in the face and they wrestled and fell to the ground with Pedro on top. Enrique appealed to Bertrand for help. As a non-royal, it would be bad form for Bertrand to kill Pedro himself. Also, he was perhaps mindful that Enrique might in future be suspicious of him as a man who had already killed one king and might not scruple to kill another. Bertrand manoeuvred the men so that Enrique was on top, saying, appropriately for a mercenary, "Ni quito rey ni pongo rey, pero ayudo a mi señor – I neither break kings nor make kings, but I help my lord." According to Mariana, Enrique then stabbed Pedro repeatedly until he died, "a thing that makes the flesh crawl".

Mariana reports that Enrique paid Bertrand 120,000 doblas, "which was a lot of money at that time" (it would buy five substantial castles), and the "benefit" of the city of Soria and several villas "for delivering Pedro to him". The "benefit" (*favor*) was evidently the tax or vassal-tribute due to the king.

After reigning for ten years as Enrique II, the first of the House of Trastámara, he was assassinated in Santo Domingo de la Calzada in 1379. He died ten days after putting on a pair of Moorish walking boots permeated with poisoned perfume, given to him by a man hired by the King of Granada for the purpose. "Thus testify very serious authors," the ever-cautious Mariana comments, "but it is also true that authors who are more prudent and serious say he died of the gout."

As with many Spanish proverbs, Cervantes found an occasion to use "I neither break kings nor make kings." Don Quijote was convinced that Dulcinea had been enchanted into the form of a country wench. Merlin advised him that the enchantment could only be broken if Sancho Panza voluntarily gave himself 3300 lashes on his naked buttocks. Alternatively, half that number of involuntary lashes would suffice. A few days later, Sancho had only managed five feeble hand slaps and Don Quijote was growing impatient, so while Sancho was sleeping Don Quijote began to take off Sancho's trousers to hasten the disenchantment process. Sancho awoke and threw Don Quijote to the ground and knelt on his chest, pinioning his hands. Don Quijote said, "What is this, traitor? You dare to make demands of your master and natural lord who feeds you?" Sancho replied, "I neither break kings nor make kings. I only help myself, for I am my own lord" (*Don Quijote II*, 60).

The Bridge of San Martín
(Toledo)

The figure of a woman can be seen carved in stone in a niche over the keystone of the central arch of the Bridge of San Martín at Toledo. This story tells why she is so honoured.

A bridge near this spot was destroyed by flood in 1203 and immediately replaced. That bridge in turn was deliberately destroyed in the 1360s for strategic reasons during a battle for the kingship between the half-brothers Pedro I the Cruel and Don Enrique de Trastámara. The present bridge, a jewel of medieval architecture restored in the 17th and 18th centuries, was built in 1390 at the order of the Archbishop of Toledo, Don Pedro Tenorio.

The archbishop hired one of the most renowned architect-engineers of that time, whose name is not recorded. The work commenced, and the people of Toledo and the archbishop watched the progress of the bridge with satisfaction. Soon, the magnificent central arch, rising to 27 metres with a 40-metre span, was completed, and it was obvious that it would be only a matter of days before the scaffolding that supported the stonework could be removed.

One night, however, the engineer seemed unusually quiet and preoccupied when he came home from the day's work. He refused to answer his wife's questions, and after his supper he left the house without telling her where he was going. He went to the bridge, where he descended a ladder and inspected the foundations of the central arch. He arrived back home pale and disturbed. His wife pressed him again for an explanation, and he hesitantly told her what the problem was.

He had unaccountably made a serious error in his calculations. He could see now that as soon as the scaffolding was taken down, the central arch would collapse, killing any workmen in the vicinity. He would be responsible for the deaths of the workers if he said nothing. If he admitted his error and dismantled the bridge, his reputation would be destroyed, and no one would ever employ him as an engineer again.

What was he to do? Of course, he couldn't let the men die, but what would he say to the archbishop? How could he explain why the bridge had to be torn down and rebuilt from scratch, when the archbishop had been impatiently urging him to complete the work as soon as possible? No matter what he did he would be ruined. He covered his face with his hands and wept bitterly.

His wife was a brave and clever woman, and she immediately saw that there was only one solution. She also knew that she had little time to do what had to be done. She waited only a moment until she could see that her husband had fallen into a troubled sleep, exhausted by his worries. Then she took a torch and went out.

The night was dark and stormy, and she passed through the deserted streets unnoticed. As the rain began to fall more heavily, she was afraid that her torch might be extinguished, and that would be fatal to her plans. She arrived at the bridge and walked trembling to the central arch, then she threw the burning torch into the complex arrangement of wooden posts and poles and ropes that made up the scaffolding. The torch sputtered briefly in the rain, but soon the flames took hold and, fanned by the wind, rose quickly. Her task accomplished, the engineer's wife ran home.

As the engineer had rightly calculated, as soon as the scaffolding burned away there was a tremendous crash of what the Toledans naturally took to be thunder. But it was the falling of the central arch of

163

the bridge. The following morning, the archbishop and the people of Toledo surveyed the damage. Seeing the burnt scaffolding, they quite understandably attributed the disaster to a bolt of lightning during the storm. The archbishop ordered the engineer to recommence the construction of the bridge, which he did with a contented mind and a heart full of gratitude to his wife.

However, the woman was troubled with feelings of guilt. On the day the bridge was dedicated and officially opened, she requested an audience with the archbishop. Fully expecting to be punished or at least scolded, she admitted that she had destroyed the bridge and explained her reason. But the archbishop, instead of castigating her, praised her cleverness and courage in saving countless lives and the reputation of her husband. And he ordered a stone carved with the figure of a woman to be placed on the bridge to commemorate her deed.

"He who would eat the kernel ..."
(Aragón)

An ambitious and violent man of short stature, Pedro IV the Ceremonious, King of Aragón 1336-1387, was an astute politician, a stern ruler of his own territory, and the dominator through battle and marriage of much of the Mediterranean. He allied himself with Enrique of Trastámara against Pedro the Cruel of Castile in the War of the Two Pedros, and was embroiled in the Hundred Years War. A skilled astrologer and alchemist, an able troubadour, a talented poet, and the author of a chronicle and a book of protocol, he outlived three wives and was survived by a fourth.

Lacking a male heir after his first two marriages, Pedro appointed his daughter, Constanza, to succeed him, ignoring the right of an heirless king's brother. This set off a rebellion among the nobles, which ended with Pedro being forced to concede a "Privilege". The following year, with the support of Cataluña, he was able to impose his will militarily on the rebels, and he acquired the second sobriquet "of the Dagger" by a dramatic gesture. Stabbing himself in the hand with the dagger he habitually wore, he tore up the paper he had signed, saying, "A Privilege that has cost so much blood should not be destroyed without the shedding of blood."

164

The irascible and unpredictable king was visiting one of his knight-vassals in Borja. As they rested during a hunt, Pedro noticed some ripe walnuts hanging from a tree and asked the knight to pick a few of the nuts and crack them for him. The knight handed the king the nuts still in their shells and quoted the 3rd-century BC Roman poet Titus Maccius Plautus: "He who would eat the kernel must crack the nut." Far from being offended, Pedro was amused, and after cracking the nuts he ordered the knight to place the cheeky response on his coat of arms as the family motto. He did so, and, so the story goes, the Nogués family coat of arms to this day bears the Latin: "Qui vult edere nuces, frangat nucem."

La Torre de la Malmuerta
The Tower of the Wrongful Death
(Córdoba)

This octagonal mudéjar-style Tower on the northeast corner of the Plaza Colón was constructed between 1406 and 1408 and remains one of the outstanding landmarks of Córdoba.

On returning from war, an ancestor of the marqueses of Villaseca was told that his wife had been unfaithful during his absence. He killed her, but later discovered that the accusation had been false. Repenting of his action, he petitioned King Enrique III for a pardon. Enrique ordered the man to build the Tower in expiation, adding, "When it's finished, you will die in it." Construction was delayed as long as possible.

If a horseman at full gallop through the archway can read the verbose dedicatory plaque, a secret door will open to reveal a great treasure. No one has collected it yet.

Two Alcaides of Antequera:
Rodrigo de Narváez and Fernando de Narváez
(Antequera)

Enrique III the Sickly, King of Castile and León (and effectively of Spain), died at the age of 27 in 1406. His brother, Prince Fernando, was the virtual king during Enrique's final years of ill health and was co-regent with Enrique's widow, Catherine of Lancaster, during the first years of the reign of Enrique's son, Juan II, who assumed the throne at the age of one year. In 1412, Fernando and Catherine split the kingdom, and he became King of Aragón as Fernando I. His grandson was Fernando II of Aragón and Castile, the first official King of Spain.

Rodrigo de Narváez was a page at Enrique's court in the service of Prince Fernando. Fernando recognised the intelligence and abilities of the young Rodrigo and soon raised him to the rank of battle leader. Rodrigo so proved his worth that when the Prince reconquered the strategically important city of Antequera in the north of Málaga Province in 1410, he installed Rodrigo as *alcaide* or governor and confirmed the sovereignty that had been granted to the city by Alfonso X nearly two centuries earlier. Rodrigo named his son "Fernando".

Rodrigo Befriends Abindarráez and Jarifa

The proud and fierce Abencerraje family formed a more or less loyal opposition among the rulers of the kingdom of Granada in the final epoch of the diminished Moorish occupation of Spain. Abindarráez was a member of this family. He and Jarifa, the daughter of the alcaide of Cártama, had grown up together in the town, and as they matured, childhood friendship evolved to love. In 1420, when Jarifa's father was transferred to Coín, they decided to marry so that they would not have to live separated by such a distance. However, Jarifa's father forbade the marriage, and the King of Granada also opposed it for political reasons.

The lovers made plans to marry in secret. As Abindarráez and a party of his friends rode by night to Coín for the early morning ceremony, they were surprised by a troop of cavalry serving Rodrigo de Narváez and taken prisoner after a brave but doomed fight against superior numbers. In the morning, Abindarráez, with tears running down his face, was brought before Rodrigo and questioned as to his name and lineage. Then Rodrigo said:

"It is not a disgrace for a seasoned warrior to weep on being captured, for the frustration of defeat and the feeling of helplessness. But for a young man, who in the heat of battle can often lose all fear of death, it is worth asking: why do you weep? Do you fear death so much?"

166

"It is not my death that I weep for, lord. I was on my way to marry the woman of my dreams, and now that my dreams have been shattered, death would be preferable to living without her. I weep for my lost dream, and because I know that Jarifa loves me so much that for us to be separated would kill her, I also weep for her death."

He went on to describe the parental and political opposition to their union and how they had planned to get around it. When he finished, Rodrigo sat in thought for a moment and then said:

"I know that the Abencerrajes are a lineage of pride and honour, and I will demonstrate that the Castilians are a people of nobility and generosity. I will release you to go and marry your bride if you swear on the hilt of your scimitar that you will return in three days and surrender yourself to me."

Abindarráez promised, and he thanked his benefactor and kissed his hand, then rode off to join his worried bride. On the third day after the wedding, he explained what had happened and that he had to return to Antequera to surrender himself to Rodrigo.

Jarifa turned pale with shock, and she was silent for a few moments while Abindarráez prepared for the journey. Then she said, "I'm going with you. I have decided to join my life with yours. We are united as one person, and we will share chains and servitude in dark Christian prisons until Allah wills otherwise. I prefer death to being deprived of your company."

Presenting himself to Rodrigo and introducing Jarifa, Abindarráez said, "My wife wishes to share my imprisonment to ease my sorrow. Now you can see why I wept when I thought I might be separated from her forever."

Rodrigo descended from his stately dais and placed his hands on Abindarráez's shoulders and said, "You have proved yourself a man of honour. We Castilians do not condemn men like you to prison. On the contrary, we praise and exalt them. You and your wife are free from this moment."

Rodrigo sent the newly-weds back to their own territory with an escort to guarantee their safe passage. At Abindarráez's request, he wrote to the King of Granada and asked him to pardon the young couple and to intercede with Jarifa's father. This was done, and Abindarráez and Jarifa were welcomed in Coín.

Fernando and the People Defy the King

The elderly Enrique IV of Trastámara, King of Castile and León (and effectively of Spain), appeared uninvited at the gate of the free and independent city of Antequera in 1470. He was accompanied by a large army, and Don Alonso de Aquilar of Córdoba was at his side. His arrival was not unexpected, as it was known that he was on his way from Málaga to nearby Archidona, and the main road passed by Antequera. Also, Don Fernando de Narváez, third Alcaide of Antequera, had learned of Enrique's plan to replace him with Alonso, and the significance of Enrique and Alonso's warlike retinue did not need to be spelled out. This was ostensibly an informal, friendly visit, but similar ruses had resulted in Enrique's political friends being installed as alcaides of other cities by threat or force.

Don Fernando was aware that he would be powerless once Enrique's Moorish guard and Alonso's troop of soldiers were inside the walls of the city. Forewarned of Enrique's intentions, he had gone to some trouble to organise an elaborate ceremony for the occasion. As the royal cavalcade stopped outside the gate, Fernando led a guard of honour out of the city to greet the king and kiss his hand, according to protocol.

"The citizens of Antequera would be grateful if Your Majesty would deign to grace our Plaza of San Sebastián with your presence so we can render our homage," said Fernando. "However, we regret that we are unable to accommodate such a large company in the city, so we invite your chaplain and an escort of fifteen to accompany Your Majesty, while the rest remain outside."

It was clear to Enrique that his plot had been discovered, but the only alternative to the planned subtle insertion of his troops into the city was to lay siege to it, and so he accepted Fernando's invitation. While Alonso kicked his heels outside the walls, Fernando closed the gate and led the royal party to the Plaza of San Sebastián. They did not stop there but continued into the Church of San Sebastián, where the stage was set for a dramatic declaration of independence.

The walls and columns and even the altar of the dimly lit church were covered in black drapery, and the nave was filled with sombre and silent citizens of the town. A catafalque stood in the transept, and on it

168

in an open coffin reposed the mummified body of Rodrigo de Narváez. The keys of the city lay possessively between the desiccated hands of the first Alcaide of Antequera. As quick to receive a subtle message as to give one, Enrique understood that this production was being staged not in homage but defiance.

A woman in widow's weeds spoke for all when she recounted the service rendered by the present aldaide, Don Fernando, to the crown. She reminded the king that Rodrigo had been Prince Fernando's right-hand man in many victorious battles, and that the Prince had rewarded him with Antequera and confirmed the city's independence. In case Enrique had missed the main point of the performance, she then gestured to the keys in Rodrigo's hands and said, "If you want to remove the keys of the city from Don Fernando in order to give them to Alonso de Aquilar, you will have to wrest them from the hands of the one to whom Prince Fernando entrusted them."

Enrique walked to the catafalque and, extending his hand over the body, said in a subdued voice, "I solemnly promise to leave the office of alcaide to Fernando in perpetuity."

The people responded with one voice: "Amen."

La Peña de los Enamorados – Lovers Peak
(near Antequera)

He clasp'd her close and cried farewell,
In one another's arms they fell;
And falling o'er the rock's steep side,
In one another's arms they died.
(from "The Lover's Rock", Robert Southey, 1798)

The 880-metre Peña rises abruptly and majestically from the vega northeast of Antequera, midway between Antequera and Archidona, to form the most imposing landmark in the area.

A Christian youth of noble lineage was captured and enslaved by a Moor. Resigned to his fate until he could be ransomed or exchanged for a Moorish captive, he gave no trouble and was trusted by his master and allowed a free run of the house. The Moor's young daughter cast her eyes on him with interest and then affection, the boy reciprocated, and they began to meet secretly as friendliness progressed to love. Some say he instructed her in the tenets of Christianity, and she was eager to convert, though Mariana doubts it.

They were only too aware that if her father discovered their relationship they would both pay with their heads. When they learned that the father had heard rumours and was suspicious, they agreed to flee to Christian territory. They set off late one night, and when daylight came and they stopped to rest at the Peña, they saw her father coming at the head of a troop of cavalry.

Climbing to the top of the mountain to escape, they heard her father call to them to come down, threatening that if they did not obey him he would give them a cruel death. This they refused to do, and the father ordered his soldiers to climb up and seize them. The boy threw boulders and rocks and sticks and whatever came to hand to fend them off. Then the father ordered crossbowmen from the nearby Moorish-held town of Archidona.

When the bowmen arrived, the young lovers knew that they were doomed. They agreed that there was only one way to escape the inevitable insults and tortures that faced them. Embracing each other firmly, they threw themselves from the peak. United in death, they were buried together.

The Marriage Bond of the Lovers of Antequera
(Antequera)

This fictional moral or exemplary tale is found in the prologue of *Relación de la vida del escudero Marcos de Obregón* (1618) by Vicente Espinel.

Two impoverished students from Antequera, probably studying at the Cátedra de Gramática in that city, were travelling to Salamanca one summer. One was bright and curious, the other lazy and careless. Perishing from thirst, they arrived at a well to refresh themselves. There they noticed a stone with gothic writing, half worn by antiquity and the passing of the animals that came to drink. A duplicated Latin inscription on the stone read: "Conditur unio, conditur unio."

170

The slower student said, "Whoever carved that was drunk or stupid. It's only ignorant people who repeat themselves."

The clever student was not content to see it so simply. He said, "I'm tired and thirsty and I don't want to go any farther this afternoon."

"Then stay here like a fool," said the other, and he continued on the road to Salamanca.

The bright one racked his brain for understanding while he cleaned the stone.

"*Unio* can mean either union or pearl," he said to himself. "*Conditur unio* means 'a union is established' or 'a pearl is formed.' I have to find out what secret is here."

Levering the stone the best he could, he raised it and found the marriage bond of the Lovers of Antequera and a pearl fatter than a nut with a necklace worth more than 4000 escudos. He replaced the stone and took another road.

Espinel used the tale to demonstrate the importance of looking beneath the surface of the main text, "because there is not a single page in the whole of my *Escudero* that does not have a specific purpose." The story smacks of fiction, but Washington Irving includes a variant in *Tales of the Alhambra* that he heard from an innkeeper in Antequera in 1829. Perhaps both derive from a traditional legend.

There was once a fountain, he said, in one of the public squares called *Il fuente del toro* (the fountain of the bull), because the waters gushed from the mouth of the bull's head, carved of stone. Underneath the head was inscribed:

En frente del toro
Se hallen tesoro.

In front of the bull there is treasure. Many digged in front of the fountain, but lost their labour and found no money. At last one knowing fellow construed the motto a different way. It is in the forehead *frente* of the bull that the treasure is to be found, he said to himself, and I am the man to find it. Accordingly he came, late at night, with a mallet, and knocked the head to pieces; and what do you think he found?

171

"Plenty of gold and diamonds," said Sancho [the guide], eagerly. "He found nothing," rejoined mine host, dryly, "and he ruined the fountain."

A local interpretation of this tradition is that the treasure in front of the bull was Antequera itself.

El Paso Honroso – The Pass of Honour
(Hospital de Órbigo, León)

In 1434, Don Suero de Quiñones placed an iron chain around his neck as a token of enslavement to his lady love. Between 12 July and 9 August, he and nine companions occupied the bridge over the Río Órbigo at Hospital de Órbigo near Astorga, León, on the Camino de Santiago. All who attempted to cross the bridge were forced to admit that Don Suero's lady was the most beautiful in the world or face combat. Beginning each day with a Mass and finishing with a feast, they challenged more than 70 knights, killing one by accident. Some years later Don Suero was killed in revenge by one of those he had defeated.

This feat of arms is one of the most famous of the Middle Ages, and Don Quijote cites it as one of the authentic examples of the practice of chivalry: "You might as well claim that the jousts of Suero de Quiñones were a joke ... Whoever denies them is completely devoid of sense and reason" (*Don Quijote I*, 49). Some modern commentators feel that Don Suero was, if not the original Don Quijote, at least one of the models Cervantes used for the creation of his hero.

The story is recounted in the 1999 US/Spain television murder-mystery mini-series *Camino de Santiago*. Hospital de Órbigo hosts a full-costumed jousting tournament each summer in commemoration of the event and as a tourist attraction.

The Pass of the Sigh of the Moor
(Granada)

In 1492, the last bastion of the Moors fell when Fernando and Isabel captured Granada from their sometime vassal Muhammad XII in the

172

final act of the Reconquest. The Moorish king's given name was Abu Abdallah, but he is popularly known as Boabdil el Chico (Small), el Chico Rey, and El Desdichado (the Unfortunate).

As Boabdil, his mother and his sorrowing entourage filed south from Granada City on their way to exile in La Alpuharra in the southeast of Granada Province, they paused at the top of the pass called Puerto del Suspiro (Sigh) del Moro for one last look back at the city. Boabdil wept and heaved a deep sigh. On hearing it, his mother said, "Weep like a woman for what you were not able to defend like a man." Or, in the (probably memory-enhanced) words of Antonio de Guevara, who was an 11-year-old page attached to Queen Isabel's court at the time and later became a prominent intellectual, "It is right that the king and his knights weep like women, because they did not fight like soldiers."

The Man Without a Shadow
(Salamanca and Navarre)

The vaulted c. 16th-century portico and recently renovated entrance to the Cave of Salamanca can be seen beneath the Plaza de Carvajal on Cuesta de Carvajal near Calle San Pablo on the south side of the city behind the cathedral and downhill from it. A secret tunnel is said to connect the Cave with the crypt of the cathedral. The Cave was closed by royal order in the 17th century "to put a stop to superstitious rumours". It was said of the famous 13th-century Scottish wizard Michael Scot:

> When in Salamanca's cave
> Him listed his magic wand to wave
> The bells would ring in Notre Dame.

During the Middle Ages, Satan himself used the Cave to hold night classes in the black arts for those studying for the priesthood at the university. The agreed payment for their tuition was that one member of the class would remain with their master as his servant when the course was finished. Don Juan de Atarrabio from Goñi in Navarre, who was pursuing both curricula, and his classmates made a plan to circumvent this.

173

After the final night of classes, the students filed out of the Cave into the bright morning sunshine. The Devil stood at the entrance, which faces east, and as each man passed him he said, "Are you going to stay with me?"

As they had arranged among themselves, each student said, "Take the one behind me."

Don Juan was at the end of the line. Satan was counting, and he knew that Juan should be the last, but when he said, "Are you going to stay with me?" and Juan replied, "Take the one behind me," Satan thought he had miscounted. He could see Juan's shadow behind him, and in the unaccustomed glare of the sunlight he mistook it for "the one behind". He brought his sword down sharply behind Juan as he passed, cutting off his shadow. Juan and the others escaped safely.

When Don Juan finished his studies at the university, he became a priest in Goñi, about 12 miles (20 km) west of Pamplona, where he lived with his mother. Of course it was soon noticed that he had no shadow, but he was a good priest and popular with the people, so they quickly got used to this slight deformity, even though it is well known that a person without a shadow cannot enter Heaven. One reason he was so popular was that he was able to make good use of the knowledge he had gained in the Devil's school. Here are two examples.

The weather had been unusually fine one year. The wheat was standing tall and thick in the fields ready to be harvested, and the local farmers were expecting a bumper crop. One day as Don Juan was about to take a siesta he noticed a huge black cloud in the distance. He said to his mother, "If that cloud comes closer, wake me up before you hear thunder."

But his mother forgot to keep an eye on the cloud, and it was looming over the town before she noticed it and woke her son. Don Juan leapt out of bed, and he heard the voice of the Devil from the cloud:

"I have some little horses that are going to trample your wheat."

The priest held a book of magic spells in one hand and a crucifix in the other and said:

"And I have some small reins that will control your horses."

The cloud burst open and poured down rain and hailstones, but through Don Juan's magic power all the rain and hail was directed into a large number of barrels that stood next to the cemetery, and so the wheat crop was saved.

174

Another time, Don Juan received a divine message in his head: the Pope in Rome was in danger and Don Juan's help was needed immediately. Satan himself in the form of a beautiful woman had so bewitched the Pope that the Pope was going to ask Satan to marry him. Don Juan called up three demons that were at his service and asked the first one, "How soon can you take me to Rome?"

The demon answered, "Fifteen minutes."

"Not good enough. And you?" he asked the second demon.

"Five minutes."

"Not good enough. And you?"

"As soon as we start we will be there," replied the third demon.

"You'll do," said the priest. "Let's go."

"What will you pay me for this?" asked the demon.

"I'll give you the uppermost part of my dinner tonight," Don Juan said, knowing what his mother planned to serve. The demon accepted this, and they had no sooner set off than they arrived at the Vatican. Don Juan knocked at the door. When the porter opened the door, Don Juan said, "Take me to the Pope immediately."

"I'm sorry, that's impossible," said the porter. "His Holiness is entertaining a visitor for dinner."

Don Juan handed the porter a staff with a cross carved on it that he had brought for the purpose.

"I want you to take this and measure the width and breadth of the table where the Holy Father and his guest are eating."

The porter did this, and as soon as he placed the staff across the width of the table after measuring the length – thereby making the Sign of the Cross – the beautiful woman gave a shriek and disappeared in a puff of smoke. The Pope realised immediately what had happened, and he asked the porter who had given him the staff and told him to measure the table.

"It was a priest at the door who wanted to come in to see you."

"Send him in now," said the Pope.

But Don Juan had already left. On the way home, he and the demon flew through a snowstorm, and when he entered the kitchen where his mother was serving his dinner, he shook the snow off his cloak.

"I didn't know it was snowing," his mother said.

"It's snowing in the Jaca mountains," said Don Juan.

"I don't believe that," his mother said.

175

"It's as true as the fact that that chicken you have roasted can sing," said Don Juan. At that, the roasted chicken sat up and began to crow.

Don Juan took a small plate and scraped off the uppermost portion of the food that was set at his place at the table. His mother had cooked a dish based on nuts, and as was her custom she had put the nutshells on the top of the food as a decoration. This is what Don Juan took outside as the payment he had promised for the demon that had flown him to Rome.

As Don Juan grew older and closer to the time when he would have to account for his life, he began to worry that he would not go to Heaven when he died because he had no shadow. However, he had noticed that when he celebrated Mass, at the moment of the Consecration his shadow appeared briefly and then disappeared again. He explained his problem to the sacristan and told him that his only hope of getting into Heaven was for the sacristan to kill him at the moment of the Consecration, when his shadow appeared.

The sacristan was horrified and refused to have anything to do with the plan. But Don Juan pressed him and wrote out a letter that explained the situation and exonerated the sacristan from any responsibility. The sacristan finally agreed to do what Don Juan wanted.

Don Juan said, "Take a big hammer, and at the moment of Consecration, when you see my shadow appear, hit me hard on the head. Then cut open my chest and take out my heart and nail it still bleeding to the door of the church. If you see a black bird take my heart, you will know that my soul has gone to Hell, but if a white bird takes it, that will be a sign that I am in Heaven."

The following morning at the Consecration the sacristan did what he had agreed, and when Don Juan was dead the sacristan cut out his heart and nailed it to the door of the church. Immediately a large flock of ravens swooped into the plaza in front of the church and began circling. But suddenly a small white dove shot straight down from Heaven, took the priest's heart in its beak, and soared straight up again until it was out of sight.

Modern Times

La Calle de la Cabeza – The Street of the Head
(Madrid)

La Calle de la Cabeza runs parallel to Magdalena, which is between Metro stations Tirso de Molina and Antón Martín in the Rastro (Market) district of southwest Madrid.

In the early 17th century, there lived in a house on Cabeza an ill-tempered and avaricious priest whose servant was fond of drinking and gambling. One day when the priest was out of the house, the servant decided to search for the money his master was rumoured to have accumulated. He had just discovered the strongbox when the priest returned and caught him in the act of breaking it open. The servant killed the priest, cut off his head, and fled to Portugal with his master's fortune.

Many years later, the servant, now passing himself off as a well-to-do gentleman, returned to Madrid, convinced that his crime had been forgotten and he would not be recognised. In a butcher's shop in the Rastro district, he saw a lamb's head on display, one of his favourite dishes. He bought the head and was carrying it home in a bag under his cloak, failing to notice that the head was leaving a trail of blood behind him.

This came to the attention of a constable, who stopped the man and asked him what he was carrying under his cloak. The servant confidently opened the bag to show him the lamb's head, but, to his consternation, it had turned into the head of the priest he had killed. He was quickly arrested, charged, found guilty and hanged in the Plaza Mayor. At the moment of the servant's execution, the priest's head changed back into the head of a lamb.

So that this miracle would not be forgotten, and as a warning to would-be murderers, King Felipe III (reigned 1598-1621) ordered a sculpture of the head of the priest to be placed on the house where he had lived and died. The neighbours complained that the image

177

frightened them, so it was removed, but the name given to the street in memory of the incident remains.

La Casa del Duende – The House of the Devil
(Madrid)

At dawn on All Souls Day in an unspecified year in the 18th century, the Confraternity of the Mortal Sin, together with the Capuchins of Patience, members of the Inquisition and Soldiers of the Faith, followed by sundry curious folk, marched on a Big House on Calle del Conde-Duque on what were then the outskirts of Madrid. The house had been built by Nicolás María de Guzmán, but it had long been untenanted, by normal people, that is, and it was now known as the Casa del Duende – the House of the Devil. The cavalcade, headed by the Bishop of Segovia, was acting in response to a complaint made by outraged residents of the district to the Tribunal of the Faith, requesting that the house be reduced to dust and salt sown over it. This is the history of the house, as related to the Tribunal.

After the house had been abandoned by the owners, it was appropriated by gamblers and revelers from time to time. They used only the ground floor of the house. One night, an argument erupted over who had won and who had lost at a game of cards. In the middle of the uproar, a dwarf suddenly entered the room through an interior door and without speaking a word angrily gestured at the gamblers to be quiet, and just as abruptly disappeared through the door.

The gamblers stationed a guard with a drawn sword in front of the door and resumed their noisy games and arguments. Again the door burst open, and another dwarf appeared, again gesturing at them angrily without speaking a word. This time the revelers leapt on the dwarf, but he vanished from their midst.

Once again the gamblers returned to their games and noisy quarrels, and the door burst open for the third time. But now a troop of twenty dwarfs armed with whips charged into the room, extinguished all the lights and beat the party-makers unmercifully until they ran terrified from the house.

The house remained uninhabited and unused until Doña Rosario de Venegas y Valenzuela, Marquesa de las Hormazas, disregarding the superstitious rumours she had heard, bought it. She cleaned and redecorated until all was in order except for the curtains and an image of the Child Jesus. When she had decided on the material and design for the curtains, she sent her butler with the measurements and description to the curtain-maker and told him to buy an image of the Child Jesus. No sooner had the butler left the house with the order than a dwarf entered with the curtains made and finished to the exact dimensions and design. The Marquesa fainted. When she regained consciousness, she found the curtains and the image of the Child Jesus all hung in their proper places. Frightened, she sent a servant for the priest. No sooner had the servant left the house than the priest, accompanied by a dwarf, arrived. The Marquesa fled the house.

A few years later, a canon from Jaén, Don Melchor de Abellaneda, laughing at the foolish stories he had heard, bought the house. One day he was writing a letter to the Bishop asking him for a book. He had just written the title of the book in the letter when a dwarf entered the room and placed the book on the table. The following day, the Canon ordered a servant to go to the church with a blank Mass card to be stamped with the official seal. Before the servant left the house, a dwarf arrived and gave the stamped card to the Canon.

The laundress of the house, Jerónima Perrín, took a load of clothes down to the River Manzanares to wash them, and left the clothes to dry next to the river. Later in the day, it suddenly began to rain heavily. Jerónima gave up the clothes for lost, but a dwarf walked into the house with the dry laundry.

Even these mysterious occurrences were not enough to frighten the Canon from the house, but there was one thing he could not tolerate. Whenever he made an error while writing, a dwarf would appear at his side to correct it. The Canon left.

The house was unoccupied for some years, except for thieves and evildoers, who used it for a gathering place from time to time. This scandalous practice and the mysterious and apparently preternatural events of the past were why the Bishop of Segovia led his dawn cavalcade to the Casa del Duende on that All Souls Day in the 18th century.

When they arrived at the house, they could see that all the doors and windows were securely closed and boarded up. However, one eagle-eyed observer swore that he could see a thin column of smoke rising

179

from one of the chimneys. The Bishop led his army of helpers in prayer while holy water was sprinkled on the walls. When this was done, the faithful attacked the doors with picks and staffs and surged into the house. They rampaged through every room, broke up the furniture, peered into every nook and cranny from the basement to the attic, but they found no living being or any sign that anyone was living there. They departed confused, silent and frustrated.

However, as soon as the Bishop's company left, the local residents saw 40 swarthy men of normal size come out of the house, shake hands solemnly, and go off in separate directions. It is said that at least these "duendes" were counterfeiters of Brazilian dobillas, who were sought by the police and condemned to death as rebels.

In any case, by the time Fernando VI owned the house in the mid-18th century, the dwarfs had abandoned it and were never seen again. The house lay derelict again for some time, and when it was eventually pulled down in the 19th century, the empty plot where it once stood continued to reek of sulphur for years afterwards.

The Holy Companion
(Galicia)

An Irishman told this story on RTÉ Radio One, the Irish national radio station, in the 1980s. He was walking the Camino de Santiago by himself, and one night at an *albergue* (pilgrim hostel) he fell into conversation with a German named Hugo, who was also alone. The Irishman suggested that since they were both alone they might walk the road together the following day.

"No, I'm sorry," said Hugo. "I've walked the Camino before, and I prefer to do it by myself."

Fair enough, thought the Irishman. The following day he was walking along the road when he noticed Hugo ahead of him in the company of another man. This made the Irishman a bit angry. Hugo refused to walk with *him*, but now he was with someone else. He spoke to Hugo that night at the albergue.

"I thought you preferred to walk the Camino alone."

"That's right," said Hugo.

"But you were walking with someone today."

"No, I was alone on the road all day."

"But I saw you," said the Irishman, "and there was a man walking along next to you."

"Ah," said Hugo. "I didn't see anyone, but I could feel a presence."

People say that if you walk the Camino alone, sometimes Santiago walks with you.

The Watch of King Juan Carlos
(Seville)

I was walking along a pedestrianised street in Seville about 11 o'clock one evening on my way to my accommodation, when a motor scooter roared up behind me, and the passenger snatched a small bag off my shoulder. I reported the theft to the police: a cheap cloth bag, a bottle of water, a guide book for the Cathedral, and a Spanish-English dictionary, total value about 12 euros. The policeman who took the report was highly incensed that I had wasted his time with such a minor complaint. I was outraged at the incident and his attitude, and for years thereafter I made my negative feelings about the city known to any Sevillano I encountered.

Their response was to shrug and admit that the city is notorious for its thieves. As an illustration, a Galician told me in 2003 that King Juan Carlos, who I admire for his genuine empathy with his subjects, had recently been offering both hands to greet a crowd of Sevillanos, and when he finished, he discovered that his gold Rolex watch was missing. Someone had stolen it off his wrist.

That story, which I regarded as an urban legend, mollified me somewhat, and I added it to my account. In 2009, however, I was told by a reliable source from Seville that the incident had really happened, and that a dogged policeman had used his underworld contacts to eventually recover the watch and return it to the king. I believe that is supposed to have happened about 2008. Unfortunately, I have been unable to find documentary evidence of either story, so perhaps they are both legends.

181

"Preparado"
(Motril, Granada Province)

This story was told to me in Motril in 2004.

A man came to live in a village in Granada Province. He was advised that everyone there had a nickname, and he should be careful what he said, because that might be given to him as a nickname.

"I'm prepared," he said, and he was known as "Preparado" thereafter.

Carreño
(Málaga)

Carreño, a famous wit in 19th century Málaga, was about to carve a stuffed turkey. His friends came to him and said, "Carreño, listen carefully. We are going to do to you exactly what you do to that turkey."

Carreño set his knife and fork back on the table, stuck his finger into the part of the bird through which the stuffing is stuffed, and sucked his finger juicily.

182

Timeless Tales

Leokadi
(Bizkaia)

The 15th-century gothic church of Santa María de Ondarroa is built on a rock overlooking the harbour. It is decorated with the only gargoyles to be found in Bizkaia, and stone figures of musicians and other humans line the roof. The entrance is level with the upper part of the town, and a walkway leads around the church. A gate has been installed that is locked at night to prevent people from making a complete circuit, so that it is no longer possible for this sort of misfortune to be repeated.

Everyone in Ondarroa knows that something terrible will happen if you walk three times around the church anti-clockwise at night, and everyone knows what happened to a teenaged girl named Leokadi when she did that. One evening, she was out with some of her friends when they were supposed to be home for the Angelus, and they dared each other to do it. They were all afraid, but Leokadi took the dare, and she walked three times around the church.

After the first circuit, her face turned white, after the second they heard chains rattling, and on completing the third Leokadi was taken up to the roof of the church and was turned into stone. To this very day, if you go to Ondarroa, you can see her face in stone, framed by sculpted chains, as part of the steeple.

Every year at midnight on the 14th of August, Leokadi comes down from the steeple dressed in black and recalls the events of the past year and tells what will happen during the festival that follows. (Actually, a dummy comes down, and a woman does the reciting.) Also on that night, witches can be seen walking down the mountain carrying torches. At the end of the festival, Leokadi says goodbye for another year and goes back up to her stone prison.

The Aqueduct of Segovia
(Segovia)

Supermodel-slim, graceful as a ballerina, and looking as fragile as a plastic toy, the majestic Aqueduct of Segovia is 2387 feet (728m) long and 92 feet (28m) high, with 167 arches, and is constructed of closely fitting blocks with no lime or mortar. A statue of the Blessed Mother graces the top level. The history books and encyclopaedias will tell you it was built by the Romans more than 2000 years ago, but when you view its lacy, delicate profile from a distance and then move closer to marvel at its massive solidity, you know that no human hand was responsible. It appeared suddenly overnight so long ago that no one remembers the year, and this is how the people say it happened.

Before the Aqueduct, servants for the wealthy and children from ordinary families had to trudge several times a day to a spring in the hills to bring water to the houses in the town. One hot day, a young girl was so fed up with the never-ending chore that she said aloud, "I would give anything to have the water brought to the door of my house."

A dark stranger dressed all in black suddenly appeared before her and said, "Do you really mean that you would give *anything?*"

"Yes, anything," she said without thinking. "I can't stand another day of this boring work."

"Would you give me your soul if I manage to bring the water to your house?" said Satan, for it is no use pretending it was not he.

"Even that," she said. But perhaps something in the old stories she had heard sounded a warning, and she added, "On one condition: I told you I can't stand another day of this chore, and so the water must be brought to the door of my house before the sun rises tomorrow morning."

"It shall be so," said the Devil, and he disappeared to prepare for the night's work ahead of him.

As the people of Segovia went to bed that night, they heard the sound of rumbles and crashes outdoors and felt the earth shake. They assumed it was a more than usually fierce thunderstorm, and they did not bother to look out their windows. But the young girl knew the reason for the noise, and she sat in her window all night watching the devils and demons, giants and Cyclopes, titans and ogres working feverishly at their Infernal master's command. As she looked on, the

184

ditches were dug and foundation stones laid, more stones were hauled from a distant quarry to be dressed on site and fitted with precision one on to another, and slowly – but all too swiftly for her comfort – the Aqueduct began to rise and take shape.

She had thought that the condition she imposed on Satan would ensure that her soul would safely remain hers. In the stories, something always happened to foil the Devil, but now she realised with a sharp stab of fear that she was going to have to make it happen. She hoped, she wished, but nothing stopped or even slowed the progress of the construction. Then she prayed to the Blessed Mother of Jesus, her mother in heaven, until she was filled and surrounded with the intensity of an appeal that would surely not go unanswered.

Keeping an eye on the minions of Hell outside, the girl could see that the Aqueduct was complete except for one stone, and the sky was still solid black. Not even a pale glow brightened the eastern horizon to announce the coming day. Satan himself was even now lifting a stone nearly the exact size and shape to fit the last hole. He tossed it as if it were a feather, flicking a chip off here, smoothing a corner there, and just as he judged it trimmed to perfection, a cock began to crow.

Satan stood still in amazement, and before he could hurl the stone to its waiting socket and so complete the work and fulfil the condition, the sun suddenly shot forth a ray of light that transfixed him, and he vanished from the face of the earth.

In the morning, when the people saw the marvel that had appeared in the middle of their town overnight, they said it was a miracle and thanked God. The girl immediately went to the priest and confessed her sin. She was forgiven and praised for her cleverness, and the truth soon emerged. Then the people said it was still a miracle, and they gave credit to God and the Blessed Mother and the young girl.

Some say that from time to time Satan visits the scene of one of his most perplexing defeats. He ponders the Aqueduct from a safe distance in the hills, trying to work out how the sun could have risen hours before nature had scheduled it to do so.

The Bridges at Soravilla and Oiartzun
(Gipuzkoa)

A stonecutter in Soravilla was trying to build a bridge over the Río Oria, but the water rose and destroyed it. He said aloud, "Only the demons of Hell will be able to help me build this bridge."

The Devil himself appeared and offered to have the bridge built before cock-crow the following morning, in exchange for the man's soul. The stonecutter agreed to the bargain, thinking that this was impossible, and 14,000 devils all named Micolás set to work. As the construction progressed rapidly, the stonecutter began to worry that he might have to pay the price after all. Fortunately, a wise woman came to him and said, "Take some salt and put it up the backside of the cock. That will make it crow."

The stonecutter did what she suggested, and when the cock crowed long before break of day, all the 14,000 devils named Micolás stopped work immediately and returned to Hell, leaving the bridge as it was.

However, all the work had been finished with the exception of one stone. When the people saw the new bridge, they noticed the gap. They fitted a stone into the waiting space, but by the following morning it had disappeared. Several times they put a stone in the hole, and each time it was gone the next day. Finally they gave up, and when you look at the bridge and see the empty space, you know the story is true.

Micaela Labaien Lasarte, aged 74, of Leiza gave that account to Juan Garmendia Larrañaga in 1988, who published it in his 1995 book *Mitos y leyendas de los Vascos*. In 1996, Fermín Leizaola Calvo, President of the Department of Ethnology at the Aranzadi Society of Sciences in San Sebastián, took me on an excursion to stone circles and dolmens in the nearby hills of Gipuzkoa. On our way back to San Sebastián, we stopped in the village of Oiartzun, not far from Soravilla. He showed me a bridge across the Río Oiartzun that had a stone missing and told me the same story about that bridge.

The Black Lake
(Burgos Province)

Sensational accounts of multiple births in several countries were circulating about the time the legend of the Seven Princes of Lara was committed to writing in the 13th century. The version of the legend of the Black Lake current in oral tradition throughout Burgos is usually attached to Doña Lambra or Doña Sancha or a Doña Urraca. The spark that set off the tragic tale of the Seven Princes of Lara was the insult Doña Lambra gave to Doña Sancha, that she had "spawned a litter of seven sons like a sow in a dung heap".

A beggar woman with five children came to the door of the Lady and asked for money. The Lady reproached her for having so many children. The beggar woman cursed the Lady to have seven children in one birth. This happened, and the Lady was so ashamed that she kept one child to raise and ordered her maid to take the other six and drown them in the river.

The Lady's husband intercepted the maid by chance and rescued the children and raised them in secret. When they were five years old he dressed them in clothes identical to those worn by the one the Lady had kept, and presented all seven at a party.

"Which one is the child that you raised?" he asked her.

She was unable to distinguish one from the others, and filled with shame she ran from the party, leapt on her horse and rode to the Black Lake in the hills above Barbadillo de Herreros. The lake, which is connected to the sea and whose bottom has never been found, took her, and since that time, whenever the seasons change, the waters churn and bellow like a bull, and no one dares to approach the shore.

A monster living in the lake has been known to devour animals that stop there to drink. The beast is covered with hair and has a head full of horns, talons like an eagle, and feet like a goat.

The Fire of Mafasca
(Fuerteventura, Canary Islands)

"Mafasca – the Leyend"
(sign on a disco in Puerto del Rosario)

A Bulgarian woman working for a hotel chain in Valencia was transferred to Puerto del Rosario on Fuerteventura. As the plane made its descent to land at the airport, she looked out the window at the bleak landscape and exclaimed, "There's been a mistake. I'm supposed to be going to Fuerteventura, not the Sahara." She cried with disappointment every day for two weeks, until she made friends with the people and came to terms with the geology.

Fuerteventura is the driest, rockiest, most desert-looking of the volcanic Canary Islands and the nearest to the African coast. The Plain of Mafasca, where this story took place, stretches southeast of the town of Antigua. It is the most desolate area of the island, with a grim and haunted atmosphere which bright sunshine and a blue sky do not relieve, making it the perfect setting for the legend of the Fire of Mafasca.

A shepherd was tending his flock in the Plain of Mafasca one night. He was hungry, and so he killed a lamb. There are no trees in Mafasca, and he needed wood to build a fire to cook the lamb. He searched until he found a grave marked by a wooden cross. He removed the cross and smashed it to kindling and used it for his fire.

It is well known that a soul cannot rest if the cross is removed from its grave, and the lost soul of the man buried there is now condemned to wander the Plain of Mafasca in the form of a blue tongue of flame.

All Fuerteventurans know the story, and many have seen the Fire. Rosa María Perclomo, who told it to me, had heard it from her grandfather, Vicente Perclomo of Tetir. Rosa has never seen the Fire, but her mother has seen it several times and described it to her. She approached it one time and passed her hand through the flame. She said it felt warm but didn't burn.

Rational scientific explanations are offered. Some say it could be methane gas or the phosphorescence from rotting organic matter, like the will-o'-the-wisp seen over marshy ground. Others suggest ball lightning, which is an electro-chemical "engine" powered by electricity from thunderclouds and using water vapour for fuel. Both appear as if out of nowhere and hover or glide a few feet above the ground and then evaporate, as the Fire of Mafasca does. But these explanations require rotting organic matter or moisture. There is little vegetation in the Plain of Mafasca, and all of Fuerteventura is very dry.

The Postman from Purgatory
(Erro, Navarre)

A woman whose husband had died married again, but she could never stop thinking about her first husband. This was well known to everyone in the town. One day a man knocked on her door, and when she asked who it was he answered, "I'm the Postman from Purgatory."

"Oh," she said. "My first husband is dead and I haven't heard anything from him yet."

"In fact," said the Postman from Purgatory, "the message I have is from your late husband, and he says that he needs one more Mass said for him so he can go to heaven, but he doesn't have the money to pay for the Mass."

The woman gave him all the money she had in the house. When her current husband arrived home, she said with satisfaction, "The Postman from Purgatory was here, and he told me that my late husband needed one more Mass to get into heaven, so I gave him all our money to open the Pearly Gates."

The husband was angry with his wife, but he wasted no time in abusing her for her foolishness. He quickly jumped on his horse and set off down the road. He encountered a traveller, who, unbeknownst to the husband, was the very man he was seeking, and asked him if he had seen the Postman from Purgatory.

"Yes," said the man. "He went up that road." He pointed to a mountain track inaccessible by horseback.

The husband dismounted and walked a distance along the indicated path without encountering anyone. He returned to where he had left his horse to find both horse and traveller gone. When he finally arrived home on foot, his wife asked him what had become of the horse. He told her that he had overtaken the Postman from Purgatory and given him the

189

horse, in order to speed him on his way to get the Mass said so that her late husband would not have to spend any more time suffering the fires of Purgatory than was necessary.

La Virgen de los Alfileritos – The Virgin of the Pins
(La Calle de los Alfileritos, Toledo)

An embroiderer was pricked by a hidden pin (*alfilerito*) at work, and her hand became infected. She went to a shrine and prayed to the Virgin, her hand was cured, and she returned to work, where she discovered the hidden pin. She removed the pin and left it at the statue of the Virgin in thanksgiving, and she continued to leave pins there until it became a habit.

One day as she was doing this, she noticed a handsome young man behind her. They became acquainted, and soon fell in love, but her parents forbade her to marry him because of the difference in their classes. The nuns at Santa Clara Convent persuaded the parents to relent, and on the day of the wedding, as she was passing the shrine, the girl left another pin. Asked why, she told the story, and this was the beginning of a custom that continues to the present day.

Girls throw pins at the statue of the Virgen de los Alfileritos, resulting in a heap of pins at the foot of the statue, and then they place the palm of the hand on the pins. If a pin sticks to the palm, it means that they will soon find a boyfriend.

The Hand and the Key of the Alhambra
(Granada)

The Alhambra is guarded by a barbican called the Gate of Justice. The visitor enters through a high arched portal whose keystone bears a carved hand, into a vestibule, and then through another portal with a key carved on the keystone. The hand is said to represent the doctrine of Islam, and the key is a symbol of the lineage of the Prophet Mohammed traced back to the House of David. Variants of a local legend give other interpretations.

A story in a Spanish children's book says that a Christian astrologer put a spell on a fair-haired Christian girl. One day the spell will be broken, and the hand will grab the key, and the Alhambra will disappear.

According to Washington Irving in *Tales of the Alhambra*, the king who built the Alhambra was a magician, and he put the complex under a spell to protect it against the hostility of the elements and the Christian enemy, and this is why it has stood intact for so long. Some day, however, the hand will grab the key, and the Alhambra will fall down to reveal hidden Moorish treasure.

"Between Pinto and Valdemoro"
(Between Pinto and Valdemoro, Comunidad de Madrid)

Pinto and Valdemoro are two dormitory communities situated in the desolate plain south of Madrid about four miles (6.5 km) apart. "Between Pinto and Valdemoro" is a proverbial expression meaning "between two stools". The isolated location of the towns and the almost featureless terrain between them lends a piquant image to the saying. This short anecdote is said to be the origin of the expression.

A man had fallen into the river that forms the border between the districts of Pinto and Valdemoro. Policemen from both towns were called to rescue him, but each decided that the river was not in his jurisdiction and the man was not his responsibility, and so the man was left to drown.

Ballads

About the Ballads

"Of course [the ballads] don't lie." – Doña Rodríguez, *Don Quijote II*, 33

"Ballads were invented to sing about notable deeds. ... Iliads without a Homer" – Lope de Vega (1562-1635).

Anonymous *romances* or ballads – narrative songs – reached the height of their popularity in the 15th century. Many were folk imitations, like the English and Scottish story ballads, of the great epics composed around the 12th century. They were shunned by educated people at first, but then imitated by literary poets from the 15th century on. Gustavo Adolfo Bécquer (1836-1870) said, "The people have been and always will be the great poets of the ages." Some of these ballads are still found in oral tradition today.

When printing was invented in the 15th century, the ballads were printed and sold individually as broadsheets and collected in books called *cancioneros*, which flourished between the 15th and 18th centuries. One large sheet folded could make a booklet of 32 pages or more. Two important printed sources of the ballads are the 1511 *Cancionero General* by Hernando del Castillo, which came out in a new edition in 1604, and the *Segunda Parte del Romancero General y Flor de Diversa Poesía*, published in 1605.

The modern ballad group Nuevo Mester de Juglaría (New Work of Balladry) continues this tradition in live performances and recordings of ballads collected from oral and printed sources. The introduction to their 3-CD compilation *El Romancero del Nuevo Mester de Juglaría* (RDQ 52212, Rama Lama Music, Madrid, 2003), which includes versions of "Gerineldo" and "Count Olinos", notes that the ballads "have remained in the collective memory as a treasure that makes us heirs of a tradition that stems from at least as far back as the 15th century, in an amazing feat of oral transmission that has survived almost miraculously to our day."

Gerineldo
(Extremadura version)

"Gerineldo, Gerineldo, Gerineldito so fine,
How I wish for three hours, when you could be mine, only mine."
"Because I'm your servant, my princess, I think you are laughing at me."
"I'm not mocking you, Gerineldo. It's only the truth that I speak."
"Then tell me the hour, my lady, your promise you will keep."
"Come between midnight and one, when my father the king is asleep."

And so at 12.30 exactly, Gerineldo puts on his silk slippers.
He steals to the door of the princess and softly to her whispers:
"Don't be frightened, my lady, have no fear, my mistress.
It's only Gerineldo, come for what you promised."
He takes her by her dainty hand; he takes her into her bed,
And there they start such actions as if they were already wed.

Exhausted by their endeavours, the lovers soon fall asleep.
The king awoke, suspicious. To his daughter's room he did creep.
There in her chamber he found them, sleeping like husband and wife.
"I'll lose the heart of my kingdom, if I take my own daughter's life,
And if I kill Gerineldo, who I raised as I would a son …
No, murder's not the solution. I know what needs to be done."

He drew his sword from its scabbard and placed it in between
His daughter and Gerineldo, to let them know they were seen.
The princess touched the swordblade and shivered at the cold steel.
"Wake up, wake up, Gerineldo. Our secret's been revealed."
"What will I do, my lady? O God, where will I go?"
"Go to my father's garden. Pick a lily and a rose."

Her father, who had been listening, met Gerineldo outside:
"Where do you go, Gerineldo, looking so pale and so white?"
"I go to your garden, my master, I go to pick roses of red,
Because my own colour has faded, then I'll return to my bed."
"You lie, you lie, Gerineldo. I know with my daughter you've lain."
"Then kill me, O my master, if my punishment is to be slain."

193

"I won't kill you, Gerineldo. I've known you all of your life.
I'll give you two an apartment, to live as husband and wife."

It happened that four months later, a great war had begun.
Gerineldo was named a captain, to fight with a battalion.
"Tell me, dear," said the princess, "how many days you'll be gone."
"Don't ask days, months or seasons, the time that I leave you alone.
It's years you will be waiting to find out if I am dead.
If I'm not home in seven years, you should find someone to wed."

For seven years she waited. Gerineldo did not return.
With her son she went as a pilgrim, the fate of her lover to learn.
On the road was a herd of cattle. She asked for their owner's name.
"They belong to the Count Gerineldo. Tomorrow is his wedding day."
To his house the princess galloped. At the gate she left her horse.
By the door she sat like a beggar. The Count tossed a coin in her purse.
"Come, come, Sir Count," she scolded. "Is that all you can do?"
"Come, beggar," said Gerineldo, "and get away with you."

"Come, come, sir," she persisted. "How little you can afford.
While in the house of my parents, you used to give much more.
Look at me, Gerineldo. Look at your own true wife.
And here look at your son, whom you can never deny."
He took her by her dainty hand. Out of the house they hurried.
"Come with me to the chapel, and there we will be married."

Count Olinos
(Also called Conde Niño)

The Count Olinos rose early, one summer Saint John's morn,
To give his horse some water, along the ocean's shore.
And while the horse was drinking, the Count began to sing:
"Who will wash my shirt, who will wash and wring
And hang it out to dry on a bush of rose or thorn?"

In the royal palace they heard his melody.
The queen said, "Listen, daughter: a mermaid of the sea."
"It's not a mermaid, mother, nor a bird you hear.
"That's the young Count Olinos; my love is drawing near."
"I will have him killed." "Then they will bury me."

She died at eleven, he died when the roosters crowed.
During the day they were both buried in their shrouds,
She as the royal daughter was placed at the altar's front,
And he as the son of a count was buried a little beyond.
From her grew an olive tree, from him an olive grove.

The queen, when she found out, ordered the trees destroyed.
The man who cut them down laboured as he cried.
She changed into a dove, he to a peacock brave.
The queen, when she found out, ordered the birds be slain.
The man who killed them wept to see such beauty spoiled.

She turned into a heron, and he to a sparrowhawk.
The heron sprang aloft and flew along the shore.
The hawk with all his speed circled her in flight.
She next became a hermitage, and he its curing fount,
To which the crippled journeyed, their healing to implore.

The queen, when she found out, quickly went to say:
"Daughter, wash my eyes, wash them without delay."
"When I was an olive tree, you ordered I be felled.
"When I became a heron, you ordered I be killed.
"And now you come to visit me, when I've become a saint."

The Lover and Death

I was dreaming a dream, dreaming about my lovers, when a woman entered my dream, whiter than snow.

"How did you get in here, love? What way did you enter, my life? The doors and windows are all closed."

"I am not your love. I am Death sent to you by God."

"Give me more time. Give me a day."

"You don't have even a day left. You have only one hour."

He put on his shoes and clothes in a rush and ran to the street where his lover lived.

"Open up, or you will never open to me again."

"But it's not the time we agreed. My father has gone to the palace, and my mother isn't asleep yet."

"Death is looking for me. Open, and I'll find life in your arms."

"Stand beneath the window where I work and sew, and I'll let down a silk rope for you to climb up. If the rope isn't long enough, I'll add my tresses to it."

She let down the rope, but it broke as he was climbing up, and Death, who was waiting below, said, "Now come with me, lover."

The Lover and the Corpse

(This is a close translation in prose of a full composite version of this ballad. The girl's parents had forbidden her to marry the young man of her choice. They ordered the suitor killed, and he has been fatally wounded.)

The morning of Saint Peter, the morning of Saint John, I was watering my horse. While the horse was drinking, I began to sing. All the birds in the world came out to listen, and people who were walking retraced their steps and stopped. "Listen to me, beautiful lady. I have 25 wounds, the least of which is mortal."

The beautiful lady was embroidering and sewing. She came down and nearly fainted. She took him by the hand and led him to a pear tree, where he died. For seven years she combed his hair and put his shoes on as if he were able to walk, and she washed his body and changed his shirt once a week. She washed his mouth with orange-blossom water, so that she would not smell death when she went to kiss him. Then one Feast of San Sebastián the tip of his nose fell off, and his bones began to separate from his flesh.

"Oh, me, what a life I have to endure! They have killed my love. Who will bury him? If I say anything to my mother, she is a woman who will talk. If I speak to my father, he will order me killed. My brothers are too young to understand about love. I'll ask my uncle the priest, who lives in Pilar.

"Uncle, my lover has died. Will you bury him?"

"Yes, you needn't cry, but I won't bury him at the door or the altar steps."

As they were burying him, she gave a sigh. Two days later she made her final confession, and the following day they buried her. One was buried in Saint Peter's, the other in Saint John's. From one grew a rose, from the other a lovely rosebush. The queen, being jealous, ordered it cut down, but the trunk remained green and blossomed again.

197

Notes

How the Basques Discovered Ireland

According to Irish mythological history in the medieval *Lebor Gabála Érenn*, the first people to arrive in Ireland were led by Cessair, granddaughter of Noah. They were killed by the Deluge forty days after they arrived. Ireland was empty for 278 years until the Partholonians arrived from "Greece". Rudolf Thurneysen (*Zeitschrift für celtische Philologie*, 13) believed that the name of the leader of these first successful residents, "Partholón", was a corruption of "Bartholomew". If this is so, and if Fabyan's account has any basis of truth (and ignoring the date given), then the first Irish people may have been Basques.

The *Lebor Gabála* is available in Spanish: *Leabhar Ghabhála: El libro de las invasiones*, Ramón Sainero Sánchez, ed., Ediciones Akal, Madrid, 1988.

How the Celts of Spain Discovered Ireland

The Tower of Hercules in La Coruña is a 223-foot (68m) second-century Roman lighthouse. Renovated in the 18th century, it is the oldest one still in operation.

San Martín Txiki and the Basajauns

This is the 4th-century bishop Saint Martin of Tours, who died 8 November 397 and was buried 11 November, which is his main feast. He destroyed pagan temples and felled sacred trees. Aetiological (causational) tales like this are the folk explanation of the transition from the pagan to the Christian culture, according to Seve Calleja in *Basajaun*, where a version of this story appears. A variant from Gipuzkoa, in which wheat is replaced by maize (which was not introduced into the Basque Country until explorers brought it from the New World), was told to the collector Juan Garmendia Larrañaga by an 88-year-old man in 1992.

The Lagoon of Antela

The Lagoon of Antela was the largest body of fresh water in the Iberian Peninsula at 4.5 x 4 miles (7 x 6 km) until it began to dry up in the 19th century for a number of reasons, including the blocking of the water flow by a French marquesa in order to raise frogs for the French market. In 1956 it was drained completely, but no trace of Antioquía was found. The lake has been refilled in recent years.

King Rodrigo and the Losing of Spain

The verse "Yesterday I was King of Spain" (my translation) is from "La Derrota de don Rodrigo" (lines 22-28), collected in *Romancero traditional de las lenguas hispánicas*, Vol. 1, 1957; p. 47. The editor notes that line 22 is frequently quoted and remains in the memory of the people. A variant of lines 22-25 is quoted in *Don Quijote II*, 26.

The section dealing with Rodrigo and the Cave of Hercules borrows and quotes liberally from Irving's *Legends of the Conquest of Spain*. Sir Walter Scott's 1811 poem "The Vision of Don Roderick" adds to the magic cloth's prophecy the Peninsular War (1810-14), in which Britain came to the aid of Spain and Portugal against France.

An excavation beneath San Ginés undertaken by Cardinal Martínez Silíceo in the 16th century revealed a cavern with bronze statues and a mass of human remains, but an intervening underground stream prevented further exploration. It is said that those who took part in this excavation fell seriously ill and died a short time later. The crypt was closed in the 19th century and the Plaza de San Ginés renamed Amador de los Ríos. Toledo had been the capital of Gothic Spain from the reign of Leovigild (568-586), replacing Tolosa. It was again the capital from Spain's inception as a kingdom in 1516 until it was replaced by Madrid in 1561.

The description of the penitence borrows and quotes liberally from Robert Southey's translation of *Crónica del Rey Don Rodrigo*, in his notes to "Roderick, the Last of the Goths". *Don Quijote II*, 33, alludes to the story. To support his argument that "behind the Cross there stands the Devil, and not all is gold that glisters," Sancho Panza points out that for all his wealth, "they set Don Rodrigo to be eaten by snakes, if the old ballads don't lie." Doña Rodríguez confirms this: "Of course they don't lie. There is a ballad that says that King Rodrigo was put, still alive, into a tomb full of toads, snakes and lizards, and after two days he said from within the tomb, in a low and sorrowful voice:

"They're eating me now, they're eating me now
In the place where I most have sinned."

Pelayo, the Saviour of Spain

Sancho Panza quotes a 16th-century versified curse on a servant who had stolen a cloak: "May you be eaten by bears, like Favila the appointed." Don Quijote explains: "He was a Gothic king, who was eaten by a bear while he was hunting" (*Don Quijote II*, 34).

Orreaga

Arturo Campión's 1877 story was inspired by the "Chant d'Altabiskar", a poem in the Basque language (*Altabiskarco Cantua*) said to have been discovered in Spain in 1794. The manuscript was accepted by some nineteenth-century French, Basque and Spanish scholars as "a genuinely contemporary document", but modern scholars are sceptical. According to Lewis Spence (*Legends and Romances of Spain*), it was "written in Basque by a Basque student named Duhalde, who translated it from the French of François Garay de Montglave (c. 1833)". *Altabiskarco Cantua* describes the massacre from the point of view of a local Basque farmer in detailed and sensational terms. The lines quoted are from Wentworth Webster's 1879 book *Basque Legends*.

Spence suggests that this famous encounter may have been merged in the "Chant d'Altabiskar" with a second battle of Roncesvalles in 824, in which two Frankish counts were defeated by Pyrenees mountain men, and an earlier battle between Franks and Basques in the reign of Dagobert I (631-638).

Atienza (*Leyendas Mágicas de España*) says that the mythical Basque personage Errolán was borrowed by the author of the Chanson de Roland. Turpín (d. 794) was Archbishop of Rheims.

Roncesvalles is the first point of welcome on the Spanish side along the main pilgrim route of the Camino de Santiago (Road of Saint

James), which runs from France to Santiago de Compostela in Galicia in the northwest of Spain.

Santiago

Medieval books and early Spanish histories preserve accounts of Saint James's life, death and subsequent activities with varying degrees of credulity. My account mainly follows the anonymous 12th-century *Liber Sancti Jacobi* and *The Golden Legend or Lives of the Saints* by Jacobus de Voragine, Archbishop of Genoa, 1275, published in English by William Caxton in 1483. In his *Historia General de España* (1592), Father Juan de Mariana gives cautious credence to some of the legends, and he defends James's presence in Spain, alive and dead, in *De adventu B. Jacobi Apostoli in Hispania* (1609).

Modern historians and hagiographers reject the tradition, said to have originated in the ninth century, that Saint James was ever in Spain dead or alive. W. Sabine Baring-Gould in *The Lives of the Saints* says that the story "does not deserve serious discussion". Samuel Butler's *The Lives of the Saints* notes that relics venerated at Compostela "were recognised as authentic by a bull of Pope Leo XIII in 1884", but their legitimacy "is more than dubious".

The English poet Robert Southey, who had little time for "Romish superstitions", belittled the legends of Santiago in the Introduction to his 1829 "The Pilgrim to Compostella: Being the Legend of a Cock and a Hen, to the Honour and Glory of Santiago – A Christmas Tale", which is a burlesque treatment of the story of the miracle at Santo Domingo de la Calzada.

And how he used to fight the Moors,
Upon a milk-white charger:
Large tales of him the Spaniards tell,
Munchausen tells no larger.

In 1992, the critic Alain Guerdat advocated the suppression of the images of Santiago Matamoros and Mataindios in the processions and churches of Spain and America. The Spanish government subsequently put pressure on the Church to remove the statue of Santiago Matamoros from the Cathedral in Compostela because "it was deemed offensive to Muslims". In 2004, the Church formally rejected any such action.

Jaun Zuria - The Golden-haired Lord

Pronunciation: the "j" is pronounced like the Spanish or the English "j" in various parts of Bizkaia. "Z" is like "s". The stress is "sur-EE-ah". Although the legend has been called "one of the untouchable dogmas" of Bizkaia (Mañaricúa, *Historiografía de Vizcaya*), it has gone through many changes between the 14th and 19th centuries. For example, in the Anglophobic climate following the rejection of the Church of Rome by "perfidious England" and the destruction of the Invincible Armada, Jaun Zuria's earlier English paternity was replaced by Scottish, Scandinavian or Irish, and in Vicente Arana's novelistic version (1887), Ordoño is killed by a woman.

My retelling is based on Antonio de Trueba's romantic literary legend in *Cuentos Populares* (1859). De Trueba borrowed freely and anachronistically from historical and legendary sources, importing real 10th-century people and events into this 9th-century legend. "Ordoño the Wicked" was Ordoño IV, usurper king of Asturias and León 958-960. Fernán González was Count of Castile c. 930-970. Jaun Zuria's great-grandson, Lope II Íñiguez Diaz, fourth Lord of Bizkaia 924-931, fought by Fernán's side against the Moors.

"Lope I Fortún 'Jaunzuria': 870-909" is first on the list of the Lords of Bizkaia in Voltes' *Tablas Cronológicas*, and he is generally accepted as having been a real person. The Battle of Arrigorriaga is said to have taken place on Saint Andrew's Day in AD 867, and this is why the Basque flag, the *ikurrin*, features the X-shaped Saint Andrew's Cross. There is no record of an Irish king of Tara named Morna.

The legend first appears in the 14th-century *Livro das Linhagens* by Don Pedro de Barcelos. In this version, Count Don Moniño of Asturias obliged the Bizkaians to pay an annual tribute of one white horse, cow and ox. Froom, exiled brother of the (unnamed) King of England, arrived in Busturia and, learning of their difficulty, told the Basques he would defend them if they made him lord. They did so, and Froom challenged and defeated Moniño. Froom's son, Fortún Froes, inherited the lordship on his death. Don Pedro apparently collected at least part of this legend from oral tradition in Busturia. Later commentators have suggested that the name "Froom" was inspired by either Fernán González or the Fomorians, mythical invaders of Ireland.

Lope García de Salazar's *Crónica de Siete Casas de Vizcaya y Castilla* (1454) and *Istoria* (or *Libro*) *de las Bienandanzas e Fortunas* (1474) include the story. Don Lope notes that Jaun Zuria's coat of arms features two blood-red wolves each with a lamb in its mouth, because when he was leaving for the battle he came across two such wolves, and he saw that as a good sign. Jaun Zuria's name was Lope, which derives from the Latin *lupus*, "wolf". Those wolves were on the coat of arms of Bizkaia from the 14th century until 1986.

In the 9th century, Bizkaia was incorporated into Castile and subject to León. Mariana (1592) says that the Bizkaians led by Jaun Zuria, "who they say was of the blood of the kings of Scotland," revolted against the León king Alfonso III the Great in 862 and defeated an army led by Alfonso's son Ordoño II. As a reward for this victory Jaun Zuria was given the lordship of Bizkaia. The cautious Mariana adds: "But who can sufficiently establish the truth of this part?"

Various sources point out that Vikings from Dublin established a base at Mundaka in the 9th century, and they trace Jaun Zuria's descent through Norwegian and Swedish kings to Thor of Thrace. His parents are named as the Irish Viking king Ivar the Snake and Princess Fargusina of Scotland, sister of King Kenneth Mac Alpine. This safely distances the Basque hero from English blood and places his descendants in the same Gothic line as the nobility of Spain.

Dueso (*Nosotros Los Vascos*) says that Jaun Zuria is a personage more imaginary than real: "An old legend says that he was born of a Scottish princess living in Mundaka, who mated with a gigantic serpent or Sugahar." Camp (*Leyendas del País Vasco y Navarra*) says that he was the son of a fifth-century Scandinavian princess imprisoned by her father to separate her from her non-royal lover, who was later executed by the king. Pregnant, she escaped and fled to the Basque Country. When she landed at Mundaka and saw the clear water of the river, she exclaimed, "¡Munda aqua!" whence comes the name Mundaka.

"Malastu" is de Trueba's version of "Malato", the name of the tree which stood in the place now marked by a stone cross erected in 1730 in Luyando. The word is probably related to *mellado* – "notched" – from the practice of driving a dagger into the trunk as a warning to invaders.

203

The empty tomb labelled "Ordoño" in the church of Santa Magdalena in Arrigorriaga is that of the centuries-later Ordoño Aguirre, a native of the town.

The Death of Lekobide

This is my free translation and retelling of "La Muerte de Lekobide" from *Leyendas del País Vasco y Navarra* by Maria José Llorens Camp; M. E. Editores, S. L., Spain; 1995.

The Death of Munso López

The theme of the vengeful spurned woman is also found in the Greek story of Phaedra and Hippolytus, Potiphar's wife in the Old Testament, the Irish "The Kin-slaying of Rónán", and the "Santo Domingo de la Calzada" chapter in this book.

The Goat-foot Lady

Modern histories trace the first six Lords of Bizkaia thus:

Lope I Fortún (Jaun Zuria) (870-909)
Manso (var. Munso) López (909-920)
Íñigo I López Ezquerra (920-924)
Lope II Íñiguez Díaz (924-931) (Famously described in the *Poema de Fernán González* as "rich in apples and poor in bread and wine;" fought with Fernán in the Battle of Hacinas, 926, though probably not against García Sánchez in 960.)
Sancho López (931-993)
Íñigo II López Ezquerra (993-1044)

Livro das Linhagens, the 14th-century source of "The Goat-foot Lady", identifies Diego López as the fourth Lord of Bizkaia, succeeded by his son Íñigo Ezquerra. "Diego López" appears to be confused with either Manso or Sancho.

The 15th-century *Bienandanzas* is the source of the previous chapter, "The Death of Munso López", in which Munso, the second Lord of Bizkaia, is rescued from the Moors by his son (by a previous wife), Íñigo Esquirra. *Bienandanzas* does not record the story of "The Goat-foot Lady".

The common element of the son, whose mother is dead or absent, rescuing his father from the Moors suggests a connection between the two stories. They may be disconnected segments of the same story, or "The Goat-foot Lady" may be a floating folk tale borrowed by a storyteller and at one time attached to "The Death of Munso López", but without other confirming sources they cannot honestly be reunited.

The Maimed Maidens of Simancas

Simancas was called Septimanca by the Romans, and the name more likely derives from *septimani* – "soldiers of the 7th legion" – or from the same element found in "Salamanca" that refers to running water.

Ramiro and Aldonza

The attractiveness of the dark-skinned Moors is proverbial. In Portugal even today, if a man appears vague or lovesick, a friend might observe, "Ha moura na costa – there is a Moorish girl on the coast", ie, nearby. This is a play on a Spanish expression referring to an impending threat: "Hay moros en la costa – there are (invading) Moors on the coast."

The Ramiro and Aldonza story is well known in Gaia. On 15 July 1999, it was performed in the town as an outdoor extravaganza called *A Lenda de Gaia* (The Legend of Gaia) by the Teatro Experimental do Porto with the support of the municipal government of Vila Nova de Gaia. The script was based on a narrative poem, "Miragaia", written in 1845 by local resident Almeida Garrett, and the account in *Livro das Linhagens*. The modern Rua (Street) de Rei Ramiro leads to the Rua do Castelo, which runs up the hill to the ruins of Alboazar's castle.

The English poet Robert Southey wrote a version in verse, "Ramiro", in 1802, based on *Livro das Linhagens*. The last two lines are:

But a heavier weight than that millstone lay
On Ramiro's soul at his dying day.

205

By the 14th century, when *Livro das Linhagens* was written, the perceived taint of Moorish blood was unacceptable in noble Christian families, so abduction legends such as this were concocted to gloss over earlier inter-marriages, which were usually politically motivated.

Fernán González, First Sovereign Count of Castile

Fact or Fiction?

Modern historians support the basic historicity of many of the events reported in the chronicles and ballads. Maiden tributes, as in the Battle of Simancas, are rooted in fact. Christian women were sent to Córdoba as wives, slaves and prostitutes until the Christians were strong enough militarily to resist.

Although the *Poema* account of the Battle of Era Degollada "contains some errors, it is basically historical" (Cruz, *Fernán González, Su Pueblo*).

"There appears to exist a basis of truth" in the incident of Sancha releasing Fernán from captivity in Navarre (Urbel, *Historia*). The Count of Lombardy is fictional, but the reference may be to intervention by Count Ramón de Ribagarza, father of Ava, wife of Fernán's son, Garcí Fernández (Urbel, *Historia*). Urbel (*García Fernández*) said that the Moorish leader Abd al-Rahman demanded that García Sánchez hand Fernán over to him. Urbel surmised that to avoid acceding to this impossible request while not to be seen refusing, as he was on nominally friendly terms with the Moors, García either turned a blind eye to Sancha's rescue or made up the story. There is also evidence that Fernán's release was conditional on his abandoning support of the usurper Ordoño IV, suggesting pressure from Sancho the (formerly) Stout of León and a temporary truce on the part of his vengeful wife, Teresa.

Following medieval sources, my account above says, "Fernán's first wife, Urraca, being dead, Teresa invited him to marry Sancha." Modern historians say that Sancha was Fernán's first wife and Urraca his second.

Saint Quirce

Quirce (Cyricus) was martyred with his mother, Julitta, in Tarsus c. 304. His feast day and the date of the battle are variously given as 16 June and 15 or 16 July. He is the patron of children, and he appeared to Charlemagne to save him from a wild boar.

"Good Count Fernán González"

In the incident of the horse and the goshawk, Sancho the Stout orders Fernán to attend the court in León. The ballad version of the story begins with and is entitled "Good Count Fernán González". This is the message sent by the king. Fernán's reply to the messenger begins, "I have no fear of the king." Menéndez Pidal quotes an anecdote in the 1598 *Floresta Española* to illustrate how well known this ballad remained in the 16th century. A Toledan lord had offended Carlos V and was ordered to appear at court on short notice. As he entered the anteroom he sang the first three lines of the ballad in a low voice: "Buen conde Fernán González, el Rey envía por vos / que vayades a las cortes que se hacen en León; / buen conde, si allá non ides, teneros han por traidor ... Good Count Fernán González, the King has sent for you / that you attend the court that he has convened in León / if you don't go he will accuse you of being a traitor ..." The page accompanying the Toledan lord interrupted with "*aunque* vayades – *although* you attend". (*Romancero Hispánico*, Vol. II, quoting Santa Cruz, *Floresta Española*, Brussels, 1598)

The Goshawk

The art of falconry was introduced into Europe by the Arabs. Goshawks (*Accipiter gentilis*) were especially prized, as the best of them were imported from northern Europe at great expense and usually did not survive long in Spain, dying of dehydration in the dry climate. The Fuero Viejo de Castilla (a *fuero* was a law passed by referendum and ratified by the lord) imposed a penalty of 70 or 100 or more sueldos for the theft, wounding or killing of a goshawk. The killing of a man was punishable by a fine of 500 sueldos.

The Church of San Andrés, Cirueña

Opposite the church of San Andrés in Cirueña, the Official College of Technical Engineers of La Rioja mounted a plaque on the wall of the Bar Xacobeo in April 2000 that reads: "Pursued by the King of Navarre, Count Fernán González sought sanctuary in the Church of Cirueña in the year 960." The altar in the present church is not broken.

The Evil Archpriest

Alfonso X the Wise's 13th-century legal code, *Las Siete Partidas* (The Seven Divisions), based on Roman law, was proclaimed the law of Castile and León in 1348 and is still used occasionally as a basis for legal arguments in Spanish courts. It includes a section dealing with canon law on the obligations of the clergy, "what they should do and what is forbidden to them". Partida I, Título VI, Ley 47 states: "No cleric of any order whatsoever should have goshawks or falcons or hunting dogs." Describing the evil archpriest as using these animals in the hunt immediately identifies him as one who flouts canon law and is thus likely to violate moral codes.

The Film

Spartaco Santoni (Fernán), Broderick Crawford (Sancho), Cesar Romero, Linda Darnell, Alida Valli, Fernando Rey, and Frankie Avalon starred in the 1963 US/Spanish film *El Valle de las Espadas / Valley of the Swords / The Castilian*, directed by Javier Setó and based on *Poema de Fernán González*.

"Widowed Before She Was Wed"

Some modern historians suspect that Sancho of Navarre was the instigator of the assassination, and he killed the Vela brothers to eliminate witnesses. This theory is supported by the fact that he soon seized Castile in the name of his wife, Munia, García's sister, realising a dream held by many previous Navarre kings. His intention seems to have been to involve himself in the politics of the kingdom of León with the purpose of turning Castile into a kingdom, which his son, Fernando I, accomplished.

Garcí Fernández and the Traitor Countess
"Self-styled Emperor of Castile"

A document dated 8 March 974 begins: "Ego Garcia Fredenandez gratia Dei comes et imperator [count and emperor] Castella ..." (Urbel, *Historia*)

The Seven Princes of Lara (or Salas)

The Spanish title is *Los Siete Infantes de Lara* (or *Salas*). The modern Spanish word *infante/infanta* (prince/princess) refers to the son or daughter of royalty, but in the Middle Ages it applied to the children of high-born nobility in general. Lope García de Salazar offers another explanation in *Libro de las Bienandanzas e Fortunas* (1474): "For that honourable death that they died they were called 'infantes'."

The story has a long literary history. An epic composed about the time of the events – "a golden age of heroic poetry", according to Ramón Menéndez Pidal – has been lost, but its text is preserved in prose form in the 13th-century *Estoria de España*. Fifteen chapters of the 14th-century *Crónica de Veinte Reyes* (Chronicle of Twenty Kings) are given to the story and fill the gaps between the ballads. Later authors such as Lope de Vega and Victor Hugo have contributed their own treatments of the subject. In *Don Quijote II*, 60, Sancho Panza quotes the line from the ballad "Don Rodrigo went hunting": "Die now, traitor, enemy of Doña Sancha."

The indefatigable Ramón Menéndez Pidal devoted a volume of 613 pages to the subject. *La Leyenda de los Infantes de Lara* was published in 1896 and revised in 1934 and 1971. An important contribution to the study of the legend is his collation of research into its historicity, which shows that most of the major events really happened and most of the participants existed. Here are a few examples.

Garcí Fernández, who founded Salas as a city in 974, was Count of Castile 970-995. The real Ruy Velázquez remains elusive, but he seems to have closely resembled his character in the story. Gonzalo Gustios existed. He was Fernán González' captain at the Battle of Hacinas (926), in which his father, Gustio González, was killed. His eldest son, Diego, was Garcí Fernández' lieutenant at the Battle of the Ford of Cascajares in 978. He had other sons, but probably not seven. He visited Almanzor in Córdoba as an ambassador in 974 or 975. Documents in Burgos signed and not signed by Gonzalo suggest that he did not take part in civic affairs between June 975 and April 992. This corresponds to the period between his protective custody by Almanzor and his release by the possibly fictitious Mudarra from Ruy Velázquez' persecution 18 years later. Almanzor's captains or field generals, Viara and Galve (Gálib, "He of the Two Swords"), were leading battles in 974.

In 1492, the heads of the princes were re-interred in a new sepulchre in the church of Santa María in Salas, and representations of the heads painted on the wall over the niche. In 1579, the Mayor of Salas opened the sepulchre. On a covering tablet was found a painting of Mudarra and his father, each with a half-ring in his hand and these joined together. Inside was a small chest containing eight heads. The heads were again examined in 1846, this time by the Chief of the Province of Burgos. The coat of arms of present-day Salas shows seven heads and Doña Sancha holding Mudarra's hand. There is an Asociación de Amas de Casa Doña Sancha in Salas. In nearby Barbadillo del Mercado, Doña Lambra's estate, stands the Hotel Doña Lambra.

In Córdoba, a house on Calle de las Cabezas (Street of the Heads) – the name dates from at least the 13th century – is said to be where Gonzalo was imprisoned. A narrow lane running off Cabezas next to the house is called Calleja de los Arquillos (Lane of the Arches) for the seven arches on which the heads of his sons were displayed.

El Cid

A primitive version of *Cantar de Mio Cid* existed as early as the 12th century. *Gesta* or *Historia Roderici*, a Latin chronicle of events in the life of El Cid, was written in 1110. The 14th-century manuscript of *Cantar* held in the National Library of Madrid was copied from a manuscript tentatively dated to 1207.

Mariana, in his 1592 *Historia General de España* (10, 4), says that as El Cid was dying, Búcar came again to besiege Valencia. El Cid wrote in his testament that the inhabitants of the city – men, women and children – were to go out and walk around the city. They did so, carrying El Cid's dead body with them, and the Moors, thinking they were being counter-attacked by superior numbers, took fright and withdrew. However, the Christians continued on to Castile and the Moors took over the city. This or a similar earlier account, presumably factual, may be the origin of the legend of the dead Cid on horseback. However, at the end of this chapter, Mariana cautiously distances himself: "Some take most of this narration for mere legend; I have recounted more things than I believe, because I neither dare to pass over in silence what others affirm, nor do I wish to state as certain what I doubt."

The episode of El Cid's beard from the 13th-century *Estoria de España*, attributed to Alfonso X the Wise, is also the subject of a ballad in Sepúlveda's 1550 collection: "Romance de el Cid y el Judío" – "En sant Pedro de Cardeña esta el Cid enbalsamado ..." The monastery of San Pedro de Cardeña was used by Franco to imprison captured enemy forces during the Civil War.

The guidebook containing the description of Jimena Gómez is *Al Destierro con El Cid* (López).

Mezquita del Cristo de la Luz

The Puerta del Sol is said to be the finest mudéjar gate in Spain. A 16th-century medallion over the archway shows the Blessed Virgin bestowing the angel-made chasuble on San Ildefonso. (See chapter "Three Miracles of Our Lady: The Chasuble of San Ildefonso".) The Puerta del Sol was built in the time of Archbishop Tenorio, who was responsible for the rebuilding of the Bridge of San Martín (see that chapter). The Mezquita del Cristo de la Luz is open to the public.

Santo Domingo de la Calzada

According to the 12th-century *Liber Sancti Jacobi*, the hanged youth incident occurred in 1090 in France, and it was Santiago who held the boy up by his feet. The resurrected chickens are absent from that version.

María Pérez the Manly

According to Mariana, Urraca was not the put-upon innocent she appears to be in the María Pérez legend. He says that Urraca was always unpopular with her Galician subjects, they objected to her marriage to Alfonso I of Aragón, and they were infuriated when she allowed Alfonso to install his own troops in Galician castles to prevent their rebelling. Her husband imprisoned her because of her "wicked and lascivious life". The Pope granted their divorce probably because they were related in the third degree: they had the same great-grandfather, Sancho the Great of Navarre. Her unpopularity forced her to abdicate in favour of her son, Alfonso VII. (He was crowned in 1111 at the age of six, though his reign is officially dated from the death of Urraca in 1126.)

The Lagarto of La Malena

As I discovered when I visited Jaén on a storytelling tour in November 2000, all the residents of the city know the legend of the lagarto, though they might not agree on some details. In his 1992 book *La Leyenda del Lagarto de la Malena y los Mitos del Dragón*, Juan Eslava Galán describes the results of a survey he carried out in the 1970s. It is curious to note that of the 280 people interviewed, 72% believe that the hide of the beast is in the church of San Ildefonso, while only 65% believe the story to be true. Galán concludes: "The legend of the lizard of La Malena originates in a myth or family of myths of battle that come from the region of India-Mesopotamia." I hold with the 65%: there is no proof that the story *isn't* true.

The Lovers of Teruel

The historicity of the story is vociferously defended by the citizens of Teruel and especially by the Instituto de los Amantes, formed "to unify criteria and improve the historical and cultural aspects of the tradition". One of the arguments most frequently presented against the veracity of the story and its setting in Teruel is that Boccaccio included a similar tale set in Florence in his *Decameron* (Day 4, Tale 8), written between 1348 and 1358, and detractors claim that the Lovers of Teruel story was plagiarised from that source. This is easily refuted. The Teruel story was in oral tradition immediately after the events, and a written edition was circulating in Italy before Boccaccio began writing his book.

Three Miracles of Our Lady

Many of these stories remain in oral circulation. Cantiga 107, for example, which tells how Our Lady saved a Jewish woman who was pushed off a cliff for alleged infidelity and then converted to Christianity, is still current in Segovia, where it is said to have happened.

The Chasuble of San Ildefonso

The imposition of the chasuble on San Ildefonso is depicted on the marble medallion above the arch of the Puerta del Sol, a relief in the Cathedral in Toledo, a retablo in and a carving over the entrance of the Jesuit church of San Ildefonso in Toledo (on Plaza Padre Juan de Mariana), and in a carving above the north entrance to the church of San Ildefonso in Jaén and on the retablo behind the main altar. Velázquez and many other painters depicted the story.

The minutes in Latin of the Tenth Synod of Toledo can be found online. Ildefonso's proposal to move the date of the Feast of the Annunciation to 18 December is the first item on the agenda, beginning "De cęlebritate festivitatis dominicę matris ..."

Muslims have a strong respect for Mary the Mother of Jesus, and the Koran mentions her frequently. Sura 3 describes the Annunciation and refers to her virginity. It was reported that when the Moors captured Toledo and converted the Cathedral into a mezquita, they took special care to protect the spot where the Blessed Mother stood.

Guzmán the Good

"Guzmán el Bueno" is found as a placename in many cities, including a Glorieta in his hometown of León. He was born where the Ministry for Justice now stands. Hostal Guzmán el Bueno is just around the corner.

213

Pedro the Cruel and Enrique the Bastard

Doña Urraca Osorio and Leonor Dávalos are buried in the Monastery of San Isidoro del Campo in Santiponce near Seville, with a suitable inscription on Leonor's tomb. The monastery was founded in 1301 by Alonso Pérez de Guzmán the Good and his wife, María Coronel, who are also buried there. The Leonor Dávalos Centre in Seville was established in 1990 to provide services for women who are victims of abuse.

The Bridge of San Martín

Rufino Miranda (*Toledo*) says that the stone carving does not depict the face of a woman: "In spite of the erosion of the stone which has taken place over the years, the mitred head of the archbishop who ordered the bridge to be restored can still be made out."

Two Alcaides of Antequera

Versions of the legend of Abindarráez and Jarifa were published in the middle of the 16th century. My account generally follows that of Antonio de Villegas in his 1565 *Inventario*. Cervantes and other writers of the period knew the story, and early in his adventures, Don Quijote confused his neighbour with Rodrigo de Narváez, Dulcinea with Jarifa, and himself with Abindarráez (*Don Quijote I*, 5).

La Peña de los Enamorados

The first written account appeared in the 15th century in relation to the Conquest of Antequera in 1410, and it is generally agreed that the story is set about that time. Mariana (1592) sandwiches it in as an aside between the beginning of the siege on 27 April and the capitulation of the city on 16 September. Apropos of his comment that the Christians posted a sentinel on the top of the Peña, he explains how the mountain got its name. Subsequent versions deviate from Mariana's telling only to add romantic touches and a variety of names for the characters.

214

The Dólmen de Menga, a 4000-year-old passage tomb on the outskirts of Antequera, is aligned east-northeast on the Peña. The rising sun at Midsummer shines from between the peaks of the Peña directly into the passage of the Dólmen.

In 2000, the Peña was declared the most important natural monument of the province of Málaga by the Environment Commission of the Junta de Andalucía.

The Man Without a Shadow

The version of the first part of this story current in oral tradition in Salamanca has Enrique, Marqués de Villena, being taught the black arts by the sacristan in the crypt of the church of San Ceprián in the 15th century.

The Cave of Salamanca is also known as the Cave of Saint Ciprian, because it once housed a shrine to the saint. Saint Ciprian of Antioch was consecrated to the Devil by his parents as an infant, and with the powers he learned to use from his infernal master he acquired a reputation as a great Magus. Later he converted to Christianity, and he died a martyr in 289. It was suggested by the 15th-century travel writer Jerónimo Münzer that the Cave might have been an oracular grotto in pre-christian times (Atienza, *Leyendas Mágicas de España*). Calleja (*Basajaun*) points out that Atarrabio is the name of a son of the goddess-witch Mari in Basque myth.

Cervantes' 1615 comedy *La Cueva de Salamanca* features a student who had graduated from the university and studied the magic arts in the Cave. Gonzalo Correas, in his 1627 *Vocabulario de refranes y frases proverbiales*, says that the Cave of Salamanca is a metaphor for the University and for Study in general, "and to this truth have been attached fabulous stories to make newcomers marvel: they say that there is a sacristy in the church of San Cebrián under the main altar, and that there magic arts are studied in secret, and that there the Marqués de Villena studied."

In an Irish parallel involving the historical-legendary Earl Gerald Fitzgerald and the mythical Donn Fírinne, the folk character Donal O'Donoghue was last in line exiting the cave and lost his shadow. Ever since then his descendants have no shadow and are known as the Black O'Donoghues (Ó hÓgáin, *The Hero*).

215

There are many stories of a Christian saint or bishop using a demon to travel to Rome to save the Pope. One variant is "Txanbenat (Jaun Benat), el Diablo y el Papa" collected in 1989 in Rentería (Larrañaga, *Mitos y Leyendas de los Vascos*). A story collected in *Waifs and Strays of Celtic Tradition Vol. 1* has the Scottish wizard Michael Scot (c. 1175 - c. 1235) flying on a demon to Rome to trick the Pope into giving him the secret of computing each year's date for the movable feast of Easter. Scot studied the magic arts in Toledo and other cities known for that speciality. He was nominated by the Pope for the post of bishop of Cashel in Ireland and only turned it down because he could not speak Irish.

The roasted chicken crowing to support a questioned statement is an international motif (see also "Santo Domingo de la Calzada" chapter).

Carreño

From *Málaga en su Literatura Oral*, Concepción Palacín Palacios, Colección Ciudad de Málaga, 1992.

Leokadi

The story of Leokadi was first told to me about 1993 by Patricia Aristondo of Ondarroa. Jaione Alkorta Aldazabal of Ondarroa, whose mother is the sister of Patricia's uncle, added details when I met her some years later.

The Black Lake

This is probably the Laguna Negra de Neila, midway between Burgos and Soria. Menéndez Pidal (*Leyenda*) apparently refers to the same lake when he identifies it as the lake of Quintanar de la Sierra. He says it is called the Lake of Doña Alambra or Ojo del Mar (Eye of the Sea).

Just 20 km to the southeast is another Black Lake, La Laguna Negra de Urbión, which figures tragically in Antonio Machado's 1912 original literary "legend", *La Tierra de Alvargonzález*.

Gerineldo

Source: Gil, Bonifacio, *Cancionero Popular de Extremadura; Colección Raíces*, Departamento de Publicaciones de la Diputación de Badajoz, 1998.
The subject matter of "Gerineldo" is inspired by the relationship between Eginardo, secretary of Charlemagne, and Emma, Charlemagne's daughter. It is probably the most popular folk ballad in Spain – some 500 examples have been collected in all parts of the country – and has been dated vaguely to the 12-16th centuries or specifically to the time of the wars with Portugal in the 14th century. The ballad is composed in couplets; I have made one line of each couplet.

One version begins with a scene from ("contaminated by", according to Bonifacio Gil) "El Rey Conde / El Conde Flores / El Conde Olinos", in which the princess first hears Gerineldo singing while watering his horse by the seashore. In the two main variants collected by Gil in Extremadura, all the couplets form a *tirada* (a succession of lines ending in the same assonance) with the endings *-ido, -illo, -iño, -irio, -ío, -iro, -igo, -isto* until the line "I'll give you two an apartment, to live as husband and wife." This is the basic, perhaps original, "Gerineldo". One of Gil's minor variants (Vol. 2, pp. 448-9) adds four lines at that point, with the endings *-ella, ella, -eta, -esa*, to bring the tale to a tragic conclusion. Gerineldo speaks first:

"But I've made a solemn promise to Christ of the Stars above
Never to marry a woman with whom I've already made love."
"Servants, come with your shotguns, bring sharpened knives for slaughter.
Kill this Gerineldo, who so insults my daughter."

My translation follows the other main variant (Vol. 1, pp. 36-7), which adds a condensed version of "La Condesita". The four lines above are omitted, and the final 20 lines continue from "It happened that four months later", all with a tirada of "a" endings: *está, ya, da, -ar, -al, -itas.* ("The only sign that indicates the fusion of two ballads is, at times, the [change in] rhyme" – Roig, *El Romancero Viejo.*) One minor variant has the king sending Gerineldo deliberately to the front lines in hopes that he will be killed.

The Lover and Death

This 15th-century ballad appeared on a poster on Metro trains in Madrid in March 2003 as part of the city's "Books on the Street" programme ("not a day without poetry").

The Lover and the Corpse

Later Basque versions of this ballad have been influenced by a verifiable event. On 8 July 1633, Pierre d'Irigaray married Gabrielle de Lohitéguy, and died on the same day. (Two years later, Gabrielle's father demanded that Pierre's family return her dowry with interest.) A ballad collected in 1870 in the Basque area of the French Pyrenees says that Pierre was killed by a poisoned nosegay sent by his bride's secret lover, and that Gabrielle kept the body of her husband in her room for seven years, in the cold earth by day and in her arms by night, bathing the corpse once a week with lemon water.

A Catalan version strays into a different ending. The lady tells a servant she will marry him if he buries the decomposing body, at which point the dead man returns to life and throws the lady and the servant off a balcony. The author draws the moral: "Two souls were lost because of parents who would not allow their children to marry those they loved."

Sources

Some of the older works listed here are available online.

(The first four books are attributed to King Alfonso X the Wise because he commissioned and published them. It is believed he wrote parts of some of them.)

Alfonso X the Wise, *Cantigas de Santa María*, Walter Mettmann, ed., Clásicos Castalia, Madrid, 1986.

Alfonso X the Wise, *La Gran Conquista de Ultramar, que mandó escribir el Rey Don Alfonso el Sabio*, Rivadeneyra, Madrid, 1858.

Alfonso X the Wise, *Primera Crónica General, Estoria de España*, que mandó componer Alfonso el Sabio y se continuaba bajo Sancho IV en 1289, Tomo I - Texto; ed., Ramón Menéndez Pidal, Bailly-Bailliere é Hijos, Madrid, 1906.

Alfonso X the Wise, *Las Siete Partidas del Sabio Rey don Alonso el Nono [sic], nuevamente Glosadas, por el Licenciado Gregorio Lopez*, en Salamanca, En casa de Domingo de Portonariis Ursino, Impressor de la Sacra Real Magestad, 1576.

Alonso, Martín, *Diccionario Medieval Español*, Universidad Pontificia de Salamanca, 1986.

Anonymous, *Milenario de Fernán González*, Junta Nacional del Milenario de Fernán González, Burgos, 1971.

Atienza, Juan García, *Leyendas Históricas de España y América*, EDAF, Madrid, Buenos Aires, México, 1999.

Atienza, Juan García, *Leyendas Mágicas de España*, EDAF, Madrid, 1997.

Avalle-Arce, J. B., *Temas Hispánicos Medievales*, Editorial Gredos, Madrid, 1974.

Ballesteros, José Pérez, *Biblioteca de las Tradiciones Populares: Cancionero Popular Gallego, Tomo I*, Madrid, 1885.

Barandiarán Irizar, Luis de, *Antología de fábulas, cuentos y leyendas del País Vasco*, Editorial Txertoa, San Sebastián, 1985. (Luis is the nephew of José Miguel, below.)

Barandiarán, José Miguel, *Obras completas*, Biblioteca de la Gran Enciclopedia Vasca, Bilbao, 1973.

Barcelos, Don Pedro Alfonso de, *Livro das Linhagens* (Book of Lineages), also known as *Nobiliario de Linajes* and *Nobiliario del Conde Don Pedro*, 14th century.

Baring-Gould, S., *The Lives of the Saints*, John Grant, Edinburgh, 1914.

Bienandanzas e Fortunas, Libro de las, see Salazar, Lope García de.

Bleiberg, Germán, *Diccionario de Historia de España*, Alianza Editorial, 1979, 1986.

Book of Saints: A Dictionary of Servants of God Canonized by the Catholic Church, The, compiled by the Benedictine Monks of St Augustine's Abbey, Ramsgate, Adam & Charles Black, London, 1922, 1966.

Butler, Rev. Alban, *The Lives of the Saints*, edited and revised by Herbert Thurston, SJ, and Norah Leeson; Burns and Oates, London, 1932-38.

Calleja, Seve, *Basajaun, el Señor del Bosque: Cuentos y Leyendas Populares Vascos*, Ediciones Gaviota, Madrid, 1994.

Camp, María José Llorens, *Leyendas del País Vasco y Navarra*, M. E. Editores, Spain, 1995.

Castillo, Rosa, *Leyendas Épicas Españolas*, Editorial Castalia, 1969.

Castro, Rubén Armendáriz, *Leyendas de Castilla*, M. E. Editores, Spain, 1995.

Catalán, Diego, *Por Campos del Romancero*, Gredos, Madrid, 1970.

Cervantes, Miguel de, *Don Quijote*; edition, introduction and notes by Martín de Riquer, RBA Editores, Barcelona, 1994. This is the edition cited in this book.

Conde, Juan Carlos et al., *Cantar de Mio Cid*, Espasa Calpe, Madrid, 1976, 1999.

Corpas Mauleón, Juan Ramón, *Curiosidades del Camino de Santiago*, El Pais Aguilar, Madrid, 1993.

Cruz, Fray Valentín de la, *Fernán González: Su Pueblo y Su Vida*, 3rd ed., Institución Fernán González y La Fundación Santa María de Bujedo, Burgos, 1988.

Cuevas, Cristobal, and Enrique Baena, *Cuentos y Leyendas Andaluces*, Editorial Arguval, Málaga, 1991.

Diccionario Enciclopédico Salvat Universal, Salvat Editores, S. A., Barcelona, 1981.

Don Quijote: for the edition cited in this book see Cervantes, Miguel de.

Dueso, José, *Nosotros Los Vascos: Mitos, Leyendas y Costumbres*, Vol. 5, Lur Argitaletxea, 1994.

Espinel, Vicente, *Relación de la vida del escudero Marcos de Obregón*, 1618.

Espinosa, Aurelio M., *Cuentos Populares de Castilla y León*, Consejo Superior de Investigaciones Científicas, Departamento de Antropología de España y América, Madrid, 1996.

Estoria de España (see Alfonso X the Wise, *Primera Crónica*).

Fabyan, Robert, *The New Chronicles of England and France*, 1516; reprinted 1811, London, with Preface and Index by Henry Ellis.

Fernández, Luis Suárez, *Historia de España: Edad Media*, Editorial Gredos, Madrid, 1978.

Galán, Juan Eslava, *La Leyenda del Lagarto de la Malena y Los Mitos del Dragón*, Universidad de Granada and Ayuntamiento Jaén, 1992.

Gallego, Mateo and Francisco Lancha, *Málaga en la Leyenda*, Editorial Arguval, 1996, 1997.

García, Jose Luis Sotaca, *Los Amantes de Teruel: La Tradición y la Historia*, Editorial Librería General, Zaragoza, 1987.

García, Reyes, and Ana María Écija, *Leyendas de Madrid*, Ediciones de la Librería, Madrid, 1998.

García Abad, Albano, *Leyendas Leonesas*, Editorial Everest, León, 1984.

Garrido, María del Carmen Díaz, text, and Jaime Montero Manso, illustrations, *Leyenda del Acueducto e Historia Resumida*, Caja de Ahorros y Monte de Piedad de Segovia, 1988.

Gea Ortigas, María Isabel, *Los Nombres de las Calles de Madrid*, Ediciones de la Librería, Madrid, 2001.

Gil, Bonifacio (1898-1964), *Cancionero Popular de Extremadura*, Colección Raíces, Departamento de Publicaciones de la Diputación de Badajoz, 1998.

Gracia, Ángel Almazán de, *Guía de las Leyendas Sorianas, Revista de Soria, nº 4*, 1994.

Holweck, F. G., *A Biographical Dictionary of the Saints*, Herder, US & UK, 1924.

Hughes, Robert, *Barcelona*, Harvill, London, 1992.

Irving, Washington, *Legends of the Conquest of Spain*. References are to the version published as part of *Spanish Papers* below.

Irving, Washington, *Spanish Papers*, ed. Pierre M. Irving, London, 1866, 1881; Vol. XVIII of 27-volume *Irving's Works, Geoffrey Crayon Edition*. This collection of previously published and unpublished pieces on Spanish themes was published after Irving's death (1859) by his son, Pierre.

Irving, Washington, *Tales of the Alhambra*, 1832; Editorial Everest, León, 1999.

Juaristi, Jon, *La Leyenda de Jaun Zuria*, Caja de Ahorros Vizcaína, Bilbao, 1980.

Larrañaga, Juan Garmendia, *Mitos y Leyendas de los Vascos*, R&B Ediciones, Donostia-San Sebastián, 1995.

Lauriño, Manuel, *Historias y Leyendas de Andalucía*, Editorial Castillejo, Sevilla, 1999.

Linhagens, Livro das, see Barcelos, Don Pedro Alfonso de.

López, Julián Pérez, *Al Destierro con El Cid*, Burgos, 1979 (3rd edition).

Mañaricúa, A. E., *Historiografía de Vizcaya; La Gran Enciclopedia Vasca*, Zalla-Bilbao, 1971.

Mariana, Padre Juan de, SJ, *Historia General de España*, Toledo, 1601 (Latin edition 1592).

Mantuano, Pedro, *Advertencias a la Historia del Padre Ivan de Mariana*, La Imprenta Real, Madrid, 1613 (2nd edition). These are Mantuano's "warnings" about inaccuracies in Mariana's *Historia*.

Martín, José Luis, *Manual de Historia de España: La España Medieval, Historia 16*, Madrid, 1993.

Mellersh, H. E. L., *Chronology of the Ancient World, 10,000 B. C. to A. D. 799*, Simon & Schuster, 1976.

Mena, José María de, *Tradiciones y Leyendas Sevillanas*, Plaza & Janes Editores, Barcelona, 1985, 1999.

221

Menéndez Pidal, Ramón, *La Leyenda de los Infantes de Lara*, 1896, revised 1934 and 1971; Espasa-Calpe, Madrid.

Menéndez Pidal, Ramón, *Romancero Hispánico*, Espasa-Calpe, Madrid, 1968.

Merino, José María, *Leyendas Españolas de Todos los Tiempos*, Ediciones Temas de Hoy, Madrid, 2000.

Miranda, Rufino, *Toledo: Its Arts and Its History*, trans. Margaret McClafferty and David Fricker, Ediciones Savir, Toledo (no date, c. 1990s).

Monteiro, Mariana, *Legends and Popular Tales of the Basque People*, Unwin, London, 1887.

Morton, H. V., *A Stranger in Spain*, Methuen, London, 1955.

Mullins, Edwin, *The Pilgrimage to Santiago*, Signal Books, Oxford, 1974, 2000.

Muñiz, Isabel, *La Leyenda de los Siete Infantes de Lara*, Publicaciones de la Institución Fernán González, Burgos, 1971.

Ó hÓgáin, Dáithí, *The Hero in Irish Folk History*, Gill & Macmillan, Dublin, 1985.

O'Sullivan, Sean, *Legends from Ireland*, Batsford, London, 1977.

Otero, Diego Vázquez, *Tradiciones Malagueñas*, Excma. Diputación Provincial de Málaga, Málaga, 1959.

Pablos, Francisco, *Centón de Leyendas y Mitos de Galicia*, Ediciones NígraTrea, Vigo, 2002.

Páez, Rafael Atencia, *La ciudad romana de singilia barba (Antequera – Málaga)*, Biblioteca Popular Malagueña, 1988.

Palacín Palacios, Concepción, *Málaga en su Literatura Oral*, Colección Ciudad de Málaga, 1992.

Parga, Luis Vázquez de, José Maria Lacarra, Juan Uria Riu, *Las Peregrinaciones a Santiago de Compostela* (3 volumes), Consejo Superior de Investigaciones Científicas, 1948; Gobierno de Navarra, Departamento de Educación y Cultura, 1992.

Perrin, Rafael Yzquierdo, *Leyendas e Historias Jacobeas*, Castilla Ediciones, Valladolid, 1999.

Primera Crónica (see Alfonso X the Wise, *Primera Crónica*).

Rodríguez-Moñino, Antonio, *Diccionario Bibliográfico de Pliegos Sueltos (Siglo XVI)*, Editorial Castalia, Madrid, 1970.

Roig, Mercedes Díaz, *El Romancero Viejo*, Ediciones Cátedra, Madrid, 1997.

Romancero Traditional de las Lenguas Hispánicas, Madrid, Seminario Menéndez Pidal y Editorial Gredos, [12 volumes] 1957-1985.

Rosal Pauli, Rafael del and Fernando Derqui del Rosal, *Noticias Históricas de la Ciudad de Loja*, 2nd edition, Fundación Ibn al-Jatib de Estudios y Cooperación Cultural, 2005, Loja.

Rose, R. Selden and Leonard Bacon, *The Lay of the Cid*, University of California Press, Berkeley, 1919.

Salazar, Lope García de, *Crónica de Siete Casas de Vizcaya y Castilla*, 1454.

Salazar, Lope García de, *Istoria* (or *Libro*) *de las Bienandanzas e Fortunas*, c. 1474.

Sepúlveda, Lorenzo de, *Cancionero de Romances*, Sevilla, 1584; edition by Antonio Rodríguez-Moñino, Editorial Castalia, Madrid, 1967.

Seymour, St. John D., *Irish Witchcraft and Demonology*, Dorset Press, New York, 1992. Originally published c. 1912.

Singul, Francisco, *Historia Cultural do Camiño de Santiago*, Editorial Galaxia, Vigo, 1999.

Spence, Lewis, *Legends and Romances of Spain*, Harrap, 1920; reprinted as *Spain*, Senate, London, 1994.

Storey, R. L., *Chronology of the Medieval World, 800 to 1491*, Simon & Schuster, 1973.

Tapis, Francisco Xavier, *Leyendas y Anécdotas de la Historia de España*, Ediciones Generales Anaya, Madrid, 1985, 1987.

Urbel, Fray Justo Pérez de, *García Fernández: El Conde de las Bellas Manos*, Ediciones de la Exema. Diputación Provincial, Burgos, 1979.

Urbel, Fray Justo Pérez de, *Historia del Condado de Castilla*, Consejo Superior de Investigaciones Científicas, Escuela de Estudios Medievales, Madrid, 1945.

Urbel, Fray Justo Pérez de, "Navarra y Castilla en el Siglo X", *Príncipe de Viana, Año V, Núm. XVII*, 1944, Diputación Foral, Institución Príncipe de Viana, Consejo de Cultura de Navarra, Pamplona.

Voltes, Pedro, *Tablas Cronológicas de la Historia de España*, Editorial Juventud, Barcelona, 1980.

Waifs and Strays of Celtic Tradition, Nutt, London, 1889.

Webster, Wentworth, *Basque Legends*, 1879; Kessinger 2004.

Yarza, Joaquín, Mariano Palacios, Rafael Torres, *Monasterio de Silos*, Editorial Everest, León, 1996.

Printed by
Brunswick Press
Dublin

224